Learning Java Programming in Clara's World

Anton Bogdanovych • Tomas Trescak

Learning Java Programming in Clara's World

Anton Bogdanovych
School of Computer, Data
and Mathematical Sciences
Western Sydney University (WSU)
Parramatta, NSW, Australia

Tomas Trescak
School of Computer, Data
and Mathematical Sciences
Western Sydney University (WSU)
Parramatta, NSW, Australia

ISBN 978-3-030-75541-6   ISBN 978-3-030-75542-3   (eBook)
https://doi.org/10.1007/978-3-030-75542-3

Cover illustration: The book cover image features the "Leaf" 3D model by Thunk3D scanner available under Creative Commons CC BY 4.0.

This Springer imprint is published by the registered company Springer Nature Switzerland AG
The registered company address is: Gewerbestrasse 11, 6330 Cham, Switzerland

Preface

Welcome to *Learning Java Programming in Clara's World*. This book is intended for a one-semester university or an equivalent high school programming course. It is equally suitable for just about anyone else who wants to start learning programming. While this text is written for students with little or no prior programming experience, experienced programmers would also benefit from the in-depth explanations, visual teaching style of this book and interesting programming challenges supplied with it.

Why Did We Write This Book?

The story of this book began ten years ago from overhearing a group of computer science students loudly talking about how much they hate programming. Hearing something like this while being deeply in love with programming made a significant impact on us and resulted in a strong feeling that something had to be done about this. Back then we were two young university academics with background in video games development and virtual reality with no involvement or experience in teaching programming. Programming was our passion and the key instrument in our daily lives. We felt a strong urge to share this passion and explain why programming is such an important tool in the twenty-first century.

After months of research into motivational techniques and existing novel methods of teaching programming, we have produced a proposal for teaching programming fundamentals that relied on similar principles (such as flow [1]) that game developers use for making players attracted to their games. We are grateful to our dean, Simeon Simoff, for trusting our passion and expertise and for allowing us to implement this proposal at Western Sydney University. Five years later, we received two national and one international awards for the teaching methodology and the visual programming framework that forms the basis for this book. The most important achievement, however, is that we have not heard students expressing their hate of programming ever since we started teaching it at our university.

Teaching Programming in a Fun Way

In this book, we are introducing the key fundamental concepts of Java programming such as loops, conditional statements, variables, expressions, methods and arrays through the eyes of a small ladybug called Clara. Clara is a fun and extremely obedient insect, who initially has very limited intelligence. Readers learn programming by making Clara move around and manipulate objects in her world. As the book progresses, Clara becomes smarter and smarter and develops her sense of touch and vision. She progressively acquires new programming skills and (together with readers) learns by tackling some of the world's greatest challenges.

Unlike many other programming textbooks that rely on solving toy artificial problems, this book explains programming concepts through real-world problems such as developing a vacuum cleaner robot, automatically patching potholes, launching rockets into space, simulating projectile motion, dynamically avoiding obstacles, delivering mail, etc. Every chapter of the book starts by presenting a challenge and then continues to explain new programming concepts with the focus on tackling this challenge. Focusing the new material explanation on these challenges helps to remind the readers of how this material is connected with the problems that they may encounter in the real world and makes it easier to relate to.

Our Teaching Approach

In order to develop the teaching methodology for this book we have reviewed and partially borrowed some of the best teaching metaphors and approaches from programming courses such as SwissEduc's "Informatik" [2] and Stanford's "Programming Methodology Course" [3] . We utilised concepts from motivational psychology [1] and applied techniques from gamification of education [4] and utilised relevant game design principles [5] to ensure that we can maintain a high level of student interest while working with programming exercises.

Our book relies on a visual teaching framework called "Clara's World". This framework uses similar principles of teaching programming in a visual way to those employed by introductory programming learning tools such as Karel [6], Scratch [7], Greenfoot [8] and Code.org [9]. Most existing frameworks and tools (i.e. Code.org and Scratch) have been developed with primary school students in mind. Our framework, however, targets university and high school students. Some frameworks (such as Greenfoot) are suitable for high school students, but they require students to memorise a large number of framework-specific commands, while in Clara's World the number of additional commands is very small, so students can concentrate on learning Java. Karel is probably the most suitable piece of software for the high school and university context, but it is underdeveloped. This is why Karel is usually employed in the first couple of introductory lectures, after which students have to switch to one of the traditional Java frameworks and abandon the highly visual approach of Karel. In contrast to Karel, this book in combination with

Clara's World helps to complete the entire first semester of a university programming fundamentals course without abandoning the visual teaching style, while allowing to maintain the required level of depth and complexity of explaining the key programming concepts.

The emphasis in this book is on making readers understand the very basic control structures that are common to all programming languages rather than immediately diving into the complexity of working with classes and objects as many other books do. The text gradually introduces readers to conditional statements, loops, methods, variables and arrays and then provides a quick overview of classes and objects towards the end. With the help of this book you will understand foundations of programming that are common for most modern programming languages, with a specific emphasis on Java (one the most in-demand languages on the market today).

We hope you enjoy learning Java in Clara's World and become as passionate about programming as we are.

Additional Online Resources

This book is supplied with digital online resources for students and educators. All programming problems presented in this book can be explored on the Clara's World website at `https://claraworld.net`.

Every programming problem covered in this book has a corresponding link to a problem template (for those readers willing to attempt the problem themselves), the link to the solution of this problem and a video recording of us solving this problem step-by-step. In addition, at the end of each chapter there is a link to exercises that readers are recommended to complete.

Instructors can be provided with a wide range of educational resources after proving their instructor status.

Digital Resources for Readers and Educators

This textbook provides free unrestricted access to online digital resources. These resources include templates and solutions for all problems presented in the book, as well as additional exercises for self study.

Students and other book readers should follow the instructions below to register on the Clara's World website and access these resources.

1. Go to `https://www.claraworld.net`
2. Select "Enter Clara's World"
3. Click "Register" and follow the on-screen instructions
4. Enter your registration details and make sure that you provide a valid email address
5. Select "Book" as the Organisation
6. Type "book2021" (without quotation marks) in the "Organisation Password" field
7. Check your inbox for the supplied email address and complete registration following the instructions you receive via email
8. Sign in with your email address and password and start using digital resources[1]

Educators can be granted access to additional resources such as lecture slides, educational videos, a large pool of exercises for every topic covered in the book, the content management and marking system, automatic plagiarism detection of submitted code and other specialised tools, facilities for registering your organisation on Clara's World, facilities for setting up your own teaching resources and exercises, admin access to your organisation, video tutorials for educators and much more.

If you are interested in using Clara's World for your programming course as an educator please send us an introductory email to educator@claraworld.net, so that we can verify your educator status.

---

[1] See Appendix A for further information about creating an account on Clara's World and using the digital resources.

Contents

About the Authors

Dr Anton Bogdanovych is a senior lecturer of entertainment computing and applied artificial intelligence at Western Sydney University, School of Computer, Data and Mathematical Sciences.

He has worked at Western Sydney University since 2007 and currently teaches "Video Game Development" and "Programming Fundamentals".

Anton's innovative approach to teaching programming fundamentals (that laid the foundations of this book) has been recognised on a national and international level. Dr Bogdanovych has been awarded the **ICT Higher Education Educator of the Year 2015** by the Australian Computer Society (ACS) and received the **International ICT Educator of the Year 2016 Award** by The South East Asia Regional Computer Confederation (SEARCC).

Since 2017 Anton Bogdanovych has been the director of academic program for the Bachelor of Entrepreneurship degree at Western Sydney University.

Anton completed his PhD in Computer Science at the University of Technology Sydney in May 2008. He is currently involved in a number of research projects related to virtual reality, artificial intelligence, robotics and motion capture.

Before starting his PhD, Dr Bogdanovych worked as a researcher and software developer in the Multiagent Systems Department in the German Research Centre for Artificial Intelligence (DFKI). The DFKI is one of the largest and most prestigious artificial intelligence research centres in the world.

Anton's industry experience with Software MacKiev (one the largest companies that produces Macintosh versions of famous Windows titles) has helped him to get familiar with programming methodologies, tools and people management techniques employed for producing large-scale commercial software. One of his products (WorldBook Encyclopedia) was preinstalled on every iMac computer sold in 2001.

Dr. Tomas Trescak holds a PhD in computer science with a specialisation in artificial intelligence from the Artificial Intelligence Research Institute, Barcelona, Spain (IIIA) of the Spanish Research Council (CSIC). For the past seven years he has worked as a senior lecturer of intelligent systems at Western Sydney University. Since 2020, Tomas has acted as a director of academic program for undergraduate studies in information and communication technology (ICT).

Tomas is an avid open-source enthusiast, contributing to existing software initiatives. He has published over 50 open-source packages for back-end and front-end development, as well as many software tools for virtual and augmented realities.

Tomas is the creator of the Clara's World framework that we utilise in this book. For his academic and software development work, Tomas has received multiple awards, among which are the **2016 Best Innovator Award** by Unearthed Association and **2015 Gold Disruptor Award** in the Best Australian ICT Educator category by the Australian Computer Society.

In his academic work Tomas seeks new ways to facilitate complex cognitive tasks in simulation, education, healthcare, cyber security and social sciences through the application of artificial intelligence. The primary focus of his research is on facilitation of creation and execution of self-adaptable, interactive normative 3D environments and their subsequent application to the fields of agent-based simulation, as well as virtual and augmented realities.

Chapter 1
Introduction to Clara's World

In this book we will be learning to program in the Clara's World programming environment that is accessible online at `http://claraworld.net`. All programming problems that this book covers are to be solved using this environment. Clara, who is an animated character (ladybug), will be the central figure of this book. All the programming problems will involve Clara in one or another way.

In Appendix A you will find a detailed explanation of how to create an account on Clara's World and how to work with problems presented in this book. We recommend that you review Appendix A, create an account on Clara's World and locate the "Book" schedule and the corresponding chapter problems before continuing reading this book. A detailed guide on how to create an account on Clara's World is available in Appendix A.2. Follow the instructions listed in this guide and make sure that you select the "Book" organisation during registration. The organisation password for the "Book" organisation is "book2021" (without quotation marks). After regis-

© Springer Nature Switzerland AG 2021
A. Bogdanovych, T. Trescak, *Learning Java Programming in Clara's World*,
https://doi.org/10.1007/978-3-030-75542-3_1

tering you will need to activate your account by following the instructions that will be sent to the email address that was provided during registration. After successful activation of your account you should be able to login to Clara's World and see the "Book" schedule. This schedule contains all problems and exercises covered in this book. Direct links to such problems will be provided throughout the book.

1.1 Meet Clara

Let us meet our hero, Clara. Clara is a ladybug, who we will be referring to as a female. At the start of this book she is rather primitive. However, as we progress through the book, Clara will be getting more intelligent. For now, all she can do is follow a small set of your commands. Clara is extremely obedient. If you ask her to do something it is guaranteed that she does it.

1.1.1 Clara's World

Clara lives in a strange discrete world that is separated into cells. These cells form streets (running horizontally) and avenues (running vertically). Clara's World keeps changing and will look different for every new problem that we have to solve. Figure 1.1 shows Clara in one of the versions of her world. The street where Clara is located at the start of an exercise will be referred to as the "first street", and the street on the opposite end of Clara's World is known as the "last street". Clara's World is usually populated with objects such as leaves, trees and mushrooms. Clara can interact with these objects by adding, removing and moving some of them.

Fig. 1.1: An Example of Clara's World.

Clara's World configuration is designed in the Clara Editor tool. After starting one of the exercises, Clara's World's original configuration will be loaded from the editor and displayed on the screen. Once Clara's World loads, you can modify it by dragging its elements around with your mouse. Figure 1.2 shows the result of moving one tree in the world from Figure 1.1.

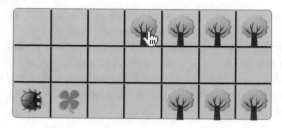

Fig. 1.2: Modifying Clara's World.

 There is a possibility of creating your own worlds in the Clara's World framework. You can experience the Clara Editor tool and experiment with creating your own worlds in the Sandbox environment available at `https://claraworld.net/link/Sandbox`.

1.1.2 Programming Clara

The state of Clara's World can be modified by instructing Clara to perform commands. The process of specifying commands that Clara must perform is called "**programming**". Commands in your program must be typed in a very precise way, otherwise Clara will not be able to understand them. If you type a command incorrectly or type something that is not a known command, Clara will not be able to follow your instructions. In this case your program will not run and Clara will report a "**compilation error**". A **complier** is a dedicated piece of software that checks your code for correctness and prepares your program for execution. Compilation errors are errors that are detected by the compiler. These are errors that prevent Clara's code from execution. Another type of errors that Clara might encounter are **runtime errors**. Runtime errors refer to illegal actions that happen during your program's execution. Examples of such actions involve attempting to walk into a tree, trying to remove a leaf that does not exist or attempting to place a leaf on top of a leaf.

Below is the list of the possible commands that Clara can execute.

Table 1.1: Clara's Commands

Command	Meaning
move()	Clara moves one step forward in the direction she is currently facing
turnRight()	Clara turns 90 degrees to the right
putLeaf()	Clara puts one leaf at her current position
removeLeaf()	Clara removes a leaf at her current position

Note that each command ends with empty parentheses "()". Using those is important for Clara to understand that what you are typing is not just some random text, but a valid command that she is expected to know how to respond to.

For Clara to respond to these commands, you need to type them in the correct place. Each practical problem in this book comes with a skeleton code. You must place your commands inside the skeleton code directly under the line that spells: "`// TODO: Write your code below`".

 Please make sure that you do not delete anything in the skeleton code, or you might run into a compilation error.

The skeleton code would typically look as follows.

```
/* PERMITTED COMMANDS
 * move, turnLeft, putLeaf, removeLeaf
 */

class MyClara extends Clara {
    /**
     * In the 'run()' method you can write your program for Clara
     */
    void run() {
       // TODO: Write your code below

    }
}
```

 If you accidentally remove something from the skeleton code, you can return the code to its original state by selecting "... → Reset Files" in the context menu that appears in the top right corner of the code editor as shown in Figure 1.3.

Further in this book we will explain all parts of this skeleton code. For now it is sufficient for you to know that your code must be placed immediately below the "`// TODO: Write your code below`" line.

Every time you instruct Clara to execute a particular command (e.g. move) Clara would act in response to this command given her current position and orientation. Each of the above commands would modify the state of Clara's world as described in Table 1.1. The `move()` command would make Clara disappear in the cell that she currently occupies and then reappear in the cell immediately next to it in the direction that Clara was facing. The `turnLeft()` command would change Clara's orientation by turning her counterclockwise by 90 degrees. The remaining two commands (`putLeaf()` and `removeLeaf()`) allow us to insert or remove leaves at the position that Clara currently occupies. Clara's environment features trees. Trees must be avoided as Clara moves around her world. It is impossible for Clara to occupy a cell that contains a tree. If Clara stands in front of a tree, trying to perform

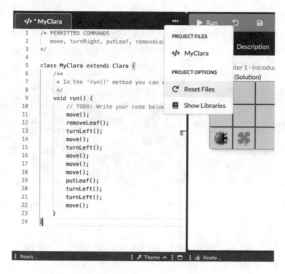

```
</>  * MyClara                              ...      ▶ Run    ↺    🖫
 1    /* PERMITTED COMMANDS              PROJECT FILES
 2       move, turnRight, putLeaf, removeLea
 3    */                                 </> MyClara            Description
 4
 5    class MyClara extends Clara {      PROJECT OPTIONS      pter 1 - Introduc
 6       /**                                                  (Solution)
 7        * In the 'run()' method you can v   C  Reset Files
 8        */                                  🖿 Show Libraries
 9       void run() {
10          // TODO: Write your code belov
11          move();
12          removeLeaf();
13          turnLeft();
14          move();
15          turnLeft();
16          move();
17          move();
18          move();
19          putLeaf();
20          turnLeft();
21          turnLeft();
22          move();
23       }
24    )|
  Ready...                     Theme ∧  □    Ready...
```

Fig. 1.3: Resetting Skeleton Files.

the `move()` command would result in a runtime error and your program would terminate.

Now that Clara and her world have been introduced, let us give some meaning to our further discussion and present a simple problem [1].

1.2 Chapter Problem: Leaf Delivery

Clara found a nice juicy leaf in the forest and wants to store it in her secure home before other bugs get to it. Clara is positioned at the bottom left corner in her world and faces east. The leaf is right in front of her in the adjacent cell. The home is represented by a box surrounded by trees. Clara must carry the leaf to the first empty cell inside this box. Once the leaf is delivered, she must step away from the leaf and hide at the back of her home. Figure 1.4 a) outlines the initial state of Clara's world and Figure 1.4 b) shows the resulting state after correct execution of your program.

Image features the "Leaf" 3D model by Thunk3D scanner available under Creative Commons CC BY 4.0.

---

[1] This book is structured in such a way that every chapter starts with a problem that we will then solve with the help of the new material that the corresponding chapter covers.

To work on this problem in Clara's World please use the following URL: `https://claraworld.net/link/C1P1`.

Fig. 1.4:   a) Initial World   b) Resulting World.

Let us now see how this problem can be solved using the aforementioned Clara commands. In order to start solving it you must open the corresponding problem on the Clara's World website (`http://claraworld.net`). After you open the website and find the problem there, you will see a window that looks similar to Figure 1.5. Let us have a quick look at what is shown there.

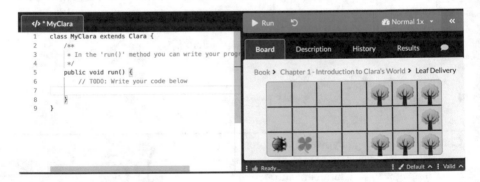

Fig. 1.5: The First Clara Problem.

1.2.1 Introducing Clara's World Framework

On the left-hand side you see a window for typing the "code" of your program for Clara to execute. At this point we will not be explaining the meaning of the text that appears there. What is important at this stage is not to delete any of this text and that you can type your commands and then execute them by pressing the "Run" button in the window that appears on the right-hand side. This window shows the current state of Clara's world. After you press the "Run" button it would be updated in response to executing your commands. Your commands must appear under the following text: `// TODO: Write your code below`. The "}" symbol must appear immediately after your last command.

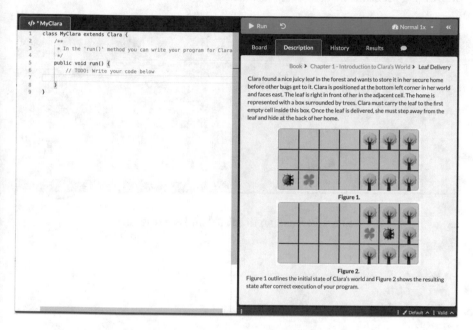

Fig. 1.6: Reading the Problem Description.

Every problem comes with a description that explains what you must achieve in solving the problem and shows an image or images that outline how the resulting state of Clara's World is expected to look on successful execution of your program. This description is available after selecting the "Description" tab in the top menu on the right-hand side of the Clara's World framework. Figure 1.6 depicts the description for our first problem. After reading the problem's description you should select the "Board" tab again, so that you can see the result of running your code.

1.2.2 Changing Clara's World Appearance

Our framework supports having different appearances for tiles and characters in Clara's World. You can choose an appearance that you prefer in the bottom right corner of the interface. Figure 1.5 shows the chapter problem using the "Default" appearance. For better readability in this book we have designed a custom appearance called "Light". An example of selecting the "Light" appearance for our chapter problem is shown in Figure 1.7. Here all visual elements (trees, Clara, leaf, empty cells) look different to what we saw when "Default" appearance was selected. Notice that the bottom right corner of Figure 1.7 now spells "Light" instead of "Default". Further in this book we will predominantly use the "Light" appearance for illustrating problems that are being discussed.

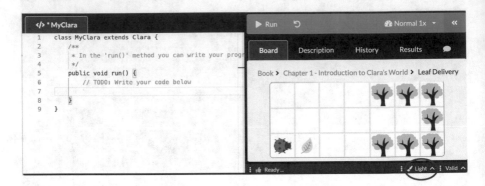

Fig. 1.7: Reading the Problem Description.

1.2.3 Working with Multiple Worlds

A good programmer should always attempt to come up with the most generic solution possible, meaning that the same code should work in many similar worlds. We will be returning to this idea multiple times further in the book. For now it is important for you to know that many problems presented in this book will come with multiple example worlds. Where multiple worlds are present, it is expected that your code correctly works with all such worlds.

Figure 1.8 shows how to select "World #2" for our chapter problem using the menu at the top. This world looks very similar to "World #1" that we saw in Figure 1.5. The only difference is some additional white space that is present due to World #2 being slightly larger.

1.2.4 Solving the Chapter Problem

What we want to produce for our first program is a set of instructions that would change the state of Clara's World from what is shown in Figure 1.4 a) to the world outlined in Figure 1.4 b). Let us think how this could be achieved. Clara currently stands at the bottom left corner. She faces east, and there is a leaf one step ahead in the direction that she faces. The first mini-task we have to complete is to pick up

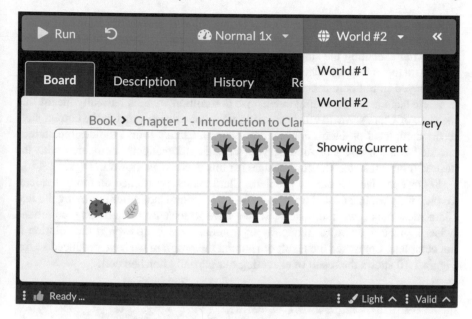

Fig. 1.8: Switching between Different Worlds.

the leaf. Clara does not have long arms, her arms are tiny, so it is not possible for her to pick it up from her current position. Thus, before she can pick up the leaf she must move to the same position where the leaf is located. Since the leaf is just one step away, we can simply type `move()` and Clara would appear on top of the leaf as shown in Figure 1.9.

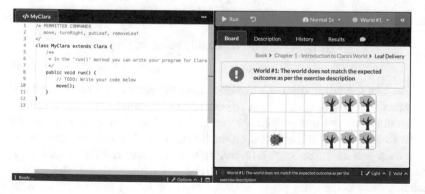

Fig. 1.9: Typing our First Command.

The code on the left-hand side of Figure 1.9 only has one command, `move()`. Notice that after this command there is a semicolon. For Clara to be able to correctly separate one command from another it is important to end every command with a semicolon. The picture on the right-hand side illustrates the result of running our code. After executing the single command in our program (move()) Clara is now located on top of the leaf. One more thing to pay attention to is the error message that is displayed in red colour above Clara's world. This error message spells: "World 1: World state is not according to exercise description", which basically means that the state of Clara's World after executing your code doesn't match the correct state of the completed problem. For each problem in Clara's World the desired state is encoded and the result of running your code is automatically compared with the desired (correct) state. The correct state for this exercise is shown in Figure 1.4 b).

Let us continue solving the problem. Clara is now positioned on top of the leaf. To pick it up we must use the removeLeaf() command. After removing the leaf Clara must make two more steps, so we have to execute the move() command twice. I encourage you to frequently try running your code even if the solution is not complete. Let us see the result of running the program we have produced so far. Figure 1.10 shows the result of executing our partially finished code.

Fig. 1.10: Running a Partially Finished Program.

Now Clara stands in front of a tree that marks the entry to her home. At this stage we want Clara to turn left, but in the list of available commands there is no command that would result in Clara performing the right turn. However, there is a way out; an alternative to turning left is turning right three times. To make her enter the home we must repeat the turnRight() command three times and then move(). After execution of the program containing these two new commands we would see Clara standing next to the entry point, but she would be facing north instead of facing east. Making Clara turn right again would make her orient to the east. Let us see how the updated code should look. To increase the readability of the code in the book, from now on we will be showing the code as text instead of showing it as an image. We will also stop displaying all the elements of the programming framework when presenting the result of running the code; instead, we will only display Clara's

World. The relevant fragment of the code we have written so far and the result of
running it are shown below:

```
public void run() {
// TODO: Write your code below
    move();
    removeLeaf();
    move();
    move();
    turnRight();
    turnRight();
    turnRight();
    move();
  turnRight();
}
```

Before we continue with solving the problem it is important to introduce you to
some advanced functionality of the Java language. Java is the name of the language
Clara can understand and is the language in which we are writing all our programs.
This language supports the functionality of creating new commands. At this point
we could actually create a new command for turning left, so that this command can
be used later. This new command would have to be "explained" in terms of a sequence of existing commands. All new commands in Java must be created outside
the curly brackets { } of the run() command, in which all our current code re-
sides. Let us see how our complete program would look after we create the new
turnLeft() command.

```
public void run() {
// TODO: Write your code below
      move();
      removeLeaf();
      move();
      move();
      turnLeft();
      move();
      turnRight();
}

void turnLeft() {
      turnRight();
      turnRight();
      turnRight();
}
```

For now, creating new commands will start with the special keyword void. We
will later learn that a command may return a value, in which case we will be using another keyword, but let us abstract away from this complexity and focus on
commands that do not return a value. In this case the keyword void means that
a command that we create does not return a value. After the keyword void we
must type the name of this new command. This name is what you choose the new

command to be known as (turnLeft in our example). It must contain no spaces. So that Clara understand that what we have typed is a command, we must add two parentheses (). For now these parentheses will have nothing inside, but later in the book we will have commands that can receive input and in this case there will be additional elements inside the parentheses. Finally, each command must be defined. By defining a command we mean that each new command must be "explained" in terms of existing commands. In the case of our turnLeft() command, it is defined as three consecutive right turns. The definition of a command must appear inside the curly brackets { } associated with this command. These curly brackets are used to show where the definition of the new command begins (the "{" bracket) and where this definition ends (the "}" bracket).

Let us finish solving the chapter problem. What is left for us to do is to make Clara complete another move() then put a leaf and step away. Below is the completed program and the result of running it:

```
class MyClara extends Clara {
/**
 * In the 'run()' method you
    can write your program
    for Clara
 */
  public void run() {
// TODO: Write your code below
      move();
      removeLeaf();
      move();
      turnLeft();
      move();
      turnRight();
      move();
      move();
      putLeaf();
      move();
  }

  void turnLeft() {
      turnRight();
      turnRight();
      turnRight();
  }
}
```

 You can see a video explanation of how to solve this problem step-by-step at https://claraworld.net/link/C1V1.

The problem is solved. If we press the "Run" button Clara would start executing your code. She would do this in a sequential manner starting from the command that appears at the top (immediately after the line //TODO: Write your code below) and would continue with the next command immediately below. The code will keep executing in this way until the last command inside the curly brackets of run() is encountered. After running this last command Clara would successfully deliver the leaf. Congratulations, you have created your first Java program!

 Exercise: Shorter code is generally easier to understand. Most programmers try to make their code as short as possible. As an exercise in producing shorter code and learning advanced interactions with Clara's World try moving one tree so that Clara's World looks similar to what is shown in Figure 1.2. After changing the configuration of Clara's World, try shortening the above code and solving the modified version of the problem by making use of the fact that moving past the edge would make Clara reappear on the other side of her world.

1.3 Revised Problem: Leaf Delivery and Reset

Creating the first program was fun. What do you think would happen if you press the "run" button again after executing your program? The answer is: nothing will happen. Clara's world will not change, and you would see an error message saying that Clara ran into an obstacle. Let us analyse why instead of repeating the leaf delivery we see this error message. The reason for such strange behaviour is the state of Clara's world. For the code you have written to work correctly Clara's environment must be in a correct state, where Clara stands in the bottom left corner of her world, faces east with the leaf being directly in front of her. However, after executing the problem the state of Clara's world would change. She would stand in front of a tree with a leaf behind her. If we look at the code we have written, we would see that the first command inside run() is move(). But there is nowhere for Clara to move because she is facing a tree. Moving into a tree is not allowed, and this is the reason why you see the error message and the program terminates when you press "run" for the second time.

Let us now create a revised version of the program, in which after delivering the leaf Clara restores her environment to its original state so that it looks like Figure 1.4 a). In this case we should be able to run the program as many times as we wish with no error messages appearing on the screen.

Resetting Clara's world to its original state does not seem all that difficult. The first thing that you probably want to do is to make Clara turn around. You can achieve this by making two left turns, but let us again create a new turnAround() command. This new command would look like this:

```
void turnAround() {
    turnRight();
    turnRight();
}
```

Similar to how we created the turnLeft() command, turnAround() must be created outside of run(). Now that we are experienced computer programmers, let us start using correct terminology. In Java, commands are referred to as *methods*. Thus, turnAround() is a new method we have created. This method must be declared (a Java term that means created) outside of the run() method. Each method has its own pair of curly brackets. The code inside these brackets is called the *body* of a method, and the part before the curly brackets (e.g. void turnLeft()) is called the method *header*. When you press the "run" button your program executes starting from the first line of code appearing inside the body of the run() method.

There is an informal agreement between Java programmers that all methods start with a lower-case letter. Names that contain multiple words are combined into one word (with no spaces), and each actual new word in it starts with an upper-case letter. Another Java specific thing that is important to understand at this stage is the fact that your entire program is also contained inside a pair of curly brackets. Let us see our latest version of the program. Your run(), turnLeft() and turnAround() methods are placed inside a pair of curly brackets that start after class MyClara extends Clara and end on the very last line of the code shown below:

```
/* PERMITTED COMMANDS: move, turnRight, putLeaf, removeLeaf
 */
class MyClara extends Clara {
/**
 * In the 'run()' method you can write your program for Clara
 */
  public void run() {
  // TODO: Write your code below
      move();
      removeLeaf();
      move();
      turnLeft();
      move();
      turnRight();
      move();
      move();
      putLeaf();
      move();
      turnAround();
  }

  void turnLeft() {
      turnRight();
      turnRight();
      turnRight();
  }

  void turnAround(){
      turnRight();
      turnRight();
  }
}
```

It is important to remember that all methods must be placed inside these curly brackets. Placing them outside would make your program incorrect and would result in an error.

The curly brackets in Java represent the beginning "{" and the end "}" of a block of code. You can use them anywhere in your code (we will later explain why this might be useful), but most of the time you will either be using them to show the beginning and the end of your method or the beginning and the end of your program.

Why is it so important to create new methods? One of the most important benefits is code reuse. If you have a feeling that a block of code might need to be repeated more than once, this means that it is a good idea to create a method around this block of code. As you will see, both turnAround() and turnLeft() will be repeated more than once in our program, so creating new commands for these is justified.

In the code above we have placed the turnAround() method as the last command inside run(). As the result of running our code Clara would deliver the leaf and would then turn around, so that she is facing west. Let us continue solving the revised version of the chapter problem. After turning around Clara must move to the leaf, pick it up and then continue moving and turning until she reaches the cell where the leaf was originally located. There she would have to place the leaf, step away and then turn around again. Below is the completed solution of the revised version of our program:

```
/* PERMITTED COMMANDS
   move, turnRight, putLeaf, removeLeaf
*/
class MyClara extends Clara {
    /**
     * In the 'run()' method you can write your program for Clara
     */
    public void run() {
        // TODO: Write your code below
        move();
        removeLeaf();
        move();
        turnLeft();
        move();
        turnRight();
        move();
        move();
        putLeaf();
        move();

        turnAround();
        move();
        removeLeaf();
        move();
        move();
        turnLeft();
        move();
        turnRight();
```

```
      move();
      putLeaf();
      move();
      turnAround();
   }

   void turnLeft() {
      turnRight();
      turnRight();
      turnRight();
   }

   void turnAround() {
      turnRight();
      turnRight();
   }
}
```

Now we have created a version of the problem in which the state before running the program is the same as after its execution. This allows us to run this code as many times as we want without receiving error messages. We encourage you to run this code a few times and modify the speed of execution in the drop down menu above Clara's world. Execution speed ranges from "Snail" to "Stellar".

 To see the solution of this problem in Clara's World please use the following URL: `https://claraworld.net/link/C1P1S`.

We have now learned the basics of programming in Clara's World. In the next chapter we continue learning more advanced constructs of the Java language.

1.4 Summary

In this chapter we learned about Clara the ladybug and practised creating programs that instruct Clara to move around her world and manipulate leaves in her environment. Clara is a very obedient insect. She never refuses to execute our commands as long as these are commands that she can recognise and they are written following the syntax of the Java programming language. At present she can only recognise four commands: `move()`, `turnRight()`, `putLeaf()` and `removeLeaf()`. By placing combinations of these commands inside the `run()` method we can make Clara follow our instructions and achieve the outcomes we desire. Clara follows our instructions by executing the commands she finds inside the `run()` method one-by-one from top to bottom. At the moment we can only achieve the outcomes we desire if the state of Clara's world exactly matches our expectations. In the following chapter we will show how to make Clara behave in a more flexible manner and will expand the vocabulary of commands she can execute.

1.5 Exercises

 Solving practical challenges is an important part of becoming a good programmer. You will find a set of practice exercises that target your understanding of the concepts covered in this chapter under the following link: https://claraworld.net/link/C1Ex.

Chapter 2
Flow of Control

In the previous chapter we learned about making Clara follow basic instructions in order to solve a simple problem. We produced code featuring a combination of the following four commands: `turnRight()`, `move()`, `putLeaf()` and `removeLeaf()`. Placing various combinations of such commands inside the `run()` method allowed us to change the state of Clara's World in the desired way and solve the problem at hand. What we have also learned is that these commands would execute sequentially, starting from the very first line inside the `run()` method until the last command there. This was empowering, but a little inflexible, because there was no mechanism to change the way our commands would execute. In this chapter we will learn the first simple mechanism of changing the execution flow (also known as the "flow of control"), so that we execute our code in a slightly more flexible manner than having to run one command after another in a sequential fashion. We will illustrate the concept of changing the flow of execution using the chapter story below.

Image features the "Cracks in asfalt road" 3D model by matousekfoto available under Creative Commons CC BY 4.0.

© Springer Nature Switzerland AG 2021
A. Bogdanovych, T. Trescak, *Learning Java Programming in Clara's World*,
https://doi.org/10.1007/978-3-030-75542-3_2

2.1 Chapter Story: Patching Roads

Performing repetitive tasks has long been imagined as something that machines could help us with. Many advocates of technological progress have been painting a future where all boring repetitive tasks are performed by machines and humans use their time and energy for doing something more creative and less trivial. Since the invention of the first steam engine we have being rapidly moving in this direction, as our technology has advanced to washing machines, industrial robots and even self-driving cars. There is, however, a lot of room left for further technological advances. One area where automation would make a lot of difference is fixing potholes on our roads. Potholes result in billions of dollars in car damage and are to blame for many car crashes and fatalities on our roads [10]. The problem is that fixing potholes is a costly and time-consuming process, while a timely repair could save funds and even lives. Researchers are working on automatic pothole detection [11], but automatically patching potholes remains an open problem. There have been, however, some developments in the area of pothole patching and even a successful patent application for a pothole repair machine [12].

Let us explain how this machine could be programmed in Clara's World. For simplicity, we would have to skip most of the technical implementation details and ignore many open problems. In her attempt to swiftly patch all the road holes, Clara will first concentrate on temporarily filling those up with leaves, replicating how road patching seems to occur in some countries.

2.2 Chapter Problem: Clara Patches Roads

Clara arrives in the city of Roadsville, which is famous for terrible roads. She decides to fix the situation and starts with the main road at the beginning of which she currently stands. The road is represented by one line of trees underneath Clara, but there are holes in this road at various places. Figure 2.1 a) shows an example of Clara's original position and the road with holes in it underneath Clara. Clara's task is to temporarily patch the road using leaves, so that it looks similar to Figure 2.1 b). At the end of each road in Roadsville (including the one Clara has to fix) there is a mushroom. Clara can use this mushroom as a road end indicator. If she encounters a mushroom, she will know that it is time to stop fixing the potholes. For simplicity, Clara can also count on the fact that each hole is one cell deep with a tree underneath.

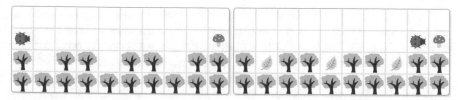

Fig. 2.1: a) Unpatched Road   b) Patched Road.

 To work on this problem in Clara's World please use the following URL:
`https://claraworld.net/link/C2P1`.

2.3 New Clara Commands

In Chapter 1 Clara was able to perform the commands shown in Table 2.1.

Table 2.1: Clara's Existing Commands

Command	Meaning
move()	Clara moves one step forward in the direction she is currently facing
turnRight()	Clara turns 90 degrees to the right
putLeaf()	Clara puts one leaf at her current position
removeLeaf()	Clara removes a leaf at her current position

With every new chapter Clara will not only solve more difficult and more interesting problems, but will also become more skilled and more intelligent. In this chapter her skills level will partially increase due to being able to execute the additional set of new commands shown in Table 2.2. Another part of her intelligence advancement comes from being able to change the flow of control, which is the key topic of this chapter.

Table 2.2: Clara's New Commands

Command	Meaning
turnLeft()	Clara turns 90 degrees to the left
treeFront()	Clara checks if there is a tree one cell in front
treeRight()	Clara checks if there is a tree on her right
onLeaf()	Clara checks if there is a leaf at her current position
mushroomFront()	Clara checks if there is a mushroom one cell in front
stop()	Terminate the execution of the program

The `turnLeft()` command will have the same functionality as the corresponding method that we created in Chapter 1 as an illustration of how new commands can be created in Java. Starting from this chapter we no longer need to define this command. Instead, it will remain in Clara's arsenal of default commands that she can execute. The following four commands (`treeFront()`, `treeRight()`, `onLeaf()` and `mushroomFront()`) will also become new standard Clara commands, but they will be working slightly differently to all the commands we saw earlier. These four new commands can be seen as sensors rather than actuators. Unlike actuators (commands that simply cause the state of Clara's World to change), sensors do not change the state of Clara's World, but help sense some aspects of this state. Actuators, such as `move()` or `turnLeft()`, simply instruct Clara to perform a particular action and do not expect any information to be reported back. These are methods that were defined to return no value (or `void`). In contrast to actuators, sensors, such as `treeFront()`, `treeRight()`, `onLeaf()` and `mushroomFront()`, simply return a value in the form of `true` or `false` in relation to a particular aspect of Clara's World. The `treeFront()` method would return the value of `true` if there is a tree immediately in front of Clara. The `treeRight()` command would return `true` if there is a tree to Clara's right. The `mushroomFront()` method would do the same for a mushroom in front. The `onLeaf()` method would return true if there is a leaf underneath Clara, and the value `false` is returned otherwise. Further in the book we will explain how working with these `true` and `false` values is supported in Java. The final new command that requires additional explanation is `stop()`. This command only works if it is used inside the `act()` method and will not work inside the `run()` method. The `stop()` command will terminate the execution of the `act()` method and the execution of the program respectively.

In all code examples within this chapter we will not be using the `run()` method, but the `act()` method will be used instead. It is, therefore, important to explain what the difference between those two methods is.

2.4 The Difference between `act()` and `run()`

In the previous chapter we wrote our code inside the `run()` method. The code we wrote inside `run()` was executed once, and then the program terminated after the execution of the last command was completed. In this chapter, however, we will be adding another method called `act()` and will be placing our code inside this new method instead of putting it inside `run()`. The difference between `act()` and `run()` lies in the fact that, instead of executing the code only once and terminating, the code that is placed inside the `act()` method will be executed again and again, until the stop() command is encountered. This means that the code placed inside `act()` will be executed in a number of iterations. Every iteration will begin with executing the very first commands inside the `act()` method and will finish after executing the last command. If there is no `stop()` command present inside `act()`

or any of other methods that are called within act(), the program would run infinitely (until artificially terminated from outside).

In every Clara's World program you are free to choose whether to use `act ()` or `run ()` for your code. It is important to remember that only one of these methods can be used in one program, meaning that you cannot have both `act ()` and `run ()` present in the same program.

2.5 Conditional Statements

Now that we have a set of new commands and can execute our program multiple times with the help of the `act ()` method, we are fully equipped to start learning new material and solving the chapter problem. *Flow of control* is the central concept of this chapter, so let us explain what it means.

In Chapter 1 we learned that the code we write will start executing from the very first command appearing at the top and will stop executing after the last command had finished running. Through running the example code from Chapter 1 we saw how our code was executing line-by-line from top to bottom. The order of command execution within the `run ()` method was linear: one command (also known as statement) was executed after another in sequence, and it was not possible to skip one of the commands. Flow of control is the order of statement execution. In this chapter we will learn how this order can be changed. The mechanism we will discuss here is the use of *conditional statements* that help to decide whether or not to execute a particular statement or to skip it. These decisions are based on a so-called **boolean** expression (also called a condition) that evaluates to `true` or `false`. When we introduced new Clara commands earlier in this chapter, we have shown that sensors such as `treeFront ()`, `mushroomFront ()` and `onLeaf ()` return exactly the values of `true` or `false`. These sensors are perfect candidates for being used inside conditional statements. In Java language, conditional statements (also known as `if`-statements) are employed for making the decision whether to execute a particular line of code or not depending on some condition being `true` or `false`. In their simplest form, conditional statements in Java have the following syntax:

```
if ( condition )
    statement;
```

In the code above the "`if`" statement is the element of the Java language known as the Java reserved keyword (an integral element of the Java language). The "condition" could be any boolean expression, meaning that it is an expression that evaluates to `true` or `false`. For now, this boolean expression will most commonly be a method call such as `treeFront ()`. The code above functions in the following manner. If the condition is `true`, the statement is executed. If it is `false`, the statement is skipped. Let us illustrate the use of `if`-statements with an example.

```
if ( mushroomFront() )
    stop();
```

Here `mushroomFront()` is the boolean condition that would be evaluated. In the situation illustrated in the picture above, `mushroomFront()` will return the value of `false` and, therefore, the `stop()` command will not be executed.

Note, that `mushroomFront()` is the command that returns a value. Its value is of boolean type, meaning that it can be either `true` or `false`. This is the first time that we encounter a command that returns a value. A detailed explanation of commands returning values and how to create such commands will be given in Chapter 8. For now, it is important to understand that there are commands that return values and that these values can be used inside `if`-statements to decide whether to execute the code that follows or not.

Some readers may find it easier to understand `if`-statements when the values `true` or `false` are explicitly mentioned similar to the code shown below.

```
if (mushroomFront() == true)
    stop();
```

The statement `if (mushroomFront() == true)` has exactly the same effect as `if( treeFront() )`, but it might be easier for some readers to relate to the former. The key difference is that in the example shown above we explicitly compare `mushroomFront()` versus `true` using the comparison operator `==`. The comparison operator tests whether the value on the left-hand side (`mushroomFront()` in our case) is equal to the value on the right-hand side (`true`). If they are equal the result of the comparison is `true` and is `false` otherwise. In the situation shown in the above picture the result of this comparison will be `true`, so the `stop()` command would execute and our program would terminate. Most readers would have no problems with understanding the above example, since they are familiar with the "if" concept of the English language and with the comparison operator from primary school mathematics. It is important to notice, however, that unlike primary school mathematics (where comparison operator would be expressed as "=") the comparison operator in Java language is "==".

Sometimes there are situations in programming when simply skipping a line of code when a certain condition is `false` is not enough and a more sophisticated conditioning mechanism is required. There are, for example, situations when we need to execute one command if the condition is `true` and another command when the condition is `false`. Such situations are supported through the use of the **else**-statement. In their general form the `else`-statements are used as follows:

```
if ( condition )
    statement1;
else
    statement2;
```

The above code functions in the following way. If the condition is true, statement1 is executed; if the condition is false, statement2 is executed. It is important to note that under no circumstances can both statement1 and statement2 be executed. Depending on the condition either statement1 or statement2 will execute, but never both. Let us illustrate the use of the else-statement with an example.

```
void act() {
      if ( mushroomFront() )
          stop();
      else
          move();
}
```

The code above uses the if-else statement inside the act() method as an attempt to start working towards solving the chapter problem. This code would make Clara move all the way from the start of the street to its end (marked with a mushroom). Remember, that placing your code inside the act() method will make it repeat until the stop() command is executed. Thus, the if-else statement will continue repeating until the mushroomFront() condition becomes true and the stop command is called as the result of sensing the mushroom at the end of the street.

At this stage we have enough knowledge about conditional statements to get us started with solving the chapter problem, so let us begin with the above code and think about how it could be extended.

2.6 Solving the Chapter Problem: Clara Patches Roads

Figure 2.2 illustrates the problem that Clara needs to solve. She appears at the beginning of an unpatched road and must patch it until the end, where she would encounter a mushroom and will then stop.

 A video that demonstrates solving this problem step-by-step is available at https:/claraworld.net/link/C2V1.

We already have the code to make Clara move until the end of the street. Let us extend it with one additional command fixRoad(). This command is something that we will define later, so for now it can be left empty. The resulting code at this stage and the state of Clara's World after running it would look as follows:

Fig. 2.2: a) Unpatched Road   b) Patched Road.

```
void act() {
   fixRoad();
   if ( mushroomFront() )
      stop();
   else
      move();
}

void fixRoad() {
}
```

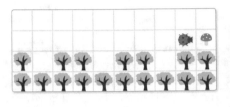

Please recall that everything we put inside the act() method is repeated until the stop() command is executed. So, Clara will first execute the currently empty fixRoad() command and will then attempt to move. These two commands (fixRoad() and move()) would continue repeating until Clara encounters a mushroom and then stop() will be executed instead of move().

Let us now think about how fixRoad() could be implemented. Given how our code is currently structured, the fixRoad() command would execute every time before Clara makes the next move. The intention behind having the fixRoad() method was to make Clara turn right before her next move and then to check whether there is a tree in front of Clara or not. Having a tree in front of Clara would mean that the corresponding segment of the road requires no patching, so Clara can turn left and continue. If there happens to be no tree then Clara would need to patch the hole in the road. The process of patching the hole does not seem straightforward at this stage, so let us create another method for this task and then think about how it could be implemented later. The code of the fixRoad() command could be written as follows:

```
void fixRoad() {
   turnRight();

   if (treeFront())
      turnLeft();
   else
      patchHole();
   }
}
```

Now the only part of our program that is left unfinished is the `patchHole()` method. This method will be executed in the situation when Clara has detected a hole in a segment of the road and is currently located on top of it (facing down). What we want to achieve within the `patchHole()` method is making a step forward, placing a leaf and then coming back to the road and orienting Clara so that she faces towards the mushroom. Thus, the `patchHole()` method could be written as follows:

```
void patchHole() {
    move();
    putLeaf();
    turnLeft();
    turnLeft();
    move();
    turnRight();
}
}
```

After defining the `patchHole()` method our solution is now complete. It is important to note that this solution would work on any road that ends with a mushroom, no matter how long the road is, how many holes are there and where these holes are located. As programmers you should always aim at writing such code that is generic, meaning that it does not just work with one particular example problem, but with many examples that match the same problem description. Such code is generally easier to understand and reuse.

The completed solution for the Clara Patches Road problem is shown below:

```
class MyClara extends Clara {
    /**
     * In the 'act()' method you can write your program for Clara
     */
    void act() {
        // TODO: Write your code below
        fixRoad();

        if ( mushroomFront() )
            stop();
        else
            move();
    }

    void fixRoad() {
        turnRight();

        if (treeFront())
            turnLeft();
        else
            patchHole();
    }
```

```
void patchHole() {
   move();
   putLeaf();
   turnLeft();
   turnLeft();
   move();
   turnRight();
}
}
```

 To see the solution of this problem in Clara's World please use the following URL: https://claraworld.net/link/C2P1S.

Hopefully, the patching roads exercise helped you to better understand how to use conditional statements in their simple form. Let us now cover this topic more extensively.

2.7 Logical Operators

Sometimes a need arises to combine multiple conditions. For example, we may require to execute a command only in situations when there is a tree in front of Clara and Clara is on a leaf. Java supports such scenarios through logical operators.

In Java there are three logical operators that are useful for working with conditional statements. These operators are "!" (logical NOT), "&&" (logical AND) and "||" (logical OR). Logical operators work in a very similar way to arithmetic operators (such as addition, subtraction or multiplication), but instead of working with numbers they work with boolean values (true and false). Logical operators also produce boolean values as the result.

Let us look at each of the logical operators one-by-one.

2.7.1 Logical NOT

Logical NOT is also known as logical negation. This operator inverts the boolean value that it is applied to. Let us have a look at an example of using logical negation. Below is the original version of a part of the chapter problem solution:

```
if ( mushroomFront() )
   stop();
else
   move();
```

The modified version of this code that uses the logical negation operator is as follows:

```
if ( !mushroomFront() )
    move();
else
    stop();
```

The latter code fragment would make Clara move when there is **no** mushroom in front of her and would make her stop otherwise. Both of these code fragments produce the same result, but the second version (that uses "!") is a more conventional way of solving the problem. It is more natural for programmers to think in which situations to move rather than to start thinking about stopping. Therefore, most programmers prefer using logical negation in their code for a situation like this.

Table 2.3: Truth Tables for Logical NOT

a	!a	treeFront()	!treeFront()
true	false	true	false
false	true	false	true

To better understand how logical negation works have a look at Table 2.3. The left-hand side of this table shows a general condition (a) and its negated version (!a). The right-hand side presents an example, where a is replaced with treeFront(). The table shows that the logical NOT operator effectively changes the boolean value to its opposite. If it applies to a value that is false, the result would be true and vice versa.

Logical NOT is a unary operator, meaning that it only requires one operand (the right-hand side) unlike the other two operators, logical OR and logical AND, which are binary operators (require both the left-hand side and the right-hand side operands). The closest example of a unary operator from arithmetic is the negative sign or "–" operator. It also requires the right-hand side only, and instead of reversing a boolean value it reverses the sign of a numeric value.

Let us provide another illustration of how the logical NOT can be used through a modification of our road patching example. Earlier we solved the road patching problem using the following code:

```
class MyClara extends Clara {
    void act() {
        // TODO: Write your code below
        fixRoad();

        if ( mushroomFront() )
            stop();
        else
            move();
    }
```

```
void fixRoad() {
   turnRight();

   if (treeFront())
      turnLeft();
   else
      patchHole();
}

void patchHole() {
   move();
   putLeaf();
   turnLeft();
   turnLeft();
   move();
   turnRight();
}
}
```

At the time of writing the above code, logical NOT has not yet been introduced. This was one of the key reasons why we had to create two methods (`fixRoad()` and `patchHole()`) for, essentially, a single purpose of patching the road when a hole was identified. Now that we know how to use "`!`" let us rewrite this code as follows:

```
class MyClara extends Clara {
   void act() {
      // TODO: Write your code below
      if ( !treeRight() )
         patchHole();

      if ( mushroomFront() )
         stop();
      else
         move();
   }

   void patchHole() {
      turnRight();
      move();
      putLeaf();
      turnLeft();
      turnLeft();
      move();
      turnRight();
   }
}
```

This new version of the code is much shorter and, therefore, much easier to understand. It is also more efficient, because in the past we had to turn right after every step to check for a potential hole in the road. With the use of the `treeRight()`

command we would only turn if there is a hole to be fixed and would keep moving otherwise, eliminating the need to turn if there is no hole.

2.7.2 Logical AND

Another logical operator (binary in this case) is logical AND. In Java, logical AND is expressed as "&&". In order for the result of `&&` to become `true` both the left-hand side and the right-hand side must be `true`. In any other case the result will be `false`. Essentially, `&&` is an operator that merges two boolean values into one, where the result would only be `true` if both of these are `true` and will be `false` in any other case. Let us have a look at Table 2.4. It covers all possible values of general a and b conditions (something that can be replaced by any command or expression that return a boolean value) and shows the result of applying the `&&` operator to those. Table 2.5 illustrates how the `&&` operator would work if applied to `treeFront()` and `onLeaf()`, which are example boolean methods that illustrate what a and b could be substituted with.

Table 2.4: Truth Tables for Logical AND

a	b	a && b
true	true	true
true	false	false
false	true	false
false	false	false

Table 2.5: Logical AND with `treeFront()` and `onLeaf()`

treeFront()	onLeaf()	treeFront()&&onLeaf()
true	true	true
true	false	false
false	true	false
false	false	false

Logical operators are very useful in conditional statements. Let us have a look at an example of using the combination of logical NOT and logical AND for testing whether Clara should keep on moving in our road patching scenario.

```
if ( treeRight() && !mushroomFront() )
    move();
```

Following the logic from the above example, Clara would only move if both `treeFront()` and `!mushroomFront()` are true. This is a compact way of making sure that Clara moves if there is a tree to her right (no hole in the road) and at the same time would not attempt to move into a mushroom if one is in front of her. Handling the situation when there is no tree to her right (a hole in the road) and patching the hole will be covered later in this chapter.

2.7.3 Logical OR

Logical OR is another binary operator that merges two boolean values into one. It has a slightly obscure syntax "`||`", but works in quite an intuitive way. Either the left-hand side or the right-hand side must be `true` for the resulting boolean value to be `true`. Only for the case when both the left-hand side and the right-hand side are `false`, the resulting value will be `false`. Let us have a look at Table 2.6. Here we show two general conditions (a and b), where a represents the left-hand side and b represents the right-hand side of the logical OR operator. Table 2.7 illustrates how this operator works for the case where general conditions a and b are replaced with `treeFront()` and `onLeaf()`.

Table 2.6: Truth Tables for Logical OR

a	b	a || b
true	true	true
true	false	true
false	true	true
false	false	false

Table 2.7: Logical OR with `onLeaf()` and `treeFront()`

treeFront()	onLeaf()	treeFront() || onLeaf()
true	true	true
true	false	true
false	true	true
false	false	false

Let us have a look at an example of using logical OR for testing whether Clara should stop or not.

```
if ( treeFront() || mushroomFront() )
    stop();
```

In the above example Clara would travel along a street, but there is a possibility of encountering both a mushroom and a tree in front of Clara, and in both such situations Clara must stop. The tree in this case would represent debris that might appear on the road. In this scenario, the use of the logical OR statement would allow Clara to stop if either a tree or a mushroom appears in front of Clara. This is very different from using logical AND, where both logical conditions must be true for the corresponding statement to execute.

2.8 Short-Circuited Operators

This is a rather advanced topic, but is still worth mentioning. The processing of logical AND and logical OR is short-circuited. Short-circuiting means that, if the left-hand side of the logical operand is sufficient to determine the result, the right-hand side operand is not evaluated.

Let us explain this point on an example. Imagine you have the following code in your program:

```
if ( treeFront() || mushroomFront() )
    stop();
```

Short-circuiting in this case would mean that if `treeFront()` is `true` then it does not really matter what the value of `mushroomFront()` is and the `stop()` command will be executed regardless of whether `mushroomFront()` is `true` or `false`. With this idea in mind Java language creators have decided not to waste processing time and not to execute the right-hand side (e.g. the `mushroomFront()` command) in such situations for optimisation purposes.

The key lesson learned here is that commands that appear on the right-hand side of a logical operator might not execute because of Java optimisation. Thus, it could be a critical mistake for a developer creating a command similar to `mushroomFront()` in such a way that it does anything else functional besides testing the mushroom and returning `true` or `false` depending on its location. As a developer you should avoid things like moves or turns or anything else that modifies the state of Clara's world within such commands simply because these world state modifications might not occur due to short-circuiting.

2.9 The Precedence of Logical Operators

Conditions can use logical operators to form complex expressions such as

```
if( treeRight() && !mushroomFront() && !treeFront() )
    move();
```

It is important to know that logical operators work in a similar way to arithmetic operators in mathematics in that they also share certain precedence rules. Similar to how multiplication has higher precedence than addition in mathematics, logical Not has a higher precedence than both logical OR and logical AND. In the case of the aforementioned example this means that !mushroomFront() and !treeFront() are evaluated first and are converted into true or false before testing the value of treeRight() and applying the logical AND operator.

2.10 Statement Blocks and Nested if-statements

Another important topic related to using conditional statements is conditionally executing multiple statements. In our earlier examples each if or else statement was responsible for conditionally executing a single line of code. Sometimes, however, it may be necessary to conditionally execute multiple lines of code. Java supports this functionality through the use of curly brackets "{...}". Enclosing a number of statements within curly brackets creates a conditionally executed statement block. Statement blocks may relate both to an if condition and to an else condition.

The statement executed as a result of an if statement or else clause could be another if-statement. These are called *nested* if-statements. In such situations an else clause is matched to the last unmatched if (no matter what the indentation implies). Curly brackets can be used to prescribe which if-statement belongs to which else clause.

To illustrate the idea of using statement blocks and nested if-statements let us imagine a situation where Clara travels along a road that may have occasional debris present (similar to what we saw in the logical OR example). This time Clara decides to act more intelligently in this situation and instead of simply stopping she would attempt to climb over the debris and then to continue patching the road until the end of it (marked with a mushroom). The code below illustrates how this behaviour modification could be implemented:

```
if ( treeFront() || mushroomFront() ) {
    if ( treeFront() ) {
        turnLeft();
        move();
        turnRight();
        move();
        move();
        turnRight();
        move();
        turnLeft();
    }
    else
        stop();
}
```

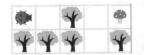

As before, we first test for either a tree or a mushroom being in front of Clara, but instead of just stopping we have another if-statement inside. This nested if-statement takes care of climbing over possible debris on the road. Inside the associated set of curly brackets there is code that would make Clara walk over a tree and then face a correct direction. Finally, there is also an else-statement that handles the scenario of Clara encountering a mushroom and stopping if she does.

2.11 Road Patching Example with Logical Operators

Now that we have explained how logical operators work, let us see how the road patching example could be modified to support Clara climbing over debris. In this new version of the road patching code whenever Clara encounters a tree on the main road she does not stop, but will climb over it. In addition, we also wanted to modify the original code so that we can illustrate the use of logical operators, nested conditional statements and statement blocks. The resulting code is shown below:

 To see the solution of this problem in Clara's World please use the following URL: https://claraworld.net/link/C2P2S.

```
class MyClara extends Clara {
    /**
     * In the 'run()' method write your program for Clara
     */
    void act() {
        // TODO: Write your code below
        if (treeFront() || mushroomFront()) {
            if (treeFront()) {
                if (!treeRight() )
                    patchHole();
                climbOverDebris();
            }
            else
                stop();
        }

        if (treeRight() && !mushroomFront())
            move();
        else {
            if (!treeRight())
                patchHole();
            if (mushroomFront())
                stop();
            else
                move();
        }
    }
```

```
void patchHole() {
    turnRight();
    move();
    putLeaf();
    turnLeft();
    turnLeft();
    move();
    turnRight();
}

void climbOverDebris() {
    turnLeft();
    move();
    turnRight();
    move();
    move();
    turnRight();
    move();
    turnLeft();
}
}
```

 A video showing solving this problem step-by-step is available at `https:/claraworld.net/link/C2V2`.

Here we have created an additional method `climbOverDebris()` to support walking over an occasional tree appearing on Clara's path. This method is called inside `act()` in situations when `treeFont()` is `true`. Note that in this updated version of the code we have created a logical condition testing for either having a tree in front of Clara or having a mushroom in front of Clara. Whenever this combined condition (`treeFront() || mushroomFront()`) becomes `true` we will either stop (if a mushroom is in front of Clara) or climb over debris (if a tree is in front of Clara).

Here the use of logical OR allows us to have a choice of either one or another condition to become true for the block of code (inside the curly brackets) to execute. This is very different from another condition featuring logical operators that appears within `act()`. In the case of the `if (treeRight() && !mushroomFront() )` condition, the associated `move()` command would only execute if there is a tree to Clara's right and there is no mushroom in front of Clara simultaneously. Only having no mushroom in front or only a tree on Clara's right is not enough. Also note the use of the curly brackets to support multiple commands being conditionally executed. We have such blocks of commands associated with `if`-statements (`if (treeFront() || mushroomFront() )`, as well as with `else`-statements (`else { if (!treeRight) ... }`). As you can see, a statement block can be associated with both an `if` and an `else` part of a conditional statement.

Exercise: The above code is, of course, a little redundant and could have been rewritten in a more compact form, but it illustrates the use of various types of conditional statements. As an exercise you should attempt shortening this code and removing unnecessary conditions.

2.12 Conditional Operator

In their attempt to reduce the amount of typing that programmers must perform, Java creators included a conditional operator (?) that can be used in your code. In general form this operator looks as follows:

```
condition ? statement1() : statement2();
```

The above code means that `statement1()` will execute if the value of `condition` is `true` or otherwise `statement2` will execute. This represents a short version of the following code:

```
if (condition)
   statement1();
else
   statement2();
```

Below is an example of how the conditional operator (also known as ternary operator) can be used for making Clara stop if there is a tree in front or move otherwise:

```
treeFront() ? stop() : move();
```

Despite the fact that using this operator results in shorter code, it is not very popular with developers because the resulting code is more difficult to understand. Most developers prefer using `if`-statements instead of the conditional operator.

2.13 Common Errors

Beginner programmers often make similar errors. Below we list the most common mistakes related to conditional statements that we often see in student code.

2.13.1 Indentation and the Use of Curly Brackets

You may have noticed that, in the code presented in this book, commands that appear inside every conditional statement are indented (moved to the right). To remind you what indentation is, here is an example:

```
if ( onLeaf() )
   removeLeaf();
```

In this example the `removeLeaf()` command starts four spaces away to the right in comparison with the associated condition (`if( onLeaf() )`. Indentation in programming is widely used for better code readability. We will provide a detailed explanation of code formatting in Chapter 4, where the use of indentation is fully explained. What we wanted to mention here is that many beginner programmers quickly grasp the idea of using indentation, but often use it incorrectly. Let us consider the example shown below:

```
if ( onLeaf() )
   removeLeaf();
   move();
```

The indentation here implies that commands `removeLeaf()` and `move()` are grouped together and that both will only execute when Clara is on a leaf. However, this is not the case. Unlike other programming languages (e.g. Python) Java does not take code indentation into account when executing your code. If there are no curly brackets present it is always assumed in Java that only the first line of code that appears immediately after the if-statement would be conditionally executed. Thus, Java "understanding" of the above code would be as follows:

```
if ( onLeaf() )
   removeLeaf();

move();
```

The `move()` command would execute regardless of the `( onLeaf() )` condition. If it is required that more than one command is conditionally executed you must use curly brackets. Below is the modified example that illustrates this idea:

```
if ( onLeaf() ) {
   removeLeaf();
   move();
}
```

2.13.2 More Formatting Errors

Another common mistake related to code formatting and indentation is illustrated by the example below:

```
if ( treeFront() )
    if (onLeaf() )
       move();
else
   stop();
```

After looking at this example many of you would see nothing wrong. Indeed, this is a completely correct snippet of Java code. The only thing that is wrong with it is incorrect indentation. The indentation above implies that the `else`-statement is associated with `if( treeFront() )`, but this is not the case. As mentioned previously, Java completely ignores indentation when your code is being executed. The principle that Java uses to decide which `if`-statement does an `else`-statement belong to is as follows: Every `else` will **always** be associated with the closest `if`-statement that is immediately above. Therefore, the `else`-statement in the above example would be associated with `if( onLeaf() )` and Java's reading of the above code would be as follows.

```
if ( treeFront() )
   if (onLeaf() )
      move();
   else
      stop();
```

2.13.3 Using Semicolons

Many of you will have noticed that almost every line in our code ends with a semi-colon. Practically speaking, semicolons are a relic of the past that Java has borrowed from other programming languages in which it was common to put multiple commands on one line and ";" helped to separate different commands. Most modern Java programmers do not put multiple commands on one line, so semicolons could have easily being discarded in a similar way as in the Python programming language. However, we do still use semicolons in Java, and some beginner programmers often get confused and incorrectly use it with conditional statements similar to the example below:

```
if ( onLeaf() );
   removeLeaf();
```

Here putting the semicolon after the `if`-statement is incorrect and would result in a **compilation error** (the kind of error that prevents your code from executing). In Java the entire `if`-statement together with the conditionally executed statements (its body) is treated as one command, and, therefore, the semicolon is not required. The correct code for the above example would have been as follows:

```
if ( onLeaf() )
   removeLeaf();
```

2.13.4 Issues with Explicit Mentioning of *true* and *false*

Earlier in this chapter we mentioned that for some programmers it may be easier
to understand conditional statements if they explicitly mention true and false
values in their code. It is completely fine to do this, but with experience many programmers grow out of this habit (mainly because using explicit true and false
values is associated with additional typing). An example we used in the beginning
of this chapter to illustrate explicit use of true is making Clara stop if there is a
mushroom in front, expressed in the following way:

```
if (mushroomFront() == true}
   stop();
```

One of the problems associated with this coding strategy is that beginner programmers often forget that, unlike mathematics, in Java language comparison of
two values (==) and assigning a value (=) are two different operators. A typical
beginner mistake would have been to code the above example in the following way:

```
if (mushroomFront() = true}
   stop();
```

This code would result in a compilation error, because instead of testing whether
the value of mushroomFront() is true or not, the above code snippet would be
trying to assign the value of true to the mushroomFront() method. Assigning a value to a method is not allowed in Java and makes little sense in general.
Thus, if you find it useful to explicitly refer to true and false inside conditional
statements, it is important to remember that the comparison operator == and not the
assignment operator = must be used in these situations.

2.14 Summary

In this chapter we learned about changing the flow of code execution. With the help
of conditional statements (also known as if-statements) we can make a decision
about whether to perform a command or not depending on a certain condition being
true or false. Clara has acquired the sense of touch and new commands among
which are sensors such as treeFront(), treeRight() and onLeaf(). With
the help of these commands she is now able to change her behaviour depending on
what she encounters in her environment.

2.15 Exercises

 Exercises that target your understanding of the concepts covered in this chapter are available at `https://claraworld.net/link/C2Ex`.

Chapter 3
Loops

Computers are very good at repetition. They can tirelessly execute a set of instructions as many times as required without losing precision or making mistakes. In solving problems with Clara you will often see the need to execute some of your code multiple times, while for other parts of your program this will not be required. In Chapter 2 we learned that placing your commands inside the `act()` method would make them repeated until a particular condition (like `treeFront()`) can be sensed within an `if`-statement, so that the `stop()` command can be used to finish your program. But what if we need to repeat something a certain number of times rather than waiting for some condition to become true? Or what if some parts of your program must be repeated and other parts not?

In this chapter we will learn about different types of loops in Java. With the help of loops we can execute a set of commands multiple times and have more control over what to repeat compared with using the `act()` method. But before exploring the theory behind loops let us start with the chapter story.

© Springer Nature Switzerland AG 2021

A. Bogdanovych, T. Trescak, *Learning Java Programming in Clara's World*,
https://doi.org/10.1007/978-3-030-75542-3_3

3.1 Chapter Story:Vacuum Cleaner Robots

Many of us imagined a future where our households are swarming with different kinds of robots. Indeed, there are many static robots around us that help with household chores, such as dish washers and washing machines, however we rarely see mobile robots that can navigate around our homes. One of the rare examples of mobile household robots are robotic vacuum cleaners (see Figure 3.1).

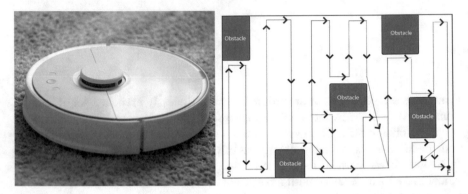

Fig. 3.1: a) Typical Vacuum Cleaner Robot   b) Robot's Navigation Chart.

In the early days of artificial intelligence developing vacuum cleaner robots was a standard mental exercise and a toy problem presented in many books, talks and lectures. It was often portrayed as a challenge that is very difficult to overcome. One of the problems that was considered to be very complicated in this domain is identifying whether there is any dirt at a particular location or not, so that the robot knows where to clean. But in reality this ended up being an artificial problem. If you recall how you would vacuum clean your home, you would realise that you do not try to locate dirt on your carpet to then walk there and clean it. Instead, you will start at one end of the area that you need to clean and would try covering the entire area in a sequential fashion until you reach the other end.

Figure 3.1 b) shows how a modern vacuum cleaner robot would perform a similar task. The robot would start at one end of the room (S) and would try to cover the area that needs cleaning by moving on a straight line from one wall to another (avoiding obstacles along the way). Once the robot reaches the wall, it will then make a step along it and will try to come back to the opposite wall. This behaviour will be repeated until the robot cleans the entire room and reaches the opposite end of the room (F).

How does this relate to Clara, you might ask? Now that we know the key principle behind vacuum cleaning, it is time for Clara to mimic this behaviour and become the vacuum cleaning super hero!

3.2 Chapter Problem: Clara the Vacuum Cleaner Robot

Clara has been partying all night. She wakes up in the morning alone in her apartment, and there is rubbish everywhere. Clara must turn into a vacuum cleaner robot and remove all the rubbish. Her apartment is a studio with only one room covering the entire flat. She is a poor ladybug and cannot afford furniture, which makes her apartment perfect for dancing and means that she does not need to worry about avoiding obstacles as she cleans. Clara's apartment is quite large. Its size is 10 metres x 10 metres.

Image features the "Saturnas vacuum cleaner" 3D model by Sergey Khanin available under Creative Commons CC BY 4.0.

 To work on this problem in Clara's World please use the following URL: https://claraworld.net/link/C3P1.

Let us look at this scenario in Clara's World. The ladybug is initially positioned in the bottom left corner of her studio apartment, as shown in Figure 3.2 a). The walls of the apartment are represented by trees. The rubbish that she must clean is represented by leaves. The leaves are spread around in a random pattern. Clara must sequentially move throughout her apartment and clean all the leaves. The result should look similar to Figure 3.2 b).

You might already have an idea about how to solve this problem using move(), turnLeft() and removeLeaf() commands that can be placed inside the act() method and be repeated until the room is clean. But how would you know when to call the stop() command to terminate your program? Let us look at the new concept that would help us with answering this question.

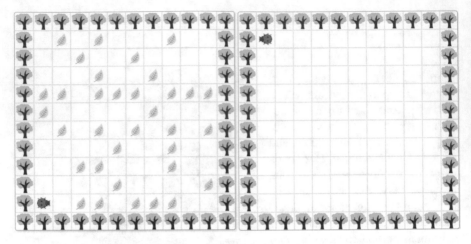

Fig. 3.2: a) Apartment before Cleaning   b) Apartment after Cleaning.

3.3 Loops

Java language offers a controlled way of repeating the execution of a set of commands via *loops*. One or more commands can be placed inside a loop structure and be repeated a desired number of times. There are two types of loops: *count-controlled loops* and *conditional loops*. Let us first look at the count-controlled loops. These are useful if you know exactly how many times to repeat something. For example, if Clara needs to turn right, she effectively has to repeat the turnLeft() command three times. In the previous chapters we have simply duplicated the turnLeft() command three times, which was not too difficult, but what if Clara needs to repeat something 1000 times? Count-controlled loops (the most common of which is a for loop) provide a much better mechanism of code repetition than simply duplicating the commands in your code like we did for turnRight().

3.4 The for Loop

In some situations (like in the scenario portrayed by the chapter problem) we know exactly how many times to repeat the code. We know the size of Clara's apartment and if we have the code for cleaning one square metre then we know that this operation would have to be repeated as many times as how many square metres her apartment contains (100 times for the apartment that is 10 metres x 10 metres). One of the constructs of Java language that allows to create a count-controlled loop is the for loop. The general syntax of the for loop is

```
for (initialisation; testing; update) {
    statement(s) to be repeated;
}
```

The `for` loop allows a programmer to initialise a loop counter, test a condition and modify the loop counter once per loop iteration all in one line of code. The first line of the loop starting with the Java reserved keyword `for` is the loop header. Note that the three parts of the loop (initialisation, testing and update) are separated by semicolons. These semicolons are compulsory and cannot be omitted (notice that there is no semicolon after the third part). Inside the curly brackets {} you should put any code that you want repeated.

Initialisation, testing and update sections can have various forms, but for our purpose of quickly solving the vacuum cleaning problem let us agree on using the following standard form for now:

```
for (int i = 0; i < numberOfRepetitions; i++) {
    statement(s) to be repeated;
}
```

Most of the time even the `for` loops created by experienced programmers would have a similar form. In this simplified version of the `for` loop the initialisation part would remain unchanged as (`int i = 0;`). The update part (`i++`) would also require no modification. The only part that would change from one loop to another is testing (`i < numberOfRepetitions`). This testing part allows the programmer to specify how many repetitions are required. Here `numberOfRepetitions` is not a Java keyword. It should be substituted by the actual number of how many times you want the code inside the curly brackets (also known as the *body of the loop*) to be repeated.

3.4.1 Examples of Using the for Loop.

Let us postpone the detailed explanation of the above code and ignore the meaning of the `for` loop's header until after solving the chapter problem. The only part of the header that should interest us at the moment is the "numberOfRepetititons". Changing the "numberOfRepetititons" to any number (e.g. 3) would make the loop repeat this many times. Below is an example of the actual Java code that uses the above template:

```
for (int i = 0; i < 3; i++) {
    turnRight();
}
```

This code is equivalent to

```
turnRight();
turnRight();
turnRight();
```

As we learned in Chapter 1, making three right turns is the same as turning left. If we assume that Clara's orientation before executing this code was similar to that shown in Figure 3.3 a) then after executing the above `for` loop her orientation would be similar to that shown in Figure 3.3 b).

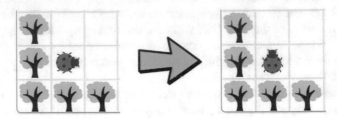

Fig. 3.3:   a) Original Orientation   b) Orientation after the `for` Loop.

Let us look at more examples of using the `for` loop. Notice that the only difference in the examples below is the number of repetitions, while the rest of the code is identical. In both examples below we assume that Clara's orientation prior to executing the code was similar to that shown in Figure 3.3 a).

```
for(int i = 0; i < 2; i++) {
    turnRight();
}
```

After running this code Clara will make two right turns (will turn around).

```
for(int i = 0; i < 4; i++) {
    turnRight();
}
```

And here Clara will make four right turns (idle turn) and her resulting orientation will be the same as her original orientation.

3.4.2 Solving the Chapter Problem with *for* Loops

Now that we have a basic understanding of how to repeat a set of Java statements with the `for` loop, it is time to start creating the program that would turn Clara into the vacuuming super hero.

A video that demonstrates solving this problem step-by-step is available at https:/claraworld.net/link/C3V1.

After we open the problem in the programming environment we would see the following template code:

```
/* PERMITTED COMMANDS
Clara: move, turnLeft, turnRight,
treeLeft, treeRight,
treeFront, onLeaf,
putLeaf, removeLeaf
JAVA: if, for */

class MyClara extends Clara {

    void run() {
    // TODO: Write your code below
    }
}
```

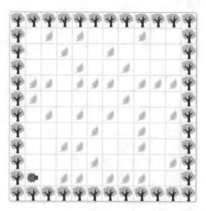

 In the previous chapters we used the act() method and have relied on it to keep repeating our code until we say stop(). This practice was useful for the simple problems we solved earlier, but starting from this chapter the problems we solve will become more interesting and more complex, so it is now time to leave this practice behind. From now on, we will no longer be using the act() method. Instead, all our commands will be placed inside the method called run(). The key difference between act() and run() is that the code placed inside run will only execute once, as if we use act() with the last command in it being stop(). The stop() command will have no effect when placed inside run().

Before rushing to solve the vacuum cleaner problem let's first think about how we could make it work? Our task now is to start moving from bottom to the top and to clean everything like a robot vacuum cleaner would do. How do you think we should start? You probably do not have an immediate answer to this question. The reason for this is that this problem is simply too complex, especially for beginners. Normally, a good approach (and that's how we solve problems in our everyday life) is to start with a large problem and identify a smaller piece of it that you can easily solve and then treat this piece (once solved) as a building block from which you are going to build the house of solving a larger problem.

What could be a smaller sub-problem that we can easily solve and that is relevant to the solution of the larger problem? How about we start with cleaning one line? If we create a dedicated method for solving this smaller problem then it will be much easier for us to solve the larger problem. Let's call this method cleanLine().

As you probably remember, creating a new method starts with the keyword `void` followed by the method name, an empty set of parentheses and then a couple of curly brackets.

```
void cleanLine() {
}
```

All the code that is related to this method has to be inside the two brackets and outside of the brackets for any other method, since you can't have a command inside a command.

Now let's think about what cleaning one line involves? We must repeat removing a leaf every time Clara is on a leaf and after this she has to move. We could have simply written the following code using `if` statements:

```
void cleanLine() {
  if ( onLeaf() )
    removeLeaf();

  if ( treeFront() )
    stop();
  else
    move();
}
```

But the above code would only work if `cleanLine()` is used inside the `act()` method. As mentioned earlier, starting from this chapter we no longer rely on the `act()` method and use the `run()` method (that executes the code inside only once and does not repeat it). If we were to use this `cleanLine()` method inside `run()` then Clara would only clean one cell and would make one move. To clean the entire line we must use a `for` loop inside the `run` method. The key question is how many repetitions would our loop require? Clara's apartment is 10 by 10, so there are exactly 10 cells in each line. One might think that 10 would be a correct number of repetitions and that the code for `cleanLine` should look like this.

```
void cleanLine() {
   for (int i = 0; i < 10; i++) {
      if ( onLeaf() )
         removeLeaf();

      move();
   }
}
```

However, if you run this code you would see that after cleaning one line Clara runs into a tree and reports an error. The reason why she runs into a tree is that she can only make 9 steps, not 10 steps on each line since before she starts moving, she already occupies one cell, so if she makes 10 moves then she would definitely run into a tree. After making 9 moves Clara would end up standing in front of a tree and the next `move()` call would make her run into a tree. One way to fix this is to change the number of repetitions to 9, but we will then run into other problems.

Instead of changing the number of repetitions we would like to show you another trick that many programmers use in similar situations. There is one way to stop Clara from ever running into a tree, which is to add a new method `secureMove()` and then use this method instead of using `move()`.

```
void secureMove() {
    if ( !treeFront() )
        move();
    }
}
```

We can now update `cleanLine()` as follows:

```
void cleanLine() {
    for (int i = 0; i < 10; i++) {
        if ( onLeaf() )
            removeLeaf();

        secureMove();
    }
}
```

Please note that the use of `secureMove()` would prevent Clara from running into a tree. The result of calling `secureMove()` on the last iteration of the `for` loop would be testing the `!treeFront()` condition, realising that it is false and then skipping the `move()` command.

Using `secureMove()` is a lazy way of solving the problem, but it is extremely effective and therefore common. Over time, as an experienced programmer, you would develop a mindset of preventing all possible errors in advance, so creating methods similar to `secureMove()` will become your second nature. The reason why `secureMove()` is powerful is that once you create it and replace every move with `secureMove()` you can guarantee that Clara will **never** run into a tree again. There is, however, a downside of this approach that lies in making unnecessary checks (testing for `treeFront()` in the last iteration of the loop), which have a slight negative impact on the performance of the program you write. There is a popular joke: "When programmers go to bed they puts two glasses on their bedside tables, one with water for the case the programmer wakes up and wants to drink and one without water for the case the programmer wakes up and does not want to drink". This joke is a reflection on a programmer's mindset of being extra careful and sometimes performing unnecessary checks and executing unnecessary code out of habit. Most of the time, having this unnecessary code poses no visible issues. You will not be able to notice slower performance in the kind of problems that we are considering in this book, but there are time-critical applications that you might be dealing with later in your career, for which optimising the program performance is critical and unnecessary commands are best removed.

Now that we have solved the problem of cleaning one line, let us get back to the larger problem of cleaning the entire apartment. Notice that now that we have created a method for cleaning one line the larger problem seems much simpler to solve than before. Our run method currently looks as follows:

```
void run() {
  // TODO: Write your code below
  cleanLine();
}
}
```

The next thing we want to do is to move to the next line and then repeat the cleaning process. Let's think how we could achieve this. The simplest way of moving to the next line from Clara's current position would have been to update our run() method so that it looks as follows:

```
void run() {
  // TODO: Write your code below
  cleanLine();
  turnLeft();
  move();
  turnLeft();
}
}
```

It looks like we are on the right track, so we might continue by calling the cleanLine() method to clean all the leaves on the second line. This would work, but notice that after executing the cleanLine() method Clara would be standing next to the tree on her left and in order for her to move to the next line she would have to turn right instead of turning left. An important thing to notice is that we have adopted cleanLine() as a logical building block that we are comfortably using without thinking how this block is implemented. Here is how our code would look after adding those steps:

```
void run() {
  // TODO: Write your code below
  cleanLine();
  turnLeft();
  move();
  turnLeft();
  cleanLine();
  turnRight();
  move();
  turnRight();
}
}
```

We keep advancing with our solution, and it is tempting to continue following a similar pattern as before. If we simply duplicate the code that we currently have inside the run() method, we would successfully clean another two lines in Clara's apartment.

```
void run() {
  // TODO: Write your code below
  cleanLine();
  turnLeft();
  move();
  turnLeft();
  cleanLine();
  turnRight();
  move();
  turnRight();
  cleanLine();
  turnLeft();
  move();
  turnLeft();
  cleanLine();
  turnRight();
  move();
  turnRight();
  }
}
```

The code above would make Clara successfully clean four lines in her apartment. If we duplicate the contents of the run method again, Clara would successfully clean eight lines. However, at this point you would probably realise that this approach is not optimal. There must be a better way of solving this problem other than repeating this rather boring pattern. What is wrong with this code above is that it is long and repetitive.

We suggest that you employ a mental exercise that we call "*the grandmother test*" in order to check whether your code is good or not. The nature of the grandmother test is as follows: take a method you have written and imagine showing it to your grandmother, who has no programming background. Imagine how you would give her a preliminary explanation of what these basic building blocks like move() and turnLeft() do and would then show her this new method you have created. Would it take long for her to understand what this method does? If the answer is "no" then your code is not ideal.

If we were to use this mental exercise with the above code, we would fail the grandmother test. What can be done to improve this code? How about we first simplify the code by giving meaningful names to some repetitive blocks of code. What keeps happening again and again in the code above is making Clara reposition to the next line after cleaning a line. There are two types of repositioning. The first type is the one we employ when Clara faces east and then starts with turning left, after which she then eventually moves to the next line and ends up facing west. And the second type is when she faces west and turns right. Let us separate these two types of repositioning into `repositionEast()` and `repositionWest()` methods. Our updated code would then look as follows:

```
void repositionToWest()
{
    turnLeft();
    secureMove();
    turnLeft();
}

void repositionToEast()
{
    turnRight();
    secureMove();
    turnRight();
}

void run() {
    // TODO: Write your code below
    cleanLine();
    repositionToWest();
    cleanLine();
    repositionToEast();
    cleanLine();
    repositionToWest();
    cleanLine();
    repositionToEast();
}
}
```

The `run()` method is now shorter and easier to understand, but there is still room for improvement. What we currently have inside the `run()` method seems quite repetitive. One good mechanism of handing something repetitive that exists in programming is loops. What we can do instead of repeating `cleanLine()` followed by various types of repositioning is to create a `for` loop. In order to do this let us closely inspect the `run` method and search for a part that can be easily repeated inside a loop. The repetitive part that looks like a good candidate for being placed inside a loop is the following code fragment:

```
cleanLine();
repositionToWest();
cleanLine();
repositionToEast();
```

This fragment allows Clara to clean two lines in her apartment. What we know is that there is a total of 10 lines in Clara's apartment, so our intuition suggests to us that repeating the above code 5 times would help us solve the problem. How do we repeat something 5 times? In the same way as we repeated the process of cleaning one leaf and then moving inside the `cleanLine()` method (with the help of a `for` loop). With this idea in mind let us update our code and make it look as follows:

```
class MyClara extends Clara {
    /**
     * In the 'run()' method you can write your program for Clara
     */
    void run() {
        // TODO: Write your code below
        for (int i = 0; i < 5; i++) {
            cleanLine();
            repositionToWest();
            cleanLine();
            repositionToEast();
        }
    }

    void repositionToWest() {
        turnLeft();
        secureMove();
        turnLeft();
    }

    void repositionToEast() {
        turnRight();
        secureMove();
        turnRight();
    }

    void cleanLine() {
        for (int i = 0; i < 10; i++) {
            if ( onLeaf() )
                removeLeaf();

            secureMove();
        }
    }

    void secureMove() {
        if ( !treeFront() )
            move();
    }

}
```

Running this code would result in the entire Clara's apartment being cleaned. Clara would make some redundant turns after cleaning the last line, but at this moment this should not trouble us too much. The most important thing is that the problem is solved. Clara's apartment is clean, and her guests are happy. They could come again tomorrow to have another party and leave a lot of rubbish behind, but now Clara has a recipe for how to clean her apartment the next day. This recipe is generic and would successfully clean all the rubbish no matter in which pattern it appears on the floor. Also note that each method present in this recipe is simple enough to pass the grandmother test.

 To see the solution of this problem in Clara's World please use the following URL: `https://claraworld.net/link/C3P1S`.

3.4.3 Elements of the `for` Loop.

Solving the chapter problem provided us with basic understanding of how to use the `for` loop. Before finishing with this concept and moving on to other types of loops, it is important to fully understand some additional aspects associated with the `for` loop concept. Let us use the following example to facilitate the explanation:

```
for(int i = 0; i < 3; i++) {
    move();
    turnLeft();
}
```

This simple loop would make Clara repeat the process of moving and turning left three times. Let us now carefully inspect each element of this loop, discuss the associated terminology and understand the advanced options that Java offers in regards to `for` loops.

3.4.3.1 Header and Body

Each loop in Java consists of a header and the loop body. The loop header is the first line "`for (int i = 0; i < 3; i++)`" that defines the logic for repeating the loop body. The header contains the following three sections: initialisation, test and update.

The body of the loop represents the code that will be repeated a desired number of times. In the example above this code is represented by two statements: `turnLeft()` and `move()`, which appear inside the curly brackets.

The principles of good coding style suggest that a loop body should always appear inside curly brackets. However, curly brackets are not compulsory. If we remove the curly brackets in the aforementioned example, this code would follow a bad coding style, but would formally remain correct and would execute without problems. The result of running the code would be different from what one might expect.

```
for(int i - 0; i < 3; i++)
   move();
   turnLeft();
```

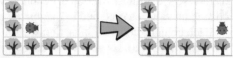

To understand the reasons for the unexpected result, let us recall that it was also not compulsory to have curly brackets after an if statement.

```
if ( treeFront() ) {          if ( treeFront() )
   move();                        move();
   turnLeft();
}                             turnLeft();
```

The two code snippets above test the same treeFront() condition, but if this condition is false, Clara would still turn left in the code snippet on the right and wouldn't turn in the snippet on the left. Having no curly brackets in the snippet on the right means that only one line (that appears immediately below the if statement header) would be conditionally tested, while all the code that follows would not be associated with the if-statement.

Similar logic applies when we work with for loops. If we rewrite the above example as follows the logic of it would not change, but the code would be easier for us to understand:

```
for(int i = 0; i < 3; i++)
   move();

turnLeft();
```

Having no curly brackets in this case would mean that only the move() command would repeat three times, while the turnLeft() command would only execute once, since having no curly brackets means that only one line of code that appears immediately after the loop header is considered to be the body of the for loop.

So far we have not paid much attention to the elements of the loop header. For solving the chapter problem it was enough for us to understand which part of the header we must change to modify the number of repetitions. Now it is time to reveal the details of other elements of the loop header.

As mentioned earlier, a loop header contains tree sections: initialisation section, test section and update section. These sections must always follow the same order and be separated by semicolons.

3.4.3.2 Loop Header: Initialisation Section

The initialisation section of the for loop (int i = 0) allows the programmer to create a so-called loop counter. This counter is needed for the computer to be able to memorise the number of loop executions. After every execution the counter would change its value as specified in the update section.

Each counter in the initialisation section should have a type (`int`), name (`i`) and the initial value (`0`). As you would have already guessed, we can use any name, type or value for this counter. The loop counter is essentially a variable that is similar to variables that are familiar to you from secondary school mathematics. We will have a detailed explanation of how variables work in programming, what is different to mathematics and which types are available in Chapter 5. Until then it is enough for you to know that most of the time we will be using integer (`int`) counters inside for loops. What you might also find useful to know is that you can change the name and the initial value of the variable.

For example, the two code snippets below have identical logic and would produce the same result:

```
for(int i = 0; i < 3; i++)        for(int k = 3; k > 0; k--)
{                                 {
   move();                           move();
   turnLeft();                       turnLeft();
}                                 }
```

But the snippet on the right would be using a different counter name (`k` instead of `i`). Other sections of the loop header would also look different in both examples. Let us continue the discussion with the focus on these differences.

3.4.3.3 Loop Header: Test Section

The test section of the `for` loop acts in the same manner as the condition section in an `if` statement. The test section describes the condition. The loop will continue repeating while this condition is true.

In the above examples the test section looks different in both loops. In the snippet on the left the loop will continue repeating until the counter `i` becomes equal to or greater than 3. In the snippet on the right the loop will stop repeating after the counter `k` becomes smaller than or equal to 0.

3.4.3.4 Loop Header: Update Section

What makes both loops in the above example repeat the same number of times (3) is the update section. The update section is the last thing to execute at the end of each loop iteration. In the above example the update section of the code snippet on the left is `i++`. This instruction tells Java to increment the loop counter (`i`) by one after every iteration. The snippet on the right employs a different strategy, instead of `i++` it uses `k--`. The `--` represents a decrement operator, so `k--` means reduce the value of the loop counter `k` by one.

The update section modifies the loop counter, which usually means increment-ing or decrementing it. It may work with multiple counters. The example below illustrates working with two counters:

```
for(int i = 0, k = 5; i > k; i++, k--)
{
  move();
  turnLeft();
}
```

Here we have two counter i and k, where the counter i is being incremented, while the counter k is being decremented after every loop iteration. The loop will continuc repeating while the value of the counter k is greater than the value of the counter i.

3.4.4 Nested Loops

Java language supports having nested loops (loops that appear inside the body of another loop). Having nested loops is a similar idea to having nested if-statements.

To illustrate the nested loops concept let us consider the example presented in Section 3.4.2. In this example we did not explicitly have nested loops, but we did have them implicitly. Let us recall that the cleanLine() method was imple-mented with a for loop inside.

```
void cleanLine() {
    for (int i = 0; i < 10; i++) {
        if ( onLeaf() )
            removeLeaf();

        secureMove();
    }
}
```

The cleanLine() method was then called within run(). Instead of creating a separate method for cleanLine() wc could have simply copied its code inside the run method as shown below:

```
void run() {
    // TODO: Write your code below
    for (int i = 0; i < 5; i++) {
        for (int i = 0; i < 10; i++) {
            if ( onLeaf() )
                removeLeaf();

            secureMove();
        }

        repositionToWest();
```

```
for (int i = 0; i < 10; i++) {
    if ( onLeaf() )
        removeLeaf();

    secureMove();
}

repositionToEast();
    }
}
```

The run() method above contains two nested for loops (followed by another loop). This is not the best code, since it would not pass the grandmother test. The code is now much more difficult to understand, because it repeats the entire loop implementation of cleanLine twice (instead of simply repeating the method name). This code, however, is completely legal in Java.

Please note that similar to what was said about nested if-statements (that you should not have more than two levels of nested if-statements) also applies to nested loops. You should not create more than two levels of nested loops or otherwise your code will become very difficult to understand.

3.4.5 The break Statement

Another topic that is important to discuss is terminating loops within the loop's body. Sometimes there are situations when it is required to terminate a loop before it has finished execution. You should actively try to avoid such situations, but on some occasions avoiding them results in bulkier code. There are two commands at our disposal: break and continue that can help with interrupting a loop.

The break statement immediately terminates a loop. After executing the break statement the loop would finish executing, the statements that appear immediately after break inside the loop body would not be executed. Program execution would continue with the statements that appear directly after this loop. It is important to note that the break statement only terminates the innermost loop where it is located. In a situation of calling the break statement inside a nested loop (e.g. inside the loop representing cleanLine() in the code above) it would only affect this inner loop, while the outer loop would continue repeating.

To illustrate how break works let us consider the example below:

```
for(int i = 0; i < 3; i++) {
    move();

    if (i == 1)
        break;

    putLeaf();
}

turnLeft();
move();
```

In this code Clara was expected to put three leaves in a line and then the loop was supposed to finish. However, the programmer has then decided to modify the code and terminate the loop using the break statement. The break statement usually is associated with some condition. In the code above this condition is i == 1. This means that the loop must be terminated as soon as the value of the loop counter i becomes "1". Notice that this has indeed worked. In the resulting world configuration we can see that only one leaf has been placed in Clara's World. Let us think about the execution of this code. When this loop starts the value of the loop counter i is "0", so Clara would make one move, would test whether the value of the counter is "1" and would not execute the break statement since it is not "1". Clara would then put a leaf, and the next iteration of the loop would start. In the second loop iteration Clara would move and then the (i == 1) test would return true, so the break statement would be called and the loop would terminate before executing the putLeaf() command. Since the loop has finished, the code that follows would start executing and Clara would turn left and would make another step forward.

In general, terminating a loop using the break statement is something that should be avoided. Only experienced programmers should utilise this practice and only in situations when using break makes the code shorter and easier to understand. If you are a beginner programmer, however, you should try to avoid using the break statement altogether. Using break by beginner programmers often leads to producing code that is difficult to understand and difficult to modify in the future.

3.4.6 The continue Statement

Another way to terminate a loop is to use the continue statement. This statement works slightly differently from break. The continue statement only skips one iteration of the loop without terminating the loop. Let us illustrate the difference between break and continue through the following example:

```
for(int i = 0; i < 3; i++) {
    move();

    if (i == 1)
        continue;

    putLeaf();
}

turnLeft();
move();
```

In this code snippet we have simply replaced break with continue. Notice that the outcome is very different. Clara placed two leaves in her world and made many more moves. The reason for this difference is that during the second iteration of the for loop (when the value of the loop counter is "1") Clara will not terminate the loop, but would simply skip all statements in the loop body that appear below the continue command and will then continue with the next iteration of the loop. As the result of this, the putLeaf() command will not be executed, but the loop itself would not terminate and would continue repeating three times, making Clara put another leaf and make one extra move. The use of continue statements is strongly discouraged by beginner programmers, since the resulting code may end up being even more confusing than code containing break statements.

3.5 Conditional Loops

Often we encounter situations when it is not exactly clear how many times we need to repeat our code. For example, if we think about the vacuum cleaner robots it becomes apparent that they are not programmed to only clean appartments of a specific size (e.g. 10 metres × 10 metres), but can successfully clean apartments of any size. Such problems (where the number of repetitions is not known in advance) can be solved with conditional loops, the most common of which is a while loop.

To give a purpose to our discussion of conditional loops let us first consider a modified version of the chapter problem.

3.5.1 Chapter Problem 2: Clara the General-Purpose Cleaner

Imagine the following situation. Clara wakes up in the morning after a party, but this time she wakes up in someone else's apartment. To make matters worse, the apartment is a mess, there is garbage on the floor everywhere. Everyone else has left, and for some reason Clara is the one who is responsible for cleaning this apartment. Moreover, this is something that will be happening to her almost every night, routinely. She would be waking up in someone else's apartment, and she is the one who has to clean it. The reason why Clara found herself in this strange situation is, of course, that she has accepted a job as a vacuum cleaner robot. In this scenario the room that Clara has to clean can be of any size (which is similar to the problem that vacuum cleaner robot manufacturers had to solve). We can no longer rely on the room being of certain dimensions; our approach to cleaning must be generic and has to work for a room of any size. How might we create a recipe for Clara that would automate the apartment cleaning task? Figure 3.4 illustrates an example apartment.

 To work on this problem in Clara's World please use the following URL: https://claraworld.net/link/C3P2.

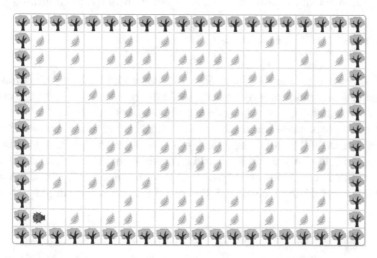

Fig. 3.4: An Example Apartment That Clara Has To Clean.

What does the fact that Clara always wakes up in a different apartment mean in terms of programming? It means that we do not know how big the apartment is. Thus, we can no longer say that `cleanLine()` must be repeated ten times nor can we say how many moves must Clara make on each line. Instead of solving this problem through repeating these actions a certain number of times in a `for` loop we have to use a different type of loop, which is called a `while` loop. The `while` loop is a conditional loop and is, in fact, a much more simple concept than the `for` loop.

3.5.2 The `while` Loop

The `while` loop allows repeating the code within the loop body while a certain condition is true. It has the following form:

```
while(condition) {
   statement(s) to be repeated;
}
```

While the `condition` is true, the statements inside the curly brackets would execute repeatedly and if the `condition` is no longer true the loop would terminate. The `while` loop is a pretest loop, which means that it will test the value of the condition prior to executing the loop body. If this condition is false before the first iteration, the loop would not execute and the statements inside the curly brackets would never be performed.

The `while` loop is very similar to an `if`-statement, so similar that some beginner programmers may confuse the two. An `if`-statement has the following form;

```
if(condition) {
   statement(s) to be executed;
}
```

The difference between `while` and `if` is that a `while` loop will continue repeating the code inside the curly brackets while the `condition` is true. In contrast, an `if`-statement will execute the code in curly brackets only once.

The simplest possible illustration of the `while` loop is the `moveToTree()` problem that we will be referring to very often in our examples. Imagine that Clara stands at the start of a street in her world somewhere and must move all the way to the end of this street. At the end of the street there is a tree (wall) that she can sense using the `treeFront()` command. Figure 3.5 illustrates this simple problem.

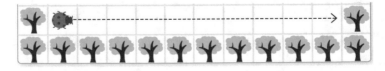

Fig. 3.5: Clara Moves to the Wall in Front of Her.

The key issue with `moveToTree` is that we don't know how far the wall is from Clara. It can be five steps away or ten steps away. We simply do not know how many steps must Clara make before she would encounter the wall, so we cannot use the `for` loop for solving this problem. However, we can easily solve this problem with a `while` loop in the following way:

```
while( !treeFront() ) {
   move();
}
```

Let us analyse how this loop executes. It is a pre-test loop (meaning that the condition will be tested before executing the loop body), so the first thing Clara would do is testing whether the condition `!treeFront()` is true. This condition would only be false if there is a tree directly in front of Clara, so at the first iteration of the loop the condition is true and we can execute the loop body. The only command we have inside the loop body is `move()`. Thus, Clara would make a step forward and the iteration of the loop would finish. Every time after finishing an iteration of the loop we test the loop condition again, so Clara would again check if there is tree in front of her. If there is no tree in front she would move again and would continue moving until there is a tree in front of her. This would successfully get her to the very end of the street as shown in Figure 3.6.

Fig. 3.6: Clara Arrives at the Wall.

When Clara reaches the end of the street she would be facing a tree, so the `!treeFront()` condition becomes `false` and the `while` loop terminates.

When creating `while` loops it is important to make sure that the loop condition would eventually become false so that the loop ends. Loops that do not end are called infinite loops. Sometimes experienced programmers create infinite loops on purpose. The simplest way to create an infinite loop in Java is to use the Java keyword `true` as the loop condition. Here is an example of an infinite loop.

```
while( true ) {
   move();
}
```

In theory, infinite loops would never terminate. In practice, they terminate if your program crashes or if you force it to stop. In Clara's World an infinite loop may lead to freezing your web browser, in which case you may have to restart it. If you are new to programming, you should avoid having them in your code. However, as you become more experienced you will start encountering situations where using an infinite loop would provide the most elegant way of solving a problem. Just remember that your loop must terminate. The easiest way to terminate a loop that is an infinite loop by design is to use a `break` statement associated with some condition. For example, we could rewrite our `moveToTree()` method as follows:

```
while( true ) {
   if ( treeFront() )
      break;
   move();
}
```

You should have noticed from the example above that similarly to the `for` loop the `while` loop may also have multiple statements inside the curly brackets. All these statements will repeat in a sequential order every iteration of the loop until the loop terminates.

At this point we have enough information about `while` loops to start solving the updated chapter problem of cleaning an apartment that has unspecified dimensions.

3.5.3 Solving the Chapter Problem with `while` Loops

We talked about the `while` loop, and now we're trying to solve the updated problem using this construct. Let us start with the code we had for solving the original version of the problem (cleaning the 10 metres × 10 metres apartment) and try to modify it.

 A video that demonstrates solving this problem step-by-step is available at `https://claraworld.net/link/C3V2`.

```
class MyClara extends Clara {
   /**
    * In the 'run()' method you can write your program for Clara
    */
   void run() {
      // TODO: Write your code below
      for (int i = 0; i < 5; i++) {
         cleanLine();
         repositionToWest();
         cleanLine();
         repositionToEast();
      }
   }

   void repositionToWest() {
      turnLeft();
      secureMove();
      turnLeft();
   }
```

```
void repositionToEast() {
   turnRight();
   secureMove();
   turnRight();
}

void cleanLine() {
   for (int i = 0; i < 10; i++) {
      if ( onLeaf() )
         removeLeaf();

      secureMove();
   }
}

void secureMove() {
   if ( !treeFront() )
      move();
}

}
```

Figure 3.7 shows the result of running this code in the new example world. As you can see, Clara has only cleaned a portion of the apartment that is 10 metres × 10 metres. Everything else is not cleaned. Let us attempt to make this code more generic, so that the entire apartment is cleaned regardless of its size. The first obvious improvement we can make to this code is updating cleanLine() by replacing the for loop with a while loop. Our intention for this change is to make Clara clean a street of any length. Here is the modified version of cleanLine():

```
void cleanLine()
{
   while ( !treeFront() )
   {
      if (onLeaf())
         removeLeaf();

      secureMove();
   }
}
```

Let us discuss what we have written here and why. The only change we made in cleanLine() is replacing for(int i = 0; i < 10; i++) with while(!treeFront()). The logic behind this change is that instead of cleaning 10 cells via the for loop we will continue cleaning one cell at a time until Clara encounters a tree in front. The cleanLine() method is, essentially, a modified version of moveToTree(), where in addition to moving Clara also attempts to remove a leaf (if there is one) on each step. Similar to moveToTree() our new cleanLine() would work for a street of any length.

One important thing to discuss is how we decided on the !treeFront() condition. The general form of a while loop's header is while(condition). The

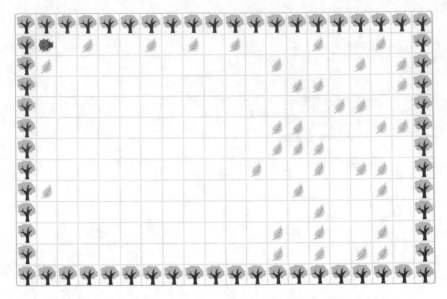

Fig. 3.7: The result of Running the Original Code for World 2.

condition that has to appear inside is a logical statement of a similar kind to those we used for the `if` statements. But what you would probably notice is that our logic when deciding on the condition for a `while` loop may seem a little backwards. When we worked with conditional statements the usual practice for us was to have something like this:

```
if ( treeFront()) {
    stop();
}
```

After having worked with conditional statements of this kind you would probably develop the kind of thinking where you search for a certain condition to become true so that you may terminate the execution of your program. This is a natural tendency of our brain to think in this way, but when working with `while` loops you have to apply this logic in a slightly different way. You may still ask yourself when would we have to stop executing the loop and the answer would be when Clara encounters a tree in front of her. However, this is not the condition that we will be putting inside the `while` loop's header. It is a common beginner's mistake to write `while (treeFront())`, but this would be wrong because what we have to put as the condition is not when to stop executing the loop, but when to continue. So what the loop header requires is the condition that represents the opposite of when to stop. Luckily for us there is a logical NOT operator in Java (`!`). With the help of the logical NOT operator you can turn a condition for when to stop into a condition for when to continue. This is the reason why in the code of `cleanLine()` above we have written `while( !treeFront() )`.

Now let us see what would happen if we run the modified code. Figure 3.8 shows the result of running the code with the updated `cleanLine()`. The result now looks much better. Clara has not cleaned all the streets (since we still rely on the `for` loop inside the `run` method), but has only cleaned 10 streets as before. Most of the leaves (not only the first ten leaves) have disappeared on the streets that Clara has cleaned. One issue that may appear slightly strange to you is that there are still leaves left alongside the vertical borders of the apartment. Why were these leaves not cleaned?

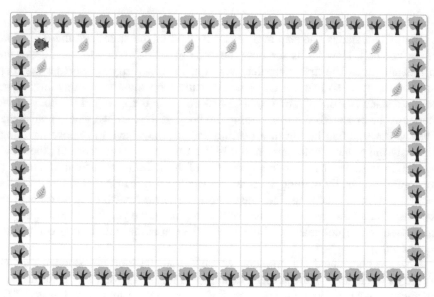

Fig. 3.8: The Result of Using a `while` Loop Inside `cleanLine()`.

If you track how Clara moves around the environment as the result of executing the updated code, you would realise that the leaves that are left are those that appear at the end of the corresponding street. Why were the leaves not removed at the end of the street? A good technique that helps with answering such questions is to do a mental exercise, where you first identify the circumstances under which the problem occurs and then make one step back. Our problem occurs when Clara reaches the end of a street. Thus, let us see what would happen just one loop iteration before Clara approaches the end of a street. The code and the illustration that appear below would help us with this mental exercise:

```
void cleanLine()
{
    while ( !treeFront() )
    {
        if (onLeaf())
            removeLeaf();

        secureMove();
    }
}
```

Here Clara stands one step away from the end of the street and there is a leaf in the last cell. Now let us see how the code of `cleanLine()` would execute in this situation. The first thing that would happen is verifying whether the loop condition is true, so that we know whether the loop must stop executing. Clara does not stand in front of a tree, so `!treeFront()` is `true` and the body of the loop must be executed. While executing the body of the loop we would realise that Clara is not standing on top of a leaf, so she does not have to remove anything. The only thing that would happen at this iteration is `secureMove()`, the result of which would be Clara standing at the end of the street (just in front of a tree). If we continue mentally running the code, we would soon realise that at this point the loop would finish executing since the condition `!treeFront()` is no longer true (because Clara now stands at the end of the street). So we will not be executing the `removeLeaf()` command, and this is why the leaf at the end of the street will not be cleaned.

Now we understand our problem, which is that the loop has stopped running before we could remove the last leaf. Problems of this sort (when a loop has finished running and we have not quite completed what we wanted) are referred to as **Off By One Bug (or OBOB)**. How could we fix this problem? The classical way of solving OBOBs is this. We must first look at the body of the loop and see which part of it we should execute again so that our problem is solved. In our example this part of the loop body is

```
if (onLeaf())
    removeLeaf();
```

Now all that is left for us to do is adding a block of code that would repeat this part of the loop body immediately after the loop. Here is how the modified version of `cleanLine()` would look if we follow this approach:

```
void cleanLine()
{
    while ( !treeFront() )
    {
        if (onLeaf())
            removeLeaf();

        secureMove();
    }

    if (onLeaf())
        removeLeaf();
}
```

As the result of running this code the `cleanLine()` method would correctly clean the remaining leaves at the end of each street. It would become our generic building block that can successfully clean a street of any length.

What is now left for us to do is to clean all the streets inside the apartment (not just the first ten). Clearly, for this to happen we must modify the code of the `run()` method and replace the `for` loop there with a `while` loop. The `run()` method currently looks as follows:

```
void run() {
    // TODO: Write your code below
    for (int i = 0; i < 5; i++) {
        cleanLine();
        repositionToWest();
        cleanLine();
        repositionToEast();
    }
}
```

What we want to achieve through modifying the `run()` method is making our solution so generic that it would work with any apartment, regardless of how many streets must be cleaned there. Being generic in this case means that our code should not only work with the two examples that we have discussed so far (10 metres × 10 metres and 18 metres × 11 metres), but must work with any kind of apartment of any size. It should even work for apartments that have fewer than ten streets.

Converting this `for` loop into a `while` loop is not as straightforward as it was in the case of `cleanLine()`. The complexity comes with the fact that we have to clean two streets at a time and the loop condition becomes difficult to figure out. Let us look at Figure 3.9, which represents the expected outcome of running our program.

If we trace Clara's movement for the provided example we would be able to anticipate that after finishing cleaning the apartment she would end up standing in the top right corner as shown in Figure 3.9. The figure provides us with a good starting point for thinking about the loop condition. Let us analyse the situation and determine what Clara could sense at this position in her world so that she knows that it

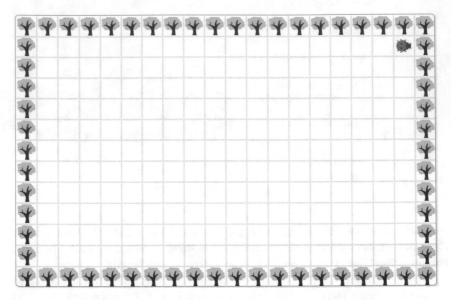

Fig. 3.9: The Expected Outcome of Executing our Program.

is time for her to stop the loop? What comes to mind is that the top right corner is unique in a sense that both treeFront() and treeLeft() can be sensed at the same time there. As we know from the previous chapter, it is possible to combine conditions using &&, so the condition under which Clara must terminate the execution of the loop should be treeFront() && treeLeft(). What we need as the loop condition, however, is to express the situation under which to continue the loop, not when to stop it, so we could rewrite our run method as follows:

```
void run() {
    // TODO: Write your code below
    while ( !( treeFront() && treeLeft() ) ) {
        cleanLine();
        repositionToWest();
        cleanLine();
        repositionToEast();
    }
}
```

Noice that we put the entire combined condition for stopping inside parentheses and then used the "!" symbol in front to convert the stopping condition into a condition for when to continue. In the following chapters we will discuss why parentheses are required and what would happen if we omit those. For now let us focus on the actual logic of the solution.

The result of running the above code is an infinite loop. Clara will clean the apartment, but will not stop. She would continue turning around and running along the last line. The key reason for not stopping after reaching the top right corner of Figure 3.9 is that Clara would not be positioned there after executing the last command in the loop's body (`repositionToEast()`). She would enter the last line from its western side, would clean it and would then turn around and move back to the western end of this street. Both `repositionToWest()` and `repositionToEast()` (due to the use of `secureMove()` instead of `move()`) are designed to work as `turnAround()` if there is a tree line above Clara. Thus, the loop body would make Clara clean the line twice and then appear at the western end facing east. This process would repeat in an infinite loop until you terminate the program.

Despite the infinite loop we are on the right track with the solution. What is required to avoid the infinite loop is simplifying the loop condition. It is easy to see that the `treeFront()` condition would become true at the end of every line that we clean, so this part does not really uniquely determine the situation in which Clara has to stop cleaning. What is unique, however, is the `treeLeft()` condition, since it would only become true once Clara reaches the upper line. Let us try rewriting the loop by simplifying the loop condition as follows:

```
void run() {
    // TODO: Write your
        code below
    while ( !treeLeft() )
    {
        cleanLine();
        repositionToWest();
        cleanLine();
        repositionToEast();
    }
}
```

Here Clara did not clean the entire apartment, as there is one last street that is left to be cleaned. The good thing, though, is that she did manage to stop on the last street and avoid the infinite loop. The situation with not cleaning the last street is similar to what we have encountered earlier (known as OBOB). There is an easy way of dealing with this situation, which is adding another `cleanLine()` call immediately after the while loop. Adding this line would help us to successfully clean the above example world.

Let us now see whether our solution is generic (meaning that it should work with an apartment of any dimensions). It is obvious that our `cleanLine()` method is generic, so our solution is then generic as far as the width of the apartment is concerned, but what about the length? We saw our code would correctly clean the example apartment of length 11 metres. Let us now look whether this code would correctly handle the earlier example (cleaning the 10 metres × 10 metres apartment). Our example comes with two different worlds, one of which represents the 10 metres × 10 metres apartment shown earlier. If you run the code below for this world, you would see that it also correctly cleans the apartment.

```
void run() {
    // TODO: Write your
        code below
    while ( !treeLeft() )
    {
        cleanLine();
        repositionToWest();
        cleanLine();
        repositionToEast();
    }
    cleanLine();
}
```

Let us discuss how this happens. What you would notice while running the code is that Clara would use `repositionToWest()` in order to get to the last street. After executing `repositionWest()` and then calling the `cleanLine()` command the entire apartment will be cleaned and Clara's World would look like the above picture. However, the loop would not terminate, since there is one more command left to execute from the loop body, which is `repositionToEast()`. Furthermore, as Clara repositioned to the west on the last street, she would not have a tree to her left now, but the tree would be on her right. What is the reason why our code would still execute correctly in this situation? The reason for this is again that we are using `secureMove()` instead of `move()` everywhere in our code. Using `secureMove()` everywhere makes it impossible for Clara to ever run into a tree. Instead of running into a tree and seeing an error on the screen Clara would simply not move, but all the turns would still execute. Let us take a closer look at the code for the `repositionToEast()` and `secureMove()` methods and mentally track what happens if we execute `repositionToEast()` when Clara is located in the top left corner of the apartment (as shown in the picture above).

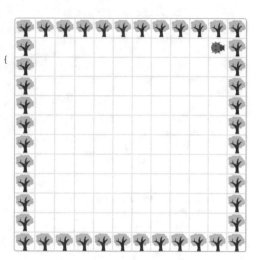

```
void repositionToEast() {
    turnRight();
    secureMove();
    turnRight();
}

void secureMove() {
    if (!treeFront())
        move();
}
```

The first thing that would happen is Clara would turn right (so she would be facing north with a tree representing the upper wall of the apartment being in front of Clara). Next, she would call secureMove(). Because there is a tree in front of Clara, the move would not happen, so running secureMove() would have no effect on Clara's World. After secureMove() Clara would turn right again, so she would now be facing east. Since repositionEast() was the last command in the body of our while loop, the current iteration of the loop would finish and the loop condition (!treeLeft()) would need to be tested in order to decide whether the loop should terminate or not. After executing repositionEast() Clara would change orientation and there now would be a tree on Clara's left, so the loop would terminate. Finally, we would execute the cleanLine() command that appears after the loop and Clara would move to the top right corner as shown in the picture above.

 To work with the solution of this problem in Clara's World please use the following URL: https://claraworld.net/link/C3P2S.

It is easy to see that because we are using secureMove() everywhere our solution would work with an apartment of any length. After reaching the upper boundary Clara would not be running into a tree, but would simply be turning around and moving to the end of the street until there is a tree on her left (and the loop can terminate). Congratulations! We have successfully produced a generic apartment cleaning program for Clara. Below is the completed solution:

```
class MyClara extends Clara {
    void run() {
        // TODO: Write your code below
        while ( !treeLeft() ) {
            cleanLine();
```

```
            repositionToWest();
            cleanLine();
            repositionToEast();
        }

        cleanLine();
    }

    void repositionToWest() {
        turnLeft();
        secureMove();
        turnLeft();
    }

    void repositionToEast() {
        turnRight();
        secureMove();
        turnRight();
    }

    void cleanLine() {
        while (!treeFront()) {
            if ( onLeaf() )
                removeLeaf();

            secureMove();
        }

        if ( onLeaf() )
            removeLeaf();
    }

    void secureMove() {
        if (!treeFront())
            move();
    }
}
```

 Exercise: If you run the above code for the apartment with the size of 10 metres x 10 metres, you would see that Clara performs some redundant operations in the last line. She would clean the last street, after which she would turn around and would walk to its opposite end attempting to clean the street again. This is not a big problem, but as a programmer you should always attempt to avoid performing unnecessary actions whenever possible. As an exercise we recommend trying to change the above solution in such a way that Clara stops after cleaning the last street and does not travel to its opposite end.

3.5.4 The do-while Loop

In addition to the `while` loop Java language also supports another conditional loop type, which is the `do-while` loop. The `do-while` loop is a *post-test* loop, which means that it will execute the loop body prior to testing the condition. Regardless of the condition (whether it is `true` or `false`) the body of the loop will execute at least once. After the first iteration this loop would behave in the same way as a `while` loop. The syntax of the `do-while` loop is as follows:

```
do {
    statement(s);
} while (condition);
```

This loop is not as commonly used as the `while` loop. It can, however, be useful and is quite elegant for situations where it is difficult to come up with a loop condition that is not equal to `false` in the first iteration of the loop.

Most of the time you will be using the `while` loop. If you are a beginner programmer then you should consider the `do-while` loop as an exotic construct that may be helpful in some rare occasions. However, as you gain more experience you should revisit this concept as in some situations it would help making your code looking more elegant. To illustrate the usefulness of the `do-while` loop let us consider the earlier example of Clara cleaning an apartment of any size. One way to implement the `run()` method for this problem could be as follows:

```
void run() {
    while ( !treeLeft() && !treeRight() ) {
        cleanLine();
        repositionToWest();
        cleanLine();
        repositionToEast();
    }

    cleanLine();
}
```

The only difference that this `run()` method has compared with the `run()` method from our earlier solution is that instead of `!treeLeft()` our loop condition is now `(!treeLeft() && !treeRight())`. The motivation for having this condition could be that we wanted to express the fact that our solution is generic and must work with apartments that have their length being an odd number(e.g. 11 metres) or an even number (e.g. 10 metres). What we wanted as the programmer of this method is for the loop to terminate after cleaning the last line. Depending on whether the number of lines to clean in her apartment is odd or even, the boundary next to the last line could either be sensed on Clara's left or on her right. There is, however, a problem with this approach. The problem lies in the fact that at the very start of the loop (when Clara is located on the first street) there will always be a tree to Clara's right. Thus, if we execute the above code snippet, the result would be similar to what is shown in the above picture (Clara would only clean the first street). The reason why only the first line would be cleaned is that the `while` loop's condition would become `false` at the start and the loop would terminate. The first line would be cleaned because of the `cleanLine()` statement that appears under the `while` loop.

One good way of avoiding this problem is to use the `do-while` loop. Here is how the code of the `run()` method could have been rewritten.

```
void run() {
    do {
        cleanLine();
        repositionToWest();
        cleanLine();
        repositionToEast();
    }
    while (!treeLeft() && !treeRight());

    cleanLine();
}
```

The use of the do-while loop in the above code allows us to execute the loop's body before testing the associated condition `!treeLeft() && !treeRight()` in the first iteration. As the result of this, Clara would successfully clean the first two lines. The condition would then be tested before deciding whether to continue with the second and all other loop iterations, but at this stage there will no longer be a tree on Clara's right.

3.6 Common Errors

Before moving on to the next topic let us also discuss the most common errors that novice programmers often have in their loops. By errors here we do not mean mistyping Java keywords, forgetting semicolons or making other similar *syntax errors* that relate to incorrect use of Java syntax. Such syntax mistakes are easy to correct, since the Clara framework is able to identify them and inform the programmer. The type of errors we would like to discuss here are so-called *logical errors*, which are much more difficult to spot in your code. Logical errors are mistakes in your solution that prevent you from achieving the intentions that you had when writing the code. In the case of logical errors you would be using correct Java syntax, so the code would be correct and the Clara's World framework would not be able to spot any errors, but the logic of the solution would be incorrect.

The Off By One Bug (**OBOB**) is one of the most common errors that deserves to be mentioned. Let us recall what it means using the following example:

```
while (!treeFront())
{
    putLeaf();
    move();
}
```

Here the intention of the programmer was to cover the entire first street with leaves. However, as the result of running this code there is one leaf missing at the end of the street. The standard approach to fixing OBOB is to repeat the relevant part of the loop body one more time immediately below the loop in the code. In our case, this relevant part would only feature one command (putLeaf()). The modified code and the result of running it is shown below:

```
while (!treeFront())
{
    putLeaf();
    move();
}

putLeaf();
```

Another common logical error that many programmers make is unintentionally creating an **infinite loop**. To illustrate this let us consider the example below:

```
while( !treeFront() ) {
    turnRight();
}
```

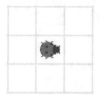

Here we see a while loop that would continue making Clara turn left until she encounters a tree in front. You may imagine that such code may be useful in scenarios where Clara is searching for a tree (and we will encounter such scenarios in the future). However, the creator of this code made a logical error, which is forgetting that there could be situations similar to the one shown in the above picture, where there are no trees around Clara. In such a case Clara would be turning infinitely (until we terminate the program). As you become more experienced you may encounter situations in which creating infinite loops is something useful, but such situations should be avoided at all cost by beginners. Creating infinite loops on purpose can be achieved using while(true), and for stopping such a loop you should use the break; statement.

The **incorrect use of a semicolon** in the loop header is the third most common error that we see in the code of our students. Let us illustrate this error using the example below:

```
for (int i = 0; i < 9; i++);
{
    move();
}
```

This error is very difficult to spot. The problem is the semicolon that appears immediately after the loop header. In Java language the entire loop (the loop body together with the header) is considered to be one command and, therefore, this semicolon is not required. Having this semicolon, however, is permitted and would not result in a syntax error. Instead of the error it would make the loop change its logic. A loop header followed by a semicolon is considered to be an empty loop. Thus, the code above would have the following meaning to a Java compiler (the program that is in charge of validating your code and preparing it for execution):

```
for (int i = 0; i < 9; i++) {
}
move();
```

Having a loop with an empty body as well as putting any block of code inside curly brackets is permitted in Java. As the result of executing this code, instead of making nine steps as the programmer intended, Clara would only make one step as shown in the above picture. The `for` loop would repeat the empty body nine times and then the `move()` command would execute only once, since it is not considered to be a part of the loop.

A similar error could also happen with a `while` loop as shown in the code below:

```
while ( !treeFront() );
{
    move();
}
```

The placement of the semicolon after the loop's header would also result in Clara making a single step forward instead of moving all the way to the end of the street.

3.7 Summary

To summarise, we have learned about a controlled way to repeat some code in your program using loops. If we know exactly how many times this code needs repeating (e.g. the size of the apartment is fixed to 10 metres × 10 metres), then the best loop type for this situation is the `for` loop. If, however, we have no explicit knowledge of how many repetitions our loop would require then we should either use the `while` or a `do-while` loop. If you are a beginner programmer then you can temporarily ignore the fact that the `do-while` loop exists. Using the `while` loop should be sufficient for beginners.

3.8 Exercises

 Exercises that target your understanding of the concepts covered in this chapter are available at `https://claraworld.net/link/C3Ex`.

Chapter 4
Coding Style and Decomposition

It may sound strange to beginner programmers, but programming is very similar to art. Very much like sophisticated art, computer programs can be beautiful and ugly or elegant and bulky. One of the important attributes that makes code appear beautiful is the coding style. Similar to how artists follow the key principles of picture composition or apply the rule of thirds, there are principles in programming, following which results in more beautiful code. In this chapter we will discuss the widely accepted coding style principles of Java programming. Following good coding style will not only make your code more pleasing to look at, but will also help you and your colleagues to understand it better and to reduce the number of errors in your programs.

Errors in programming code (also known as bugs) are a part of daily life and should not be feared; however, there are situations when errors may become too costly and should be avoided. In the chapter story below we would like to introduce a couple of such scenarios and to illustrate how following the principles of good coding style can help with preventing code bugs.

© Springer Nature Switzerland AG 2021
A. Bogdanovych, T. Trescak, *Learning Java Programming in Clara's World*,
https://doi.org/10.1007/978-3-030-75542-3_4

4.1 Chapter Story: Consequences of Errors in Code

This chapter's story is a tale from one of our programming lecturers, Mikhail. The story dates back to the Cold War times, the period of fierce rivalry between the United States and Soviet Union. Both countries focused on achieving technological and military domination, and Mikhail was at the forefront of the space exploration race on the Soviet Union's side. He worked on developing software for one of the experimental rockets during the early space exploration days (before humans began to travel into space). An important piece of work he had to complete was making sure that if something goes wrong with the rocket it will not fall back to Earth causing major damage. Since there were no humans on board, the approach back then was to initiate self-destruction in case of any potential critical problem. Mikhail's code, of course, was classified and he never showed it to us, but he explained the key high-level principles of how he has written it. Early computers struggled to process all the necessary data in real time, so they heavily relied on so-called "lookup tables" – manually produced computational results for various key rocket parameters during the first minutes of its flight. An analytical team was in charge of computing these parameters and populating the table with correct data.

What is interesting for our purposes here is how self-destruction was initiated. Let us have a look at the following code that provides a high-level overview of the self-destruction initiation procedure:

```
void integrityTest() {
   if ( height != desiredHeight(flightTime) )
     integrityTestFailure();
   else
   if ( airPressure != desiredPressure() )
     integrityTestFailure();
   ...
}

void integrityTestFailure() {
   initiateSelfDestruct();
}
```

Here methods such as `desiredHeight()` and `desiredPressure()` are used to obtain the data from lookup tables and compare it with currently observed parameters. The rocket is destroyed if any of the lookup table values does not match the corresponding live observation.

This code worked absolutely fine for the first launch of the rocket. Programmers have tested it for errors and analysts have verified all their computations multiple times to make sure that the values in the lookup tables are correct.

Some time later a decision was made to replace the engine on the rocket and install a more powerful new engine on it. Mikhail checked his code, and it seemed like there was no need to change anything there. Just a few seconds after launch the rocket exploded, blowing up hopes, dreams and quite a lot of money spent on the project. What could have gone wrong?

Let us think about what happened. The code was working fine, and the first launch was a big success. But after installing a more powerful engine the rocket exploded. Could the simple snippet of code shown above be responsible for this? The code looks completely fine, but let us recall what has been mentioned about `desiredHeight()` and `desiredPressure()` methods. These methods would first extract the corresponding value from a lookup table and would then compare it with the current observation. But when a more powerful engine is in use the height of the rocket would be increasing more rapidly than when the old engine was used. After some time the difference between the observed height and the desired height extracted from the lookup table would go beyond the acceptable threshold, so the `integrityTestFailure()` method would be activated and the rocket would be destroyed.

It appears that the values in the lookup table were not updated to account for the more powerful engine being installed. This mistake could, of course, be blamed on the analysts, but the programmer could be blamed as well. Had there been a note in the code somewhere stating that any engine changes should result in updating the lookup table values, there would have been no accident. What we see through this example is how important it is not to only write code for our computer to understand, but also to insert reminders and provide detailed explanations to humans who would be in charge of maintaining and modifying this code. The above story is not about the code being correct, it is about good coding principles.

Further in this chapter we will focus on principles for writing good code. As you saw from the space rocket example, good code is code that is written in such a way that people who end up maintaining it are aware of all potential problems and can detect those quickly within the code. Before getting into the details of how to create good code, let us have a look at an example of what very bad code looks like.

4.1.1 What Is Bad Code?

There is more to bad code than the lack of comments or forgetting to emphasise potential critical issues. What is considered to be one of the key features of bad code today: is having the code written in such a way that it is difficult to understand. This idea may seem obvious today, but in the early 1990s, when the authors of this book were university students, it was actually trendy in the software developer community to deliberately write code in a complex and obscure manner. Many programmers demonstrated their overcomplicated solutions with pride, challenging others to decipher their solutions. It was widely believed that the value of a programmer would increase if he or she is able to produce such code that no other person is able to understand, because being able to write their code in such a way made them indispensable. This trend, however, was very short lived. As we started working on large projects and in large teams, it became apparent that modifying existing code happens more frequently than writing new code. Important team deadlines became more common, and also more common became scenarios when an "indispensable" programmer has gotten sick just before a critical team deadline, forcing other team members to fix bugs in their obscure code. Very quickly such "cowboy coders" were out of fashion, as their coding style was negatively impacting on productivity.

To demonstrate to you what bad code is and why it is difficult to handle have a look at the code fragment below and try to guess what this code does:

```
class MyClara extends Clara
{
    public void run() {
    while(!mushroomFront()){
    if (treeFront()){
    turnLeft();
    while (treeRight()) {
    move();
    }
    turnRight();
    move();
    move();
    turnRight();
    while (!treeFront()) {
    move();
    }
    turnLeft();
    }
    else
    move();
    }
    }
}
```

This solution happens to be smaller than many other problems we have solved in this book. It is, however, much more difficult to read than all other solutions that we have encountered. The reason is that when producing this code we deliberately violated all the key principles of writing good code. This solution has no comments, no indentations and no decomposition. If you are curious about what this code actually does and how an improved version of this solution is supposed to look, you can have a look at Section 4.2.3.1.

4.2 Key Principles of How to Write Good Code

As many things in computer science, the principles mentioned here come from experience. Many mistakes (similar to the one explained in our chapter story) had to be made for these principles to emerge. The principles of writing good code are as follows:

1. Write programs that are understandable by humans
2. Comment your code
3. Use readable names

4. Use methods for repetitive blocks or those that are longer than 15 lines
5. Use correct formatting
6. Follow a consistent notation

Writing programs that are understandable for humans is by far the most important rule. At first sight, it may sound self-explanatory, but this rule was widely neglected a few decades ago. Authors of this book vividly remember the times in the early 1990s when it was fashionable to write such code that no other human (except for the person who wrote it) could understand. Many programmers were competing with each other in their ability to put as much logic as possible into a single line of code. It was a common belief back then that programmers capable of creating such obscure code would find themselves in a unique position of intellectual superiority and would become indispensable at their workplace. However, as the complexity of programming projects has increased and the size of the programming teams started to grow, the trend started to change.

Imagine yourself in a position of a software manager. The day of a critical deadline has arrived. Today is the day of the release of the software product that your team has been working on for an extended period of time. Final checks are being done, and the team of testers makes sure that there are no critical issues (such as a crash or a freeze) present in the release. Suddenly, one of the testers reports that under certain conditions the software crashes. A release has been postponed. The code of the problematic component has been written by one of the cowboy coders, who likes to show his superiority by overcomplicating the code. Unfortunately, the cowboy coder is quite ill and is unable to help with fixing the bug. Everyone else shakes their heads saying that they are unable to understand this code. As the manager in this situation you have to learn from this experience and make a decision that would help to prevent similar scenarios happening in the future. The logical choice for the manager in this case is to prohibit such obscure coding practices or even to fire the cowboy coder.

Thus, the first principle of writing good code is, in fact, the important philosophical pillar of all the remaining principles. Writing good code is all about making sure that the code can be quickly understood by all members of your team. Commenting the code, using readable names, breaking it down into methods, using correct formatting and following a consistent notation are all related to writing programs that are understandable by humans. Let us continue exploring these principles.

4.2.1 Comments in Code

Adding comments to your code is an important part of making your code easier to understand. Below is an example of a typical comment you would find inside the exercises supplied with this book:

```
/*
 * MyClara is a subclass of Clara. Therefore, it inherits all
     methods of Clara:
 *
 * PERMITTED COMMANDS:
 * Actions: move(), turnLeft(), turnRight(), putLeaf(),
     removeLeaf(), stop()
 * Sensors: onLeaf(), treeFront(), treeLeft(), treeRight()
 * JAVA: if, else, while, for, !, &&, ||
 */
```

This comment mainly provides an explanation to the programmer about permitted commands. Creating a comment in Java is very simple. Anything that is located between /* and */ is considered a comment and will not be treated as code. Notice that there are valid commands such as move() and turnLeft() present inside this above comment; however, they will be ignored by the compiler, will not be treated as code and will not be executed. The additional "*" characters present in the above comment are there for decorative purposes only and don't have any functional meaning. Below is an example of a comment that doesn't feature those additional characters:

```
/*
Any text...
As long as you need...
Can be put in-between those characters and the machine will just
    ignore it.
Even if you put something like:
move(); turnLeft(); move();
It will still be ignored
Because those comments are intended for humans, so that they
    better understand your program.
*/
```

4.2.1.1 Single Line Comments

Despite comments being very useful for understanding programming code, commenting is not something that many programmers enjoy doing. Often comments are inserted after substantial chunks of code have been already written and tested. To simplify and to speed up the commenting task, Java language offers the concept of single-line comments. Single-line comments are popular with programmers because adding those only requires typing two characters "//", not four characters like for multiple-line comments. This only works for a comment that fits on one line.

Single-line comments could start at the very beginning of the line or could appear to the right of the line of code. It is not generally good practice to add comments immediately to the right of the line of code, but it is acceptable. Examples of single-line comments are shown below:

```
// Sometimes you don't have much to say
System.out.println("I have nothing to say!");

// If your comment fits in one line then use "//".
// Java compiler will ignore everything to the right of "//".

move(); // turnLeft(); and the rest of this line is a comment

// In the line above move() will be executed, but not turnLeft()
```

Single-line comments are useful for very short explanations or for attracting attention to critical blocks of code. Single-line comments are a popular choice with programmers for testing the consequences of removing a particular line of code. Instead of actually removing the line of code it can simply be "commented out". With this approach it becomes easy to return back to the original code if removing the line did not achieve the desired result. A more common approach, however, is to use multiple-line comments for this purpose, because testing the results of removing multiple lines of code happens more frequently than "commenting out" one line.

As a finishing remark about commenting your code we would like you to spend a minute thinking about the chapter story (of the self-destroyed rocket). One of the problems with Mikhail's code (according to his own admission) was the lack of comments. Had there been a comment mentioning that lookup tables must be updated in case of any changes of the rocket engine, there would have been no disastrous outcomes. It is important to remember that our code is not only written for the computer to execute, but also for our team members (and ourselves). It must be written in such a way that critical things are well explained within comments, so that if we have to look at this code again a few years later we would immediately notice critical issues and will act accordingly.

4.2.1.2 What to Comment

Personal computers have been with us for quite some time. During those years, through trials, errors and outright disasters (similar to the above story of Mikhail), we have established a number of guidelines in regards to what should be commented in computer code. Below is the list of recommendations related to code commenting:

- Always explain what your program (or its part) is expected to do at the top of the corresponding file.
- Explain what every methods does as well as its pre-conditions, post-conditions, parameters and return values.
- Put a comment before every long block inside a method.
- Important blocks that may cause issues (e.g. do not forget to update the lookup table) or code that may be difficult to understand must be commented.

To illustrate and discuss these guidelines let us consider a correctly commented example of the Clara cleaner problem from Chapter 3. Figure 4.1 serves as a reminder about the requirements of problem, which is to clean an apartment of the specified dimensions (10 metres x 10 metres).

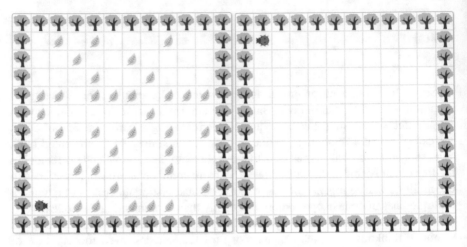

Fig. 4.1: a) Apartment before Cleaning   b) Apartment after Cleaning.

4.2.1.3 Clara Cleaner Problem with Comments

The code below shows the same solution of the problem as discussed in Chapter 3, but this time with comments. Notice that in the past the place were we were supposed to insert our code was marked by the following comment line:

```
// TODO: Write your code below
```

 To see this problem in Clara's World please use the following URL: https://claraworld.net/link/C4P1.

Now that you have an understanding that this line was a comment that helped you find where to write your code, you should remove this line. It does not serve any other practical or informative purpose, so removing it would help to reduce the number of lines that require attention.

Let us have a look at the code below. It starts with a brief explanation of a high-level approach to solving the problem, followed by comments for every method detailing its key function and an explanation of the associated pre-conditions and post-conditions.

Pre-conditions are important aspects of the required state of Clara's World that are expected to be satisfied for the method to work correctly. Post-conditions refer to the changes in Clara's World resulting from executing a given method.

```
/*
 * In this problem Clara must clean her apartment of leaves.
 * It is known that her apartment is 10 cells x 10 cells in size.
 * She must move in a sequential fashion (line-by-line).
 */
class MyClara extends Clara {
    /*
     * The run() method is the starting point of the program.
     * We will continue to repeat cleaning 2 streets at a time
     * until we hit a tree on Clara's left.
     */
    void run() {
        for (int i = 0; i < 5; i++) {
            cleanLine();
            repositionToWest();
            cleanLine();
            repositionToEast();
        }
    }

    /*
     * Clean one line from all leaves.
     * Pre-condition: located at the line start not facing a wall.
     * Post-condition: located at the opposite end facing the wall.
     */
    void cleanLine() {
        for (int i = 0; i < 10; i++) {
            if ( onLeaf() )
                removeLeaf();

            secureMove();
        }
    }

    /*
     * Reposition to next line to the west of Clara
     * Pre-condition: located at the end of a line facing a wall.
     * Post-condition: located at the next line not facing a wall.
     */
    void repositionToWest() {
        turnLeft();
        secureMove();
        turnLeft();
    }
```

```
/*
 * Reposition to next line to the east of Clara
 * Pre-condition: located at the end of a line facing a wall.
 * Post-condition: located at the next line not facing a wall.
 */
void repositionToEast() {
   turnRight();
   secureMove();
   turnRight();
}

/*
 * Move forward and avoid crashing into a tree.
 */
void secureMove() {
   if ( !treeFront() )
      move();
}

}
```

4.2.2 Code Indentation

Good coding style is not only about commenting your code. Similarly important is giving your methods and variables (something we will learn about in Chapter 5) good meaningful names, as well as to use correct indentation. Indentation refers to using white space to separate and emphasise blocks of code with a particular goal of attracting attention to code elements that are more important than other.

Attracting attention to important elements of your code is important for being able to understand the code quickly. The human brain seems like a perfect mechanism, but in reality it is far from being perfect. Due to its imperfection our brain needs constant simplification and emphasising. To illustrate this, we would like to suggest you perform a simple exercise. Please try to solve it quickly and pay attention to how much time you had to spend on it and how correct your answer was. You are expected to spend less than 20 seconds on this task. The exercise is as follows:

Brain Teaser: *Read the sentence below and count the number of "f" letters in that sentence.*

FINISHED FILES ARE THE RESULT OF YEARS OF SCIENTIFIC
STUDY COMBINED WITH THE EXPERIENCE OF YEARS.

Try reading the text carefully and focus on counting the letters. How many "f"s did you count? Do you remember what the text was about?

This exercise does not seem very complicated. The text is rather short, and given the perfect brain of yours it would not be too difficult to complete it and produce the perfectly correct answer. However, if you are similar to many other people who have attempted this exercise, you would appreciate that it is a little more challenging that it appears, and the answer you come up with is very likely to be an incorrect one.

The correct answer is six. To convince you that this is the case, let us have a look at the same text presented in a slightly different way.

Finished Files are the result oF years oF scientiFic study
combined with the experience oF years.

You would probably agree that this task became much simpler and it is almost impossible to make an error while solving it after each "F" letter has been emphasised. This example is a good metaphor for explaining why code indentation is used in programming. It helps to emphasise your attention on elements that are important and allows you to quickly skip large chunks of code that you are not interested in. Code indentation has a similar effect to emphasising letters in the above example.

To explain what indentation is let us consider the run() method from the Clara cleaner example shown below:

```
void run() {
    for (int i = 0; i < 5; i++) {
        cleanLine();
        repositionToWest();
        cleanLine();
        repositionToEast();
    }
}
```

Indentation in this case refers to placing additional spaces for every line inside a method, for every line inside an if-statement and for every line inside a loop. A part of indentation is also making sure that curly brackets for every loop, method or if-statement align. In this example, the code inside the run method is "tabbed away", meaning that there are four additional spaces in front of every line. A similar approach is followed for the code inside if-statements and loops (four spaces are placed in front of every line of code located inside of those). In any programming editor (including Clara's World) you can achieve this effect by pressing the "tab" key, which will add the four space characters.

4.2.3 Decomposition

One of the most important aspects of creating good code is to follow the principle of problem decomposition. Problem decomposition means breaking a large problem down into smaller and more manageable sub-problems and producing the problem solution using different levels of abstraction. This definition probably sounds confusing, so let us try to explain this principle on an example.

4.2.3.1 Example: Hurdle Race

In this example Clara trains to participate in in the Olympic Games as a champion in hurdling. Hurdling is the sport that involves running and jumping over obstacles at speed. Unlike traditional hurdling, where all obstacles have the same height, the height of hurdles in Clara's World can vary. Hurdles can be located anywhere in Clara's World. Clara trains for running hurdle races of various distances. For her training she prepared a number of racing tracks, where the end of the track is always marked with a mushroom. Figure 4.2 a) shows Clara's initial position before the start of the race, while Figure 4.2 shows her final position.

 A video that demonstrates solving this problem step-by-step is available at `https:/claraworld.net/link/C4V1`.

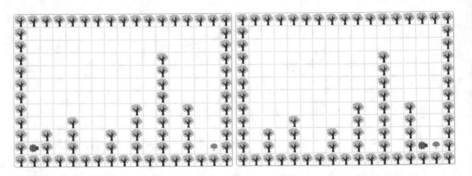

Fig. 4.2: a) Start of the Race   b) Finish of the Race.

 To work on this problem in Clara's World please use the following URL: `https://claraworld.net/link/C4P2`.

If you attempt to solve this problem in one go by starting to type sequences of `move()`, `turnLeft()` and `turnRight()` commands inside the `run()` method, you are most likely going to struggle with solving it. As the counting letters example above showed you, our brain is not perfect and it sometimes struggles with solving very simple tasks. However, we have developed tricks to handle the brain's imperfection, and decomposition is one of them. This is the step that we intuitively follow without even noticing in our daily life, but it is a step that many beginner programmers have difficulties with when it comes to explaining this approach to a machine while writing code.

Exercise: Try solving the hurdle race problem without decomposition and then return to this chapter and compare your solution with the solution shown below. Reflect on this experience while reading the remainder of this chapter.

Let us consider how you would be explaining the process of running a hurdle race to a child, who has never seen such a race before. You would probably say something like: "You need to keep running until you encounter a hurdle in front of you, then you get over the hurdle and then you repeat this process until you are at the finish line". This is exactly what decomposition is all about, a process of taking a larger problem and solving it as a sequence of smaller steps.

The high-level natural language solution presented above is called an **algorithm**. When solving a programming problem, it is always a good idea to first think of an algorithm and then to start thinking about how to turn it into code. It is more common in programming to present algorithms as a number of short steps rather than sentences in free form. Thus, let us present this algorithm in a more common form.

Hurdle Race Algorithm

---

1. Walk to next hurdle
2. Climb over a hurdle
3. Repeat until a mushroom is in front

For solving this problem using Java code we now simply need to convert this algorithm into Java code. An important lesson you should have learned from problem decomposition is that, instead of placing your entire solution inside the run () method, it is better to break it down into smaller sub-problems such as walking until next hurdle, climbing over a hurdle and repeating this until there is a mushroom in front. The part of this process that is most uncomfortable for a beginner programmer is that in doing so we would need to operate with methods that do not yet exist, meaning that we would need to adopt a mentality where we first use the method for solving a problem and then define what this method does.

Let us try to apply what we have learned about decomposition so far to solving the hurdle race problem. We will begin by converting the above algorithm into valid Java code inside the run () method. The first thing we would want to express is making Clara finish the race after encountering a mushroom in front. This task seems very simple. All that is required is a simple while loop that looks as follows:

```
public void run() {
    while ( !mushroomFront() ) {
        move();
    }
}
```

This code would work in the situation with no hurdles present, but in our race this is not the case. Thus, the next step is climbing over hurdles, and this is where decomposition starts to emerge. Clara does not know where the hurdles will be

located, but she can sense being right in front of one by using the treeFront ()
command. With the help of treeFront () we can produce the following high-
level solution:

```
public void run() {
    while ( !mushroomFront() ) {
        if ( !treeFront() )
            move();
        else
            climbHurdle();
    }
}
```

Clara will climb over hurdles whenever there is a tree in front and will be moving
otherwise. If we repeat this logic until Clara encounters a mushroom, she would
then be able to correctly run her race. But what is climbHurdle ()? There is
no such command known to us yet? This is the part that may be uncomfortable to
beginner programmers, as climbHurdle () is a method that does not yet exist,
but a method that we would need to define later.

A simple rule we would recommend beginner programmers to follow is **the rule
of two seconds**. If you are solving a problem or a sub-problem, try thinking about
solving it for two seconds. If a clear solution does not come to you within this time
then it is a sign that you should apply decomposition, meaning that you should break
this problem into smaller sub-problems and then solve these independently.

With the rule of two seconds in mind let us try to think about defining what
climbHurdle () means. If you are a beginner programmer, you would probably
not have a definite answer within two seconds. Therefore, let us simplify this problem by breaking it down into two separate pieces: climbing on top of a hurdle and
climbing down a hurdle. The following code could be used for making this happen:

```
void climbHurdle() {
    climbUp();
    climbDown();
}
```

Again, we had to solve the climbHurdle () problem by using methods that
do not yet exist. This means that both climbUp () and climbDown () must be
further defined. An important thing that we were able to achieve with decomposition
is that we no longer need to think about the larger problem (running the hurdle race).
We can now fully concentrate on programming climbUp () and climbDown ().
These problems can be seen as being completely independent of the main problem.

Let us try applying the two second rule for solving the climbUp () problem.
This problem can be defined as Clara standing in front of a stack of trees, having to
go on top of this stack. Most of you should have a solution idea after thinking about
this problem for two seconds. All that is required is to turn left and then continue
moving while there is a tree on Clara's right. If you were to do this, it is similar
to placing your right hand on a wall and continue climbing up until you no longer
sense the wall with your right hand. Once Clara reaches the point when there is no

tree to her right, she must turn right and make a step, so that she is positioned on top
of the stack of trees. Java code for solving this subproblem is shown below:

```java
void climbUp() {
    if ( treeFront() )
        turnLeft();

    // keep my hand on the right wall and follow it
    // while it's there
    while ( treeRight() ){
        move();
    }

    turnRight();
    move();
}
```

Now only one last piece of the puzzle is left unsolved. The `climbDown()`
method must be defined. With climbing down a hurdle we follow a similar approach
to climbing up, but we can no longer rely on the trees on Clara's side. On her way
down the hurdle Clara would also have trees on her right, but a tree would still be
there when she is all the way down the hurdle. What she must rely on instead is
sensing a tree in front of her. Clara would finish her climb down the hurdle as soon
as she senses a tree in front. Below is a Java solution of this problem:

```java
void climbDown() {
    move();
    turnRight();

    while ( !treeFront() ) {
        move();
    }

    turnLeft();
}
```

The very last command (`turnLeft()`) in the `climbDown()` method requires
explanation. Without having this line Clara would move one step forward (so that
that she is no longer immediately on top of the tree stack), would turn right (towards
the bottom of her world) and would continue moving down until she reaches the
bottom (sensed by a `treeFront()` command). Clara would have successfully
climbed down the hurdle by now. Why do we require the `turnLeft()` command
after this? The reason for having to turn left is that correct decomposition requires
the code on all levels of abstraction to correctly connect. In our case this means that
we expect Clara to face east after climbing over a hurdle. Since climbing over a
hurdle consists of climbing up and climbing down, we must ensure that Clara faces
east within `climbDown()`. This is why the `turnLeft()` command is required.

So far in our solution we haven't been using comments. Commenting code is
not only something that is necessary for commercial programmers, working jointly
on large projects. It is actually even more helpful for beginner programmers. Us-

ing comments develops good habits and can help a lot with avoiding errors or with finding issues in your code faster. Comments can also greatly help beginner programmers learning to use decomposition. To illustrate this, let us get back to the need for adding the `turnLeft()` command in `climbDown()`. The absence of a comment explaining what are the expected pre-conditions and post-conditions for `climbDown()` is what could have made it difficult for many beginner programmers to realise that turning left is required. Earlier in this chapter we discussed that every method we create should have a comment in front, explaining what this method does, as well as what are pre-conditions and post-conditions. Following the advise would have helped us not to forget adding `treeLeft()`, because facing east would have been the post-condition of the `climbDown()` method. Checking the validity of your program on higher levels of abstraction means that, whenever a method is being used, its expectations regarding pre-conditions and post-conditions are met. Let us now add comments to our code and see the complete solution.

```
class MyClara extends Clara {
    // To run the hurdle race we need to move forward
    // forward or jump hurdles until we see a mushroom.
    public void run() {
        while ( !mushroomFront() ) {
            if ( !treeFront() )
                move();
            else
                climbHurdle();
        }
    }

    // Makes Clara climb over a vertical line of trees.
    // Pre-condition: Stands in front of hurdle, faces east
    // Post-condition: Stands behind the hurdles, faces east
    void climbHurdle() {
        climbUp();
        climbDown();
    }

    // Climbs up a hurdle.
    // Pre-condition: Stands in front of hurdle, faces east
    // Post-condition: Stands on top of the hurdle, faces east
    void climbUp() {
        if ( treeFront() )
            turnLeft();

        // follow the right wall while it's there
        while ( treeRight() ){
            move();
        }

        turnRight();
        move();
    }
```

```
// Cimbs down a hurdle.
// Pre-condition: Stands on top of the hurdle, faces east
// Post-condition: Stands behind the hurdle, faces east
void climbDown() {
    move();
    turnRight();

    while ( !treeFront() ) {
        move();
    }

    turnLeft();
}
}
```

 To see the solution of this problem in Clara's World please use the following URL: `https://claraworld.net/link/C4P2S`.

4.2.4 Naming Conventions

You will have noticed that all the methods in the above example seem to follow a similar naming convention. The convention we followed there is the standard for Java developers and is called the "camel case notation". The reason for this name is that methods (and later variables) named this way look similar to a camel with sudden humps. The humps represent capital letters indicating the start of the next word. Let us see some examples of method names that correctly follow this notation.

```
move();
turnRight();
climbHurdle();
```

Here, the first letter of every method name is lower case. If a method name is composed of multiple words, each word (except for the first one) should start with an upper-case letter.

4.3 Summary

In this chapter we have learned about principles of writing good code. To summarise, good code must read like good English, be easy to understand, have comments and follow the camel case naming convention for methods and variables.

We have also learned about code decomposition. Decomposition helps us to tackle complex problems by breaking them down into smaller subproblems (implemented as methods). Before solving a problem it is important to think of an algorithm and then use it for solving the problem.

Decomposition can be also useful for making your code easier to read and quicker to understand. One way of making this happen is to avoid methods that are very long. Below is a summary of decomposition guidelines that we recommend you to follow:

1. Each method you create should solve one problem
2. Each method should be 1–15 lines of code
3. Give methods good names
4. Each name should give a clear idea about the purpose of the method
5. Your code must read like good English, so that humans can easily understand it
6. Have comments for every method
7. Blocks of code that repeat more than once should be placed inside a method

4.4 Exercises

 Exercises that target your understanding of the concepts covered in this chapter are available at `https://claraworld.net/link/C4Ex`.

Chapter 5
Variables

Clara continues her development into an advanced insect. She now has a sense of touch and can recognise a tree in front of her or a leaf underneath. With the help of conditional statements she can vary her behaviour depending on what she can sense. Through the use of loops it is possible for Clara to repeat some of her actions a desired number of times. She can also create new commands and use them in her problem-solving endeavours. In this chapter we will introduce variables. With the help of variables Clara will get a significant boost in her abilities. She will now be able to memorise various events and even count different things in her world.

Image features the "The Big Bang Theory Living Room" photograph by dronepicr available under Creative Commons CC BY 2.0.

© Springer Nature Switzerland AG 2021
A. Bogdanovych, T. Trescak, *Learning Java Programming in Clara's World*,
https://doi.org/10.1007/978-3-030-75542-3_5

5.1 Chapter Story: The Friendship Algorithm

A popular sitcom "The Big Bang Theory" features a character called Sheldon
Cooper, who lacks basic social skills. In Season 2 Episode 13 Sheldon needs to
use the university's super computer for his research. He finds out that Barry Kripke
is in charge of allocating access to this computer. Unfortunately for Sheldon, Barry
tends to only grant access to his friends. Sheldon decides to become Kripke's friend.
However, his initial attempt to befriend Barry fails. In a true scientific manner Sheldon decides to conduct additional research in a public library on the topic of making
friends. He finds a relevant book in the children's section and translates it into the
friendship algorithm shown in Figure 5.1.

 A video featuring the corresponding part of the Big Bang Theory episode
is available at `https:/claraworld.net/link/C5VSheldon`.

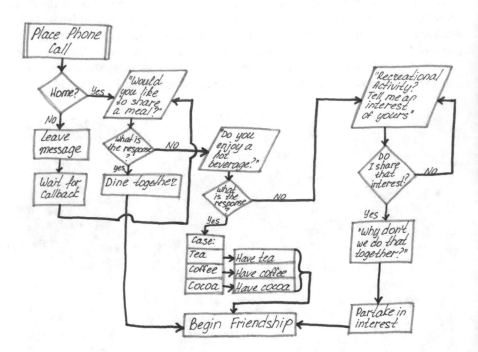

Fig. 5.1: Friendship Algorithm.

Following this algorithm Sheldon attempts to establish friendship with Barry
over the phone and employs the above flowchart. He discovers that Barry is at home,
so he asks him whether Barry would like to share a meal with Sheldon. He receives
a negative response from Kripke and continues following the flowchart by asking

him whether he would enjoy a hot beverage. After receiving another negative response Sheldon continues with the final part of the algorithm, where he asks Barry for an example of a recreational activity that they could do together. Unfortunately for Sheldon, neither of the activities named by Barry represent a shared interest. Sheldon did not take into account the fact that there could be no shared interest, and he is stuck in an infinite loop where he continues to ask Barry: "tell me an interest of yours". One of Sheldon's friends (Howard) comes to the rescue and corrects the algorithm. In the corrected version of the algorithm (shown in Figure 5.2) the loop only repeats six times. After six repetitions Sheldon must select the least objectionable activity (LOA) from the list of Barry's interests and then propose to engage in this activity together and partake in the interest. This should result in establishing friendship. After identifying rock climbing as the least objectionable activity Sheldon eagerly starts searching for rock climbing lessons on the Internet.

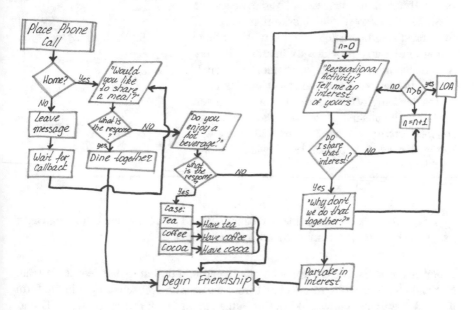

Fig. 5.2: Corrected Friendship Algorithm.

The flowchart shown in Figure 5.2 is one of the few ways to represent an algorithm. In Chapter 4 we showed how algorithms can be described with pseudocode. Using flowcharts is another common form of illustrating algorithms. In this example we have blue rectangular boxes that represent commands (methods) that can be performed. The diamond shaped boxes are conditional statements that can result in true (yes) or false (no). Red arrows illustrate the execution flow.

A substantial portion of this algorithm is quite straightforward as it contains a simple sequence of actions. The most interesting part for our purposes is requesting an interest from a potential friend in a loop and then selecting the least objectionable activity. What makes this part interesting is the fact that selecting the least objectionable activity would require using some kind of memory. This is something we do not yet know how to do.

5.2 Chapter Problem: Selecting the Least Objectionable Activity

Sheldon Cooper must become friends with Barry Kripke. He has developed the friendship algorithm and follows it while talking to Barry over the phone. The final part of this algorithm (shown on the right) requires asking Barry for one of his interests. If one of the interests received matches one of Sheldon's interest, the algorithm succeeds. If the interest does not match, Sheldon must continue asking until Barry provides six interests. If there is no match after six attempts Sheldon must analyse the interest received and select the least objectionable activity (LOA) from the interests given by Barry. The matching interest or the least objectionable activity is what Sheldon and Barry will do together as an important step towards becoming friends.

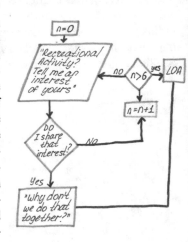

 To work on this problem in Clara's World please use the following URL:
https://claraworld.net/link/C5P1.

For this problem Clara will not be moving around or manipulate leaves. Instead, she would be required to receive input from the user and present output in the form of text. We will learn how to do all this in the remainder of this chapter. Let us start presenting the new material that is necessary for solving the chapter problem by explaining how Clara may memorise something using variables.

5.3 Variables

You may be familiar with the concept of variables from mathematics. Variables in programming are very similar and are probably much friendlier. In programming variables are predominantly used for storing data of a particular type and not so much for defining and solving equations (which is also possible). In simple terms, a variable is a box (a place in your computer's memory) that has the following three characteristics: **name**, **type** and **value**. Figure 5.3 illustrates this simple idea.

Fig. 5.3: A Variable as a Box.

Let us have a detailed discussion about each of the three characteristics of a variable in details before showing examples of how they are used.

5.3.1 Variable Names

Variable names in Java use a similar notation and similar principles to method names. A variable name must start with a letter or underscore "_". It is not permitted in Java for the first character of a variable name to be a digit. A variable name may only contain alphanumeric characters (digits 0–9 and letters a–z or A–Z), underscores (_) and the dollar sign ($). The dollar sign is rarely used in Java.

It is important to remember that, similar to method names, variable names are also case sensitive. This means that `itemsPurchased` and `itemspurchased` would be treated by Java as two separate variables.

Similar to method names, variable names cannot include spaces. Another limitation on naming variables is that a variable name (as well as a method name) cannot be one of Java's reserved keywords. Table 5.1 presents the list of all such keywords that are not allowed to be used as variable or method names.

Table 5.1: The List of Java Reserved Keywords

abstract	assert	boolean	break
byte	case	catch	char
class	const	continue	default
do	double	else	enum
extends	false	for	final
finally	float	goto	if
implements	import	instanceof	int
interface	long	native	new
null	package	private	protected
public	return	short	static
strictfp	super	switch	synchronized
this	throw	throws	transient
true	try	void	volatile
while			

In addition to the aforementioned strict limitations there are also variable naming conventions. Not following these conventions does not represent an error, however, following them helps to adhere to good coding style and should be respected. As per Java variable naming conventions, variable names should be descriptive and it should be clear from the variable name what purpose a particular variable serves. Below is an example of a fragment of code that declares variables for computing bank account balances:

```
double a = 32.58; // against Java conventions
double accountBalance = 1500.23; // following conventions
```

Here the variable called "a" does not violate the strict rules of the Java language, but it violates Java conventions, as the name of the variable is not descriptive. The name "accountBalance" is a much better choice, since the purpose of this variable is much clearer. When programming in Java you should always attempt to make your code easier to understand, and using descriptive variable names is an important part of this. The code that contains descriptive variable and method names can be considered to be self-documenting, meaning that it is easy to understand what this code does without having to read the comments.

Another important convention for naming variables that should be respected is using the so-called camel case notation. Camel case notation was respected in the above example for declaring the `accountBalance` variable. The essence of this notation is that variable names that consist of multiple words should use upper case letters for the first letter of every word (excluding the very first word) and lower case letters for everything else. Java methods should also follow the camel case notation. In general, it is also expected that variable names predominantly contain nouns, while method names should also contain verbs.

5.3.2 Variable Types

The second characteristic of a variable is its type. When declaring a variable in Java its type must be explicitly specified. The type of a variable determines which type of values a variable can store. If we continue with our metaphor of a variable being a box, we may say that a variable's type would determine the size of the corresponding box. Java language comes with eight data types embedded in the language (called primitive data types). The most commonly used primitive data types are shown in Table 5.2.

Table 5.2: Commonly Used Primitive Data Types

`int`	- stores integer values
`double`	- stores real values
`boolean`	- stores logical values (`true` or `false`)
`char`	- stores characters

In the above table the first two data types (`int` and `double`) are used for storing numeric values. A variable of type `int` would store integer numbers, while variables of type `double` store real numbers. The `boolean` data type allows programmers to store logical values. These values are limited to only one of the two possible options (`true` or `false`). Finally, the `char` data type helps to store individual characters. Each variable of the `char` type can store one character.

Unlike mathematics, in programming it is important to explicitly differentiate between real and integer numbers. One of the reasons for this is that in programming we often need to count repetitions (e.g. inside `for`-loops), and it is useful for the variables responsible for counting these repetitions to be integers. When dealing with integer numbers we can easily obtain the next number after, say "3" (being "4"), which is much more difficult when dealing with real numbers. The next real number after "3" simply does not exist. One may argue that the next number is "4", while it could also be "4.1" or "4.01", etc. Another reason for explicitly differentiating between different types of numbers is the memory footprint (size of the box) associated with a variable. Table 5.3 shows an exhaustive list of all primitive data types responsible for numeric values, the range of values that each type covers and the associated memory footprint. Each variable you declare is stored in the memory of your computer. This memory is a limited resource, and you should always attempt to minimise the amount of memory that your program uses. As you see from Table 5.3, the memory footprint varies between 1 byte (for variables of type `byte`) and 8 bytes (for variables of type `double`).

Table 5.3: Primitive Data Types, Range and Memory Usage

`byte`	1 byte	Integer values in the range - 128 to +127
`short`	2 bytes	Integer values in the range -32,768 to +32,767
`int`	4 bytes	Integer values in the range -2,147,483,648 to 2,147,483,647
`long`	8 bytes	Integer values in the range -9,223,372,036,854,775,808 to 9,223,372,036,854,775,807
`float`	4 bytes	Real numbers in the range $3.40282347 \times 10^{38}$ to $1.40239846 \times 10^{-45}$
`double`	8 bytes	Real numbers in the range $1.7976931348623157 \times 10^{308}$ to $4.9406564584124654 \times 10^{-324}$

The choice of a numeric data type should be made depending on whether it is expected for the corresponding variable to store numbers with a decimal point or not and on the expected range of values for this variable. If numbers after the decimal points are required (for example, if you will be computing account balances and want to represent dollars and cents), then either `double` or `float` types should be used. The range of possible values depends on the problem that your code is solving. For example, if you need to count the number of people that live on planet Earth then you have no other choice but to work with the `long` data type. Other types (such as `double` or `float`) would not be suitable because they operate with numbers that contain a decimal point, while all other data types that work with integer numbers (such as `byte`, `short` and `int`) are limited to values that are smaller than the number of people currently living on our planet.

Apart from the eight primitive data types Java also contains one special data type embedded in the language. This data type is "`String`". The `String` data type is used for storing fragments of text. The fact that this is a special data type and not a primitive data type is apparent from the first letter "S" being upper case. All primitive data types in Java start with a lower-case letter, while all special data types are expected to start with an upper-case letter.

5.3.3 Variable Values

Each variable is always associated with one value. It is possible in Java to declare a variable without specifying its value. In such situations Java would automatically assign the values of such variables to be the default value for the particular data type. The default value for most numeric types is 0. The default value for the boolean type is `false`. The default value for `char` is `'\u0000'` and the default value for String is "`null`". As one would expect, possible values of a variable are restricted by the range of values associated with a particular type (for numeric type ranges see Table 5.3).

Values of type `String` that appear in Java code must be enclosed in quotation marks, such as `"this is a String value"`, while values of type `char` are enclosed within apostrophes (`'c'`).

5.3.4 Declaring Variables

Variables can be created (declared) by specifying the type of a variable followed by a space (or a number of spaces) and then specifying the name of the variable. Each variable declaration must end with a semicolon. Below are some examples of valid variable declarations:

```
int x;
byte inches;
short month;
int speed;
long timeStamp;
float salesCommission;
double distance;
```

It is common for each variable to be declared on a separate line. However, Java also permits declaring multiple variables of the same type within one line of code. Specifying a data type followed by multiple names separated by commas will create multiple variables of this type. The example below creates five variables (v1, v2, v3, v4 and v5) of type int:

```
int v1, v2, v3, v4, v5;
```

5.3.5 Assigning Variable Values

When declaring a variable you can immediately assign its value after the "=" symbol. The code example below illustrates declaring two variables and assigning their values:

```
int a = 2;
```

a   2

```
double b = 4.7;
```

b   4.7

The images on the right-hand side illustrate these variable using the box metaphor. After executing the above code the corresponding boxes would be assigned with the values that appear on the right-hand side of the "=" operator. It is important to notice that the box associated with the b variable is twice as large as the box of the a variable. This reflects the fact that a variable of type dobule occupies twice as much memory (8 bytes) than a variable of type int (4 bytes).

Variable values can be assigned anywhere in your program's code (not only during initialisation). If you are assigning a value of a variable that has already been declared, you no longer need to specify its type. The example below shows how a value of variable a can be reassigned after making Clara turn left:

```
int a = 2;
turnLeft();
a = 7;
```

Running this code would result in the variable x first created with the initial value of 2. After turning left this value would then be changed to 7. The statement a = 5 has a slightly different meaning to what you are used to seeing in mathematics. In programming "=" is always an assignment operator (used for assigning a value) and nothing else, while in mathematics it is often a comparison operator. Below is an example of a code fragment that may initially make little sense to you and may even seem wrong if you are not used to seeing variables outside of mathematics:

```
int a = 2;
a = a + 1;
```

Your initial reaction to this code might be to protest and argue that the last statement makes absolutely no sense, as the value of a cannot be the same as a + 1. The above code, however, is perfectly valid, because "=" is not a comparison operator, but an assignment operator. It is used for assigning a value to the variable (a) on the left-hand side. When computing the new value of a it is perfectly normal in programming to refer to the current value of a and do computations with it. The right-hand side of the a = a + 1 equation extracts the current value of a (2) and increments it by one. The result (3) is then stored inside a. In the process of running this code variable a would first be initialised with the value of 2 and would then be updated to the value of 3.

You may ask whether comparison similar to mathematics is at all possible in programming. The answer, of course, is: "yes". The key difference from mathematics is that comparison in Java looks different from in mathematics. The comparison operator is "==", not "=". The example below illustrates how comparison works in Java. Here we first declare the variable result and assign its value to 9. We then perform a comparison within an if-statement to test whether the value of the variable is 1. If the value happens to be 1, Clara would then turn left.

```
int result = 9; // assigning a value of 9
if ( result == 1) { // testing the value
    turnLeft();
}
```

In this example Clara would, of course, not turn left because the value of result is not 1. The value of result would remain being 9 and will not change.

5.3.6 Variable Visibility

Variables can be declared inside any of your methods and even within the body of your program and outside of any methods. Each variable that you declare is only known (visible) inside the pair of curly brackets within which it was created. Within this set of curly brackets each of your variables must have a unique name. Trying to declare multiple variables with the same name (within the same set of curly brackets) would result in a compilation error.

The code example below shows declaring two variables with different visibility. One of them (a) is declared outside of any methods, but inside the body of the program (within the main set of curly brackets {}). This variable would be visible everywhere inside the program and inside all of its methods (run() and swapValue()). The second variable (b) is declared inside the run() method and, therefore, is only known there. Attempting to use it (by calling int d = b;) within swapValue() would cause a compilation error because variable b is not known inside this method. Another problem in the code below is the last line (int a = 10;) inside the run() method. Here we are attempting to declare another variable a, but this variable name has already been used. There is another variable called a that was declared just above the run() method that is also visible within run(). It is illegal in Java to have multiple variables with the same name, so this line would cause a compilation error and the program, therefore, will not run.

```
public class MyClara extends Clara {
    int a = 5;

    void run() {
        double b;
        int a = 10; // would result in a compilation error
    }

    void swapValue() {
        int c = a // would work
        int d = b; // would result in a compilation error
    }
}
```

5.4 Receiving User Input from Keyboard

Variables in programming are frequently used for receiving data from the user and memorising this data within the program. The simplest form of receiving user input is letting a user type something from the keyboard within a dialog window. Clara's World framework supports the following three methods of receiving keyboard input:

- readInt – enter an integer value
- readDouble – enter a real value
- readString – enter a text value

The aforementioned commands are methods that receive input and return output. An extended discussion of such methods will be provided in Chapter 8. What is important to understand at this stage is that Java supports methods that receive input and return a value and that such values are returned as variables. Below are some examples of receiving keyboard input and storing it within variables. The text that you type inside parenthesis (such as "Enter text here: ") will be the text displayed at the top of the corresponding dialog window.

```
String textInput = readString("Enter text here: ");
int intInput = readInt("Enter an integer number: ");
double realInput = readInt("Enter a real number: ");
```

As the result of running this code you will see three dialogs appear on the screen as shown in Figure 5.4. They will appear one-by-one, and code execution will pause until you type in a value of the correct type and press "OK".

The values you type inside the text entry field would be memorised in the textInput, intInput and realInput variables correspondingly.

Fig. 5.4: Dialogs for Keyboard Input.

5.5 Console Output

Another important piece of functionality of Clara's World (and Java in general) is printing text on the screen. Java programs feature the environment called "console". This environment allows programmers to display the output of their programs. In many Java frameworks, console appears as a separate window. In Clara's World, console is simply a part of the screen of the main window of your program. Producing console output in Java is possible via the following two commands: `System.out.print` and `System.out.println`. The difference between these two commands lies in the fact that the latter command would result in printing the text to console and would ensure that everything that is printed after appears on the new line. In contrast, everything that is printed after a `System.out.print` command would start printing on the same line.

Let us see a combined example that illustrates using keyboard input and console output. In this example we ask the user to enter their first and last name and then greet the user.

 A video of solving a simplified version of this problem is available at `https:/claraworld.net/link/C5V1`.

```
public class MyClara extends Clara {
    void run() {
        System.out.println("Programming is great fun!");
        String firstName = readString("Enter your first name: ");
        String lastName = readString("Enter your last name: ");
        System.out.print("Hello, ");
        System.out.print(firstName);
        System.out.print(" ");
        System.out.print(lastName);
    }
}
```

In this program we received user input and stored it in two `String` variables (`firstName` and `lastName`). The values of these variables are then printed on the screen. The fact that we are printing a value of a variable rather than some text (e.g. "firstName") is reflected by not using quotation marks in the corresponding lines of code. Whenever we do not use quotation marks inside the parentheses of `System.out.print` or `System.out.println`, Java assumes that we are requesting to print the value of a variable with the name that appears inside parentheses. If this name exists, the value will be printed, or otherwise a compilation error would be reported. If we run the above code and enter "John" for first name and "Smith" for last name, the output of the program would look as follows:

```
Programming is great fun!
Hello, John Smith
```

Let us now see another example that illustrates working with numeric variables. The code below asks the user to enter two integer numbers and prints the sum of these numbers:

```
public class MyClara extends Clara {
   void run() {
      int n1 = readInt("Enter n1: ");
      int n2 = readInt("Enter n2: ");
      int sum = n1 + n2;
      System.out.println(sum);
   }
}
```

Running the above code and entering 3 (for n1) and 4 (for n2) would result in the output of 7.

5.6 Friendship Algorithm: Memorising Interests

Now that we have a basic understanding of variables and how to work with them for receiving user input and printing output on the screen we can start solving the chapter problem (friendship algorithm). Let us begin by producing the code for memorising six interests and printing those on the screen. Memorising six interest would require six variables. Since what we want to memorise is text (not numbers or characters) these variables must be of type String. The code below shows the solution of this simplified problem:

 You can see a video explanation of how to solve this simplified problem at https://claraworld.net/link/C5V2.

```
public class MyClara extends Clara {
   // Initialise 6 variables that will store user interests
   String inter1, inter2, inter3, inter4, inter5, inter6;

   // Text prompt for the interest entry dialog
   String dialogMessage = "Tell me an interest of yours: ";
```

```
void run() {
    enterUserInterests();
    printUserInterests();
}

/*
 * Request 6 user interest in the String form
 * and save those into our variables
 */
void enterUserInterests() {
    inter1 = readString(dialogMessage);
    inter2 = readString(dialogMessage);
    inter3 = readString(dialogMessage);
    inter4 = readString(dialogMessage);
    inter5 = readString(dialogMessage);
    inter6 = readString(dialogMessage);
}

/*
 * Print user interests that are stored in variables.
 * variables interest 1 - 6 must be initialised
 */
void printUserInterests() {
    System.out.println(inter1);
    System.out.println(inter2);
    System.out.println(inter3);
    System.out.println(inter4);
    System.out.println(inter5);
    System.out.println(inter6);
}
}
```

We have separated the solution into two parts that are handled by the corresponding methods. The `enterUserInterests()` method is in charge of receiving user interests, and `printUserInterests()` displays those on the screen. For storage of user interests we use the variables `inter1`, `inter2`, ..., `inter6`. We have also created an additional `String` variable (`dialogMessage`) for memorising the "Tell me an interest of yours: " message that would appear in every text entry dialog.

Try running this code and entering some of your interests as input values to the program. See how these values are displayed on the screen. Are these values printed correctly?

The code we have written does not look optimal. Notice how the code inside `enterUserInterests()` and `printUserInterests()` appears repetitive. An experienced programmer would look into this code and would immediately feel that this code could be shortened with the use of loops. However, using loops in this code is not possible since every line inside the aforementioned methods is using a different variable name. Further in this chapter we will show how we could optimise this code so that the use of loops would become a possibility.

5.7 Mid Point Example

Let us take a short break and practise a little more with variables before producing the complete solution of the friendship algorithm. In the next simple (and more visual) exercise our goal will be to find the centre of the street where Clara is positioned and to place a leaf at the middle of this street as shown in Figure 5.5. As often happens in this book, in solving this problem we aim at developing a general-purpose solution that would not only work for the example world shown below, but one that would work for a street of any length.

To work on this problem in Clara's World please use the following URL:
https://claraworld.net/link/C5P2.

Fig. 5.5: a) Initial State   b) Final State with a Leaf in the Middle.

Exercise: This problem could be solved without using variables through manipulating many leaves. We encourage you to try doing this and enrich your problem-solving capabilities in this way.

Let us discuss how this problem can be solved with variables. A simple strategy that could be employed is to make Clara walk until the end of the street and count how many steps she makes (the length of the street). After reaching the end of the street, Clara should then turn around and walk half the number of steps that she memorised as the street length. As the result of doing this she would appear at the street centre. She should then finish by placing a leaf and stepping away. The code below shows a Java implementation of this algorithm:

```
class MyClara extends Clara {
    public void run() {
        int steps = 0;

        // Go to the end of the street and count steps
        while ( !treeFront() ) {
            move();
            steps = steps + 1; // steps++;
        }
```

```
System.out.println("steps = " + steps);

// now we know how long is the street
// if we divide this length by 2
// then we know how many steps we need
// to get to the middle of the street
steps = steps / 2;
System.out.println("steps to middle = " + steps);

// now turn around
// and keep going back
turnAround();

// All we have to do now - is to move in a for loop
// and repeat it for the numer of times that equals
// to the length of the street divided by 2
for ( int i = 0; i < steps; i++) {
    move();
}

// We are done. Put that leaf down
putLeaf();

// and step away
if ( !treeFront() )
    move();
}

void turnAround() {
    turnRight();
    turnRight();
}
}
```

 You can see a video explanation of how to solve this problem step-by-step at https://claraworld.net/link/C5V3.

The key part of this solution is to use the variable steps for counting the number of steps Clara makes until the end of the street. At the start of our program we declare this variable and assign its initial value to 0. Selecting appropriate initial values for your variables is quite important. In our case the choice of 0 for the initial value of steps is due to the fact that Clara has not started moving and, therefore, the length of the street at this stage is 0.

After declaring and initialising the variable we then work with it inside a while loop. Clara will make a step (move()) every loop iteration until she encounters a tree in front. In parallel with moving, Clara would also be increasing the value of the steps variable by one after every step she makes. Incrementing a variable by one can be achieved in two different ways. We could do this by executing the following code `steps = steps + 1`. An alternative way is to replace this line by `steps++`. If you uncomment the `steps++` command, remove the part of the line to its left and then run the code, you will see no difference in the outcome. This is because `steps++` is the so-called shorthand for incrementing a value by one. Java has a number of such shorthands integrated into the language aiming to reduce the amount of typing for operations that are common in many solutions. We will have a detailed look at these in Chapter 6.

After executing the `while` loop, the `steps` variable would contain the number of steps Clara made until the end of the street. Next in our solution we print the value of this variable on the screen and then divide it by two. We could have created an additional variable for storing the result of this division and memorising how many steps Clara must make so that she appears at the middle of the street. However, you should always try to reduce the memory footprint of your code and not use additional variables where you can avoid doing so. In our case, the `steps` variable has served its purpose for storing the length of the street and can now be reused for storing the number of steps to the street centre.

The final important part of our solution is making Clara turn around and then move the same number of times as the updated value of the `steps` variable. In our code we do this within a `for` loop. Now that you have learned about variables you should understand `for` loops better. What happens inside the parentheses of a `for` loop is: a) declaring and initialising a variable (`int i = 0;`), b) introducing a condition for when to continue iterating the loop (`i < steps`) and c) increment-ing the loop counter (`i++`). The `for` loop in this code looks a little different from the loops we had before. Instead of the loop testing part containing a number and looking like `i < 10`, we used a variable. The effect of using a variable is that the value of this variable would be extracted at run time and then used in a similar way to how the number `10` would have been used. In our case this helps us to dynami-cally compute the number of steps that Clara must make to end up at the centre of the street and make this work on a street of any length.

After arriving at the street centre Clara places a leaf and steps away. In our at-tempt at coming up with a generic solution we are also making sure that there is no tree in front of Clara and that stepping away is a possibility. There could be a tree in front of Clara in a situation when the street is very short.

The solution is complete. Try running it and selecting different example worlds to make sure that it is indeed generic and works with all the supplied examples.

 To see the solution of this problem in Clara's World please use the fol-lowing URL: `https://claraworld.net/link/C5P2S`.

The last thing we would like to focus your attention on is the fact that a `for` loop is a specific case of a `while` loop. We could have easily rewritten that part of the code containing the `for` loop as follows:

```
int i = 0;
while (i < steps) {
    move();
    i++;
}
```

This code is equivalent to its `for` loop version below:

```
for ( int i = 0; i < steps; i++) {
    move();
}
```

Despite them being equivalent, it is preferable to always use the `for` loop for situations when we need to repeat something a known number of times and a `while` loop for situations when the number of repetitions is not known in advance. This helps to improve the readability of your code. The `for` loop implementation is more compact (which means less typing), and seeing a `for` loop in your code would implicitly communicate to the person reading it that the number of repetitions is know in advance (helping to understand the code quicker).

5.8 Friendship Algorithm: Finding LOA

We are now fully prepared for tackling the friendship algorithm. For the sake of simplicity we can assume that Sheldon only has one interest (physics) and is not interested in anything else. Our task is to receive six user interests and if none of them directly matches Sheldon's interest (physics) we would have to select the least objectionable one and print it on the screen. If we convert the relevant part of the diagram from Figure 5.2 into pseudocode, we would obtain the following high-level algorithm:

```
Memorise my interest (assume only 1)
Repeat 6 times:
   Request user interest
   If the interest matches mine then
     stop repeat and nominate LOA
   otherwise
     Memorise user interest
     Compare each user interest with mine
   Find LOA by comparing all interests
Initiate LOA
```

It is difficult for us to establish a good heuristic for how Sheldon would select the least objectionable activity (LOA). It is also not the purpose of this chapter to go deep into simulating Sheldon's cognitive processes. As a simple compromise we could come up with an approach that works. What we could employ is a simple high-level approach, which is to count the number of letters in each user interest and compare this number with the number of letters contained in Sheldon's only interest (physics). The least objectionable activity would be the one with the most similar number of letters to the word "physics" (which contains 7 letters). If one of the user interests, for example, is "horse riding" (12 letters) and another interest is "ventrilo-quism" (13 letters) then the distance between "horse riding" and "physics" would be 5 letters (12 – 7) and the difference between "ventriloquism" and "physics" would be 6 letters (13 – 7). Between the two aforementioned activities, therefore, "horse riding" would be the least objectionable one. For computing the distance between two activities in this way we have developed the `activityDistance` method that is supplied with the skeleton code for this problem. The implementation of this method is shown below:

```
int activityDistance(String activity1, String activity2) {
    int retVal = 0;

    if ( activity1.length > activity2.length )
        retVal = activity1.length - activity2.length;
    else
        retVal = activity2.length - activity1.length;

    return retVal;
}
```

This method relies on study material that we have not yet covered (about methods that receive input and return output). It will be covered in Chapter 8. What is important for you to understand is that this method receives two variables of type `String` as input and returns the distance between these two strings. The distance is obtained by counting the length of each `String` representing an interest and returning the resulting distance as the output of the method. This method can then be used for comparing "physics" with each of the interests provided by the user (the person on the other side of the phone) and selecting the interest with the smallest possible distance as the least objectionable activity (LOA). It is possible for multiple interests to have the same distance to "physics". In this case any of those can be nominated as LOA. The simplest strategy is to nominate the first such interest.

The high-level algorithm we showed above for finding the least objectionable activity has one serious problem: it requires six variables. Because of this, it is difficult to employ loops for receiving user interests. It is good that we only need to process six user interests in our search for the least objectionable activity. Imagine that we have to process hundreds of interests instead of six. We would then need to declare hundreds of variables and hundreds of similar-looking `readString` calls in our code. It is common in programming to have to process hundreds of items, and there is a way to do this without declaring so many variables. Let us see how our algorithm could be optimised so that we can use loops for processing the input and are not required to create a unique variable for each interest entered by the user.

The optimised version of the friendship algorithm implementation employs a coding pattern that is quite common in programming. Having to deal with six variables in our initial implementation prevented us from shortening the code and employing a loop for its repetitive parts. What is important to understand is that we do not actually need to store all six interests, since we only need to select the least objectionable activity as the result. Instead of storing all the interests we can memorise only the best candidate for being the least objectionable activity. We can then receive the next user interest and see whether it is a better candidate or not. If it happens to be a better candidate, we would then treat it as such; if not, we would then request the next interest. The pseudocode of the optimised algorithm for identifying the LOA is shown below:

```
Memorise my interest (assume only 1)
Set LOA to nothing
Repeat 6 times
   Request user interest
   If interest matches with mine then
      stop repeat
   otherwise
      Compare interest with current LOA
      If interest is a better LOA candidate
         Memorise interest as current LOA
Initiate LOA
```

Let us now see how this algorithm could be translated into Java code. We would require the following variables:

```
String   sheldonInterest = "Physics";
String   loa = "nothing";
int      loaDistance = 500;
```

Here `sheldonInterest` is the variable that stores the only interest of Sheldon and will be used for comparison with user interests. The `loa` variable will be used in our code for storing the best LOA candidate. We would also need to memorise the distance between Sheldon's interest and the current LOA candidate, so that we can perform quick comparisons. The variable responsible for this is `loaDistance`. In the above code we have initialised this variable with a value of 500. The reason for doing this is to make sure that we start with a large enough number, so that the corresponding distance for the very first interest we enter is smaller and it becomes LOA. This point will become clearer as we progress with the implementation.

 You can see a video explanation of how to solve this problem step-by-step at `https://claraworld.net/link/C5V4`.

Now that we have created variables supporting the LOA selection, we can introduce the `for` loop that will handle entering user interests and finding the LOA. We will be using the `readString` command for entering one of the user interests. Each time we receive a new interest, it will be stored in the same variable (`currentInterest`). Within the loop body we would then need to decide whether this interest is a good candidate for becoming the LOA or not. The code of this loop is shown below:

```
for (int i = 0; i < 6; i++) {
    String prompt = "Tell me an interest of yours: ";
    String currentInterest = readString(prompt);
    int currentDistance = activityDistance(currentInterest,
        sheldonInterest);

    if (currentDistance < loaDistance) {
        loaDistance = currentInterestDistance;
        loa = currentInterest;
    }

    if ( currentInterest == sheldonInterest )
        break;
}
```

The important part of the above code is computing the distance between the currentInterst (that we received from the user in the current iteration of the loop) and sheldonInterest (physics). After computing this distance we check whether this distance (currentDistance) is smaller than the distance that was stored within loaDistance (which represents the distance between sheldonInterest and the current LOA candidate). If it is smaller, then we found a new LOA candidate and should store it in loa and update the distance in loaDistance. Otherwise we simply ignore the currentInterest and continue with the next iteration of the loop. It is important to note that because we have initialised loaDistance with a very high number (500) the if (currentDistance < loaDistance) statement will return true for whatever text we type as the first interest of the user (if this text does not exceed 500 characters, which is unlikely). In this way we can make sure that the first interest will temporarily become the LOA and will remain so until a better candidate emerges. It is also important to mention that if the user happens to enter "physics" as one of the interests we must stop our search for LOA, since "physics" would directly match Sheldon's only interest and no further search will be needed. Termination of our search is achieved by executing the break; command. In chapter 3 it was mentioned that this command should be avoided for better code readability. Here, however, we see one of the examples where the use of this command is justified.

The complete solution of the friendship algorithm is shown below. In order to test how our code works we also print the values of each interest and the associated distance.

```
class MyClara extends Clara {
    public void run() {
        String  sheldonInterest = "Physics";
        String  loa = "nothing";
        int   loaDistance = 500;

        System.out.println("Perhaps, we can share a recreational
            activity together?");
```

```java
// We will request the interest of the user 6 times
// If our interests happen to match (physics is entered)
// then we exit the loop and stop asking (break call)
for (int i = 0; i < 6; i++) {
    // Memorise user input in currentInterest
    String prompt = "Tell me an interest of yours: ";
    String currentInterest = readString(prompt);
    int currentDistance = activityDistance(currentInterest,
        sheldonInterest);

    // Let's print the distance on the screen
    System.out.println(currentInterest + ": distance = " +
        currentDistance);

    // Update the stored least objectionable activity if
    // found one with a shorter distance
    if (currentDistance < loaDistance) {
        loaDistance = currentDistance;
        loa = currentInterest;
    }

    // Stop the loop if the user types "Physics"
    if ( currentInterest == sheldonInterest ) {
        leastObjectionableActivity = sheldonInterest;
        break;
    }
}

// If no interest matches "Physics" we have to present LOA
if ( loa != sheldonInterest )
    System.out.println("Your "+ loa + " interest strikes me
        as the least objectionable one.");

System.out.println("Let us do " + loa + " together!");
}

// This is a method that returns a variable.
// It calculates how close two activities are to one another
// by comparing the number of characters in each activity
int activityDistance(String activity1, String activity2) {
    int retVal = 0;

    if ( activity1.length > activity2.length )
        retVal = activity1.length - activity2.length;
    else
        retVal = activity2.length - activity1.length;

    return retVal;
}
}
```

To see the solution of this problem in Clara's World please use the following URL: `https://claraworld.net/link/C5P1S`.

If we enter the following interests: "miniature trains", "coding", "3D chess", "comic books", "flags" and "watching Star Trek" as user interests we would receive the following output.

```
Perhaps, we can share a recreational activity together?
miniature trains: distance = 9
coding: distance = 1
3D chess: distance = 1
comic books: distance = 4
flags: distance = 2
watching Star Trek: distance = 11
Your coding interest strikes me as the least objectionable one.
Let us do coding together!
```

As you see, the above code would correctly select "coding" as the interest with the smallest distance to "physics". Since for replacing the LOA it is required for the distance to be smaller than what has been already memorised, we would not select "3D Chess" despite the fact that it has the same distance to "physics".

5.9 Summary

In this chapter we have introduced the concept of variables. Variables give Clara memory and allow her to remember events that happen and facts that become known. With the help of variables Clara can count leaves in her environment and even simulate the friendship algorithm from The Big Bang Theory sitcom. In the next chapter we will continue learning about variables and focus on how variables can be used for doing simple calculations.

5.10 Exercises

 Exercises that target your understanding of the concepts covered in this chapter are available at `https://claraworld.net/link/C5Ex`.

Chapter 6
Expressions

Now that Clara can use variables she has rapidly advanced in her abilities. Variables gave her memory. She can now memorise various events that had happened and later recall these memories and use them in her decision-making. In this chapter we will further advance Clara's abilities. We will teach her some mathematics. In particular, we will be covering the use of arithmetic operations. We will also teach her how to handle situations when Clara must act in response to an event that has (or has not) happened in the past.

© Springer Nature Switzerland AG 2021
A. Bogdanovych, T. Trescak, *Learning Java Programming in Clara's World*,
https://doi.org/10.1007/978-3-030-75542-3_6

6.1 Chapter Story: Letterboxes with Flags

In the United States of America there is an interesting tradition related to letterboxes. Many letterboxes have a flag attached. This flag is used as a form of communication between the mailbox owner and the mail delivery person. This communication can happen in two different ways. The mailman raises the flag after inserting incoming mail into the letterbox, as a signal that can be see from the owner's house, indicating that there is new mail. This flag can also be used as a form of communication from the house owner to the mailman. House owners can insert their outgoing mail into the letterbox and then raise the flag. This flag then becomes a signal for a mailman driving or walking past this house, indicating that there is some outgoing mail that needs to be collected and delivered to the post office (where it will be sent out).

This simple metaphor of a flag as a communication instrument is widely used in programming. We use flags to memorise whether a particular event has or has not happened. Flags in programming are represented by boolean variables. Let us now present the chapter problem that employs this technique.

6.2 Chapter Problem: Using Flags

Clara has successfully acquired a working holiday visa to the USA. While travelling around the country, meeting new people and having fun, Clara decides to work in mail delivery. She finds herself in the small town of Claraville, consisting of ten houses. In Claraville there is a small lane leading to every house. At the beginning of each lane there is a letterbox. Clara must learn how to work with letterbox flags. Based on whether the flag is set or not she must decide whether to pick up mail or to deliver some advertisement brochures to the street where she is at. It is a rainy day today, so instead of leaving the mail inside the letterbox Clara decides to take it all the way to the owner's house (under the roof). She must leave the flag correctly set depending on whether she delivered mail (flag is up) or collected mail (flag is down).

 To work on this problem in Clara's World please use the following URL: https://claraworld.net/link/C6P1.

Let us see how this problem looks in Clara's World. Clara is located at the beginning of the first street in her town and must walk until the end of the last street as shown in Figure 6.1. Her town is organised in such a way that every small street starts on the western side (left edge of Figure 6.1) and the houses are located on the eastern edge. The first street starts at the southern edge (bottom) of Figure 6.1.

 You can see a video explanation of how to solve this problem step-by-step at https://claraworld.net/link/C6V1.

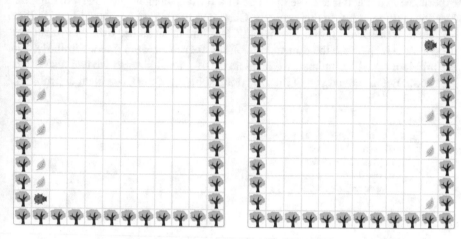

Fig. 6.1: a) Before Mail Delivery   b) After Mail Delivery.

The scenario shown in Figure 6.1 a) illustrates the case of Clara having flags set on the second, third, fifth and ninth streets. On those streets she would put the flag down and would then collect the outgoing mail. On all other streets she would set the flag up and would deliver mail (illustrated by placing a leaf at the end of the street). The result should look similar to Figure 6.1 b).

6.3 Boolean Variables

The aforementioned letterbox flag did not only become a widespread visual metaphor for email clients, but also a conceptual metaphor for programming with boolean variables. The term "flag" is often used in programming as a reference to a variable of type `boolean`. Such variables allow programmers to create a memory of a certain event happening (or not happening) during a program's execution. A boolean variable can have one of the two possible values: `true` or `false`, which are Java reserved keywords, meaning that the words `true` and `false` are part of the Java language. Below are some examples of assigning values to boolean variables:

```
boolean b = true;
boolean p = b;
```

Let us practise using boolean variables through solving the chapter problem.

6.4 Solving the Chapter Problem

Repurposing of existing code is quite common in programming. Let us gain some experience in doing this and use the code of the Clara cleaner solution from Chapter 3 as the starting point. In this problem Clara had to traverse her world line-by-line and clean it of leaves. In the case when Clara had to clean her own apartment we used a for-loop, since the dimensions of her apartment were fixed. Similarly, for the problem of delivering mail we have a city of a fixed size, so we can also use a for loop. Let us remind you of the for-loop solution of the Clara cleaner problem.

```
class MyClara extends Clara {
   void run() {
      for (int i = 0; i < 5; i++) {
         cleanLine();
         repositionToWest();
         cleanLine();
         repositionToEast();
      }
   }

   void repositionToWest() {
      turnLeft();
      secureMove();
      turnLeft();
   }

   void repositionToEast() {
      turnRight();
      secureMove();
      turnRight();
   }

   void cleanLine() {
      for (int i = 0; i < 10; i++) {
         if ( onLeaf() )
            removeLeaf();
         secureMove();
      }
   }

   void secureMove() {
      if ( !treeFront() )
         move();
   }
}
```

This code would result in Clara moving from the bottom to the top of her world, cleaning all the leaves along the way. It will only work correctly if Clara's World is of size 10 x 10, which matches the dimensions of Claraville in the mail delivery problem.

The first important point of difference that we have to address is that in the mail delivery problem each street starts at the western edge (left), while in the Clara cleaner case we were moving in a zigzag fashion, starting the next street immediately after the end of the previous street. Thus, we have to change the way Clara repositions to the next street, making sure that after repositioning she always appears at the western edge. To make this happen, let us remove the `repositionToEast()` and `repositionToWest()` methods and replace them with a method called `reposition()`. We will need to update the `run` method to reflect this change. Apart form using `repositionToEast()` and `repositionToWest()` the `run()` method currently uses `cleanLine()`. The name `cleanLine()` is no longer practical, because Clara needs to deliver mail rather than cleaning streets. We are reusing existing code and could have left the old name there, but it is a bad practice to keep names that do not reflect the task at hand. Let us call this method more appropriately, such as `deliverMail()`. The modified parts of the program would then look as follows:

```
void run() {
    for (int i = 0; i < 9; i++) {
        deliverMail();
        reposition();
    }
    deliverMail();
}

void reposition() {
    turnAround();

    while ( !treeFront() ) {
        move();
    }

    turnRight();
    move();
    turnRight();
}
```

Now the `reposition()` method makes Clara return to the start of the street before moving to the next street. Because of this change we had to modify the `for`-loop in the `run()` method. Instead of making Clara clean two streets at a time she now delivers mail to one street at a time, so the loop repeats nine times. Similar to how we discovered that we had to do one fewer reposition in the Clara cleaner scenario because Clara occupied one of the streets at the start of program execution, here we also need to reposition nine times instead of ten. But we still need to deliver mail to ten houses, and this is why the `deliverMail()` method is repeated once more after the loop.

Implementing the `deliverMail()` method is the part of the problem where we must use boolean flags. Boolean flags are only needed when, depending on whether some event has or has not happened, we are required to modify Clara's behaviour. If this behaviour can be enacted immediately after the event then there is no need for employing boolean flags. These flags are only useful if the reaction to the event has to be postponed. In the case of the mail delivery problem, Clara would have to decide whether to deliver mail or not depending on whether she saw a flag at the start of the street or not. This decision cannot be made immediately after sensing the flag. Clara has to see the flag first, remember whether it was up or down, walk until the end of the street and only then decide about mail delivery depending on what she saw before. Let us implement this using boolean variables.

```
void deliverMail() {
   boolean isFlagUp = false;

   if ( onLeaf() ) {
      isFlagUp = true;
      removeLeaf();
   }

   while ( !treeFront() ) {
      move();
   }

   if ( isFlagUp == false)
      putLeaf();
}
```

In the above solution of the `deliverMail()` method we have employed a variable called `isFlagUp`. It is a good practice to have the names of all boolean variables start with the prefix "`is`". In this way your code will read like good English, which is one of the key requirements of good coding style. The `isFlagUp` variable has been given an initial value of `false`. The `deliverMail()` method starts with Clara standing at the start of the street, where the mailbox would be located. At this stage she can sense whether a flag is up or not by testing whether there is a leaf (representing the flag in our scenario) present at Clara's current position. Therefore, the value of the `isFlagUp` will be changed to `true` if Clara happens to be on a leaf. In this situation (Clara being on a leaf) the flag on the letterbox has been raised by the owner, so we can immediately act upon collecting the outgoing mail. This act is not visualised, but what we would have to visualise is lowering the flag after picking up the mail. This is achieved by calling the `removeLeaf()` method. Many beginner programmers would have written the following code:

```
if ( onLeaf() ) {
   isFlagUp = true;
   removeLeaf();
}
else
   isFlagUp = false;
```

This, however, is a redundant solution. The else clause is not required. We were able to eliminate those two extra lines in the solution shown earlier by cleverly assigning the initial value of the isFlagUp variable to false. If Clara happens to be on a leaf when the mailDelivery() method is called, the value of the isFlagUp variable would change to true, but if Clara is not on a leaf, it would remain the same as the default value (false) that it was initialised with. Thus, there is no need to reset it to false when Clara is not on a leaf.

After memorising what Clara sensed about the flag at the start of the street in the isFlagUp variable, she would need to move until the end of the street (to the house) and only then would she be required to check whether to deliver mail or not. In making this decision Clara would have to rely on her memory of sensing the flag, as in our scenario she is only expected to deliver mail if there was no flag at the start of the street. Below is the complete solution of the mail delivery problem:

```
class MyClara extends Clara {

    void run() {
        for (int i = 0; i < 9; i++) {
            deliverMail();
            reposition();
        }

        deliverMail();
    }

    void deliverMail() {
        boolean isFlagUp = false;

        if ( onLeaf() ) {
            isFlagUp = true;
            removeLeaf();
        }

        while ( !treeFront() ) {
            move();
        }

        if ( isFlagUp == false)
            putLeaf();
    }

    void reposition() {
        turnAround();

        while ( !treeFront() ) {
            move();
        }

        turnRight();
        move();
        turnRight();
    }
```

```
void turnAround() {
    turnLeft();
    turnLeft();
  }

}
```

 To see the solution of this problem in Clara's World please use the following URL: `https://claraworld.net/link/C6P1S`.

Using boolean flags for memorising events is a very common technique in programming, so it is important that you understand the above solution.

6.5 Variables and Literals

Now that we have gained more experience with boolean variables and assigning values to them, let us cover more material related to assigning values to other types of variables. Values assigned to variables in Java code are called literals. This term refers to variables of any type regardless of whether we are working with numeric or text values. Some examples of literals are shown below:

```
int    i = 23; // 23 is an integer literal
double  d = 2.4; // 2.4 is a double literal
boolean b = true; // b is a boolean literal
String s = "Hello"; // "Hello" is a String literal
char   c = 'a'; // 'a' is a char literal
```

A data type that is a little challenging with assigning variables in Java is `float`. This type (also called single precision) covers numbers that have up to seven digits after the decimal point. It is a memory compact version of the type `double` (also called double precision) that covers numbers having up to 15 digits after the decimal point. What makes `float` more challenging in relation to literals is the fact that the following line in Java would result in a compilation error:

```
float pi = 3.14159;
```

The reason for this strange behaviour of the Java compiler is that 3.14 is considered a `double` literal, not a `float` literal. By default Java assigns the type `double` to all numbers with a decimal point. Ensuring that a number is treated as a `float` can be achieved by adding the letter "f" next to the number as shown in the code snippet below:

```
float pi = 3.14159f;
```

Literals representing text are another special case. Java has two data types for handling text. For storing a string of text we use the `String` type, and for storing individual characters we use the `char` type. `String` literals in Java must be enclosed inside quotation marks `""`, and character literals are to be placed inside apostrophes `' '`. It is important to remember that boolean literals require no apostrophes or quotation marks, since `true` and `false` are Java reserved keywords. Below are examples of `boolean`, `String` and `char` literals:

```java
boolean b = true;
String s = "Hello, World!";
char c = 'a';
```

6.6 Working with Keyboard Input

Another important aspect of working with variables is dynamically specifying their values. In many programming languages (including Java) this is supported by typing variable values from keyboard. The classical Java ways of obtaining data from the keyboard will not be covered in this book, since they are not supported in our programming framework. Here we will discus Clara's World specific methods of data entry.

As shown in Chapter 5, our framework supports entering data in the form of `String` or `int` using the following methods:

- `readString()` – supports entering the value for a variable of type `String`
- `readInt()` – supports entering the value for a variable of type `int`

The above methods return a variable as their output. Methods that return output and receive input will be further discussed in Chapter 8. For now it is only important to remember the syntax of using these new methods for variable input. The examples below will help you with this task:

```java
int i = readInt("Enter the value of i: ");
String s = readString("Enter the value of s: ");

System.out.println("The values are:");
System.out.println(i);
System.out.println(s);
```

If you run this code you will see the windows shown in Figure 6.2 appear. These windows will not appear at the same time. The window shown in Figure 6.2 a) will appear first. After you enter the value of "i" and press "OK" you will see the window shown in Figure 6.2 b). Only after you enter the text in both windows will you see the output printed to console. The console output should appear immediately below Clara's World. If you enter the data shown in Figure 6.2, you should see the following output of your program:

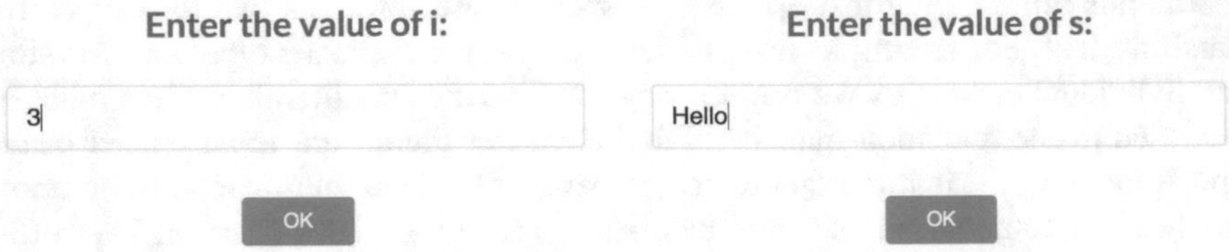

Enter the value of i: **Enter the value of s:**

| 3| | | Hello| |

OK   OK

Fig. 6.2: a) Number Entry   b) String Entry.

```
The values are:
3
Hello
```

The `System.out.println` command prints the corresponding text and then moves to the next line, making sure that everything that is printed to console next would appear on the next line. There is an alternative command that allows to continue printing on the same line. This command is `System.out.print`. Let us have a look at the code shown below:

```
int i = readInt("Enter the value of i: ");
String s = readString("Enter the value of s: ");

System.out.print("The values are: ");
System.out.print(i + ", ");
System.out.print(s);
```

This code would produce the following console output:

```
The values are: 3, Hello
```

Apart from mentioning the fact that we now have one line of text due to using `System.out.print` instead of `System.out.println`, it is also important to note that the use of the "+" character in `System.out.print(i + ", ")` helped us to concatenate two lines. Every time the "+" character is used and a `String` value is located to either side of it (left or right), the Java compiler assumes that "+" is a concatenation operator that must combine two strings together. In the case when one of these values is not a `String`, Java will try to automatically convert such a value into a `String` and then perform the concatenation. The result will be different if both sides are numbers. In this case "+" will be treated as an addition operator. Let us look into operators in more detail.

6.7 Arithmetic Operators and Expressions with Variables

Computer science originated from mathematics, so many mathematical concepts are supported within programming languages. Java is not an exception to this rule.

Classical arithmetic operators that you find in algebra are present in Java as well. Similar rules that apply in mathematics will also automatically apply in Java.

As our programming problems grow in complexity we require computations to be performed with variables. Such computations are called expressions. An expression in Java is a combination of terms and operators. Terms can be:

- variables: like a
- literals: like 7
- method calls: like readInt()

Below are some examples of Java expressions. Both expressions use the addition operator. In the first case we are adding two variables, while in the second case we are adding an integer literal to a variable.

```
int sum = a + b;
a = b + 3;
```

In Java we can use most of the arithmetic operators present in algebra, but some of them have a slightly different meaning. Table 6.1 shows the key arithmetic operators present in Java.

Table 6.1: Arithmetic Operators in Java

Operator	Meaning	Type	Example
–	Subtraction	Binary	nominalCost = totalCost - tax;
+	Addition	Binary	totalCost = nominalCost + tax;
*	Multiplication	Binary	tax = nominalCost * taxRate;
%	Remainder	Binary	remainder = value % 5;
/	Division	Binary	discountedPrice = originalPrice / 2;

In the table above the type of all operators is listed as "Binary". This simply means that each operator must have two operands (requires the left-hand side and the right-hand side). The arithmetic operators listed in the table work as one would expect in algebra (with small exceptions). Similar to algebra, it is an error to try to divide any number by zero. When working with two integer operands, the division operator requires special attention.

Let us have a look at each of these operators in details.

6.7.1 Subtraction

Subtraction in Java works similar to mathematics. Some examples of subtraction in Java are

```
int sub = a - b; // subtraction of two variables
System.out.println(sub - 5); // subtracting a literal
int c = -a + b; // negative sign
```

In the last line of the above code we have used the "–" operator as the negative sign rather than subtraction operator. Similar to mathematics, expressing the negative sign in this way is also valid in Java.

6.7.2 Addition

Addition in Java works exactly like one would expect in mathematics.

```
int a = b + c; // addition of two variables
System.out.println(c + 3); // adding a literal
int sum = 5 + 10; // adding two literals

// using a Java method (readInt) inside an expression
int sum = a + readInt("Enter the number you want to add to a:");
```

Notice that in the last line of the above example we have an expression that utilises a Java method `readInt()`. In this case the expression can only be computed at runtime, after the user enters the value end presses the "OK" button in the corresponding dialog.

6.7.3 Remainder

If you have used a calculator before, you might have used the "%" symbol for computing percentages. In Java, however, this symbol represents the remainder operator. The remainder operator works the same way as in mathematics. Remainders in Java only apply to integer (int) numbers and variables. Remainders in programming are used quite frequently. Examples of using the remainder operator are shown below:

```
int r1 = 13 % 2;
int r2 = 8 % 5;
System.out.println("r1 = " + r1 + ", r2 " + "= " + r2);
```

The result of running the above code is as follows:

```
r1 = 1, r2 = 3
```

Let us provide a quick explanation of what a remainder is for those readers who find the above result confusing. The remainder operation in arithmetics is related to division and represents what is left over after dividing one integer number by another. In simple terms, if you want to compute x % y, you would first need to find the closest number to x (but smaller than x) that divides by y without a decimal point in the result. Let us call this number "z". The remainder can then be computed by subtracting the value of z from x: `remainder = x-z`.

Let us see how the remainder is computed on an example. Imagine that we must compute `int r = 43 % 8`. The way we compute it is as follows:

```
int r = 43 % 8 => 43 = 8 * 5 + 3 => r = 43 - (8*5) = 3
```

Here we first find the number that is closest to 43 (but smaller than 43) that divides by 8 without a decimal point in the result. This closest number is 40, because 40/8 = 5 (no decimal point). The remainder is then computed by subtracting this number from 43. Our answer is 3.

Another way to explain the remainder is to say that 3 is a part of the number 43 that prevents it from dividing by 8 without having a decimal point in the result.

6.7.4 Division

Division in Java works slightly differently depending on the type of arguments you divide. The most simple case is when we divide two real numbers (float or double). An example of real number division in Java is shown below:

```
int a = 7.0 / 2.0;
```

The value that will be stored in the variable a after running the above code is `3.5`. This is exactly what one would expect. We received this result because we have explicitly forced Java to treat 2 and 7 as real numbers of type double by writing "2.0" and "7.0".

Dividing the same two numbers, however, would work very differently if one of them is an integer. Let us now consider the following code:

```
int a = 7 / 2;
```

You might expect that the outcome would be the same (3.5). But you would be wrong. If both numbers involved in a division are integers, Java automatically assumes that the expected result must be an integer number, so the result stored in the variable is is 3.0. In our case it is explicitly stated that the result is to be stored in a variable of type int, but even if we change it as follows there will be little difference:

```
int a = 7;
double b = a / 2;
```

The example above represents one of the most confusing sides of Java division. The way Java would execute this code is as follows: Java would compute 7 / 2 (obtaining 3.5). After checking that both 2 and 7 are integers, Java would make an automatic assumption that the expected result should be of type `int`, so it would convert the result of division (3.5) into an integer number by losing everything after the decimal point. It is important to note that Java would never round up, but would simply ignore the number after the decimal point. The result of division at this stage would be 3. Now the result of division must be copied into the variable (b) that appears on the left-hand side of the expression. This variable, however, is now of type double. Instead of storing 3.5 as the value of b, Java would simply turn the integer number from the previous step (3) into a double. The value stored in the variable b after running this code will be 3.0.

One of the lessons learned from the above example is that we must ensure that at least one of the numbers involved in a division is of type double or float if we do not want to lose the numbers after the decimal point. The following code would result in correctly assigning the value of 3.5 to the variable b:

```
int a = 7;
double b = a / 2.0;
```

Here the expression a / 2.0 is not treated as integer division because 2.0 is a double literal.

6.7.5 Variable Casting

Adding ".0" to an integer number involved in a division is one way to force the division to be treated as a double division (instead of integer division). This option, however, does not always exist. Let us consider the following example:

```
int a = 7;
double b = 2;
double c = a / b;
```

In this example the value of c will end up being 3.0 due to integer division, because both a and b are integer numbers. The problem we have here is that we no longer have a number that can be easily converted into a double by adding ".0" to it. However, Java provides us with an alternative called variable casting. We can artificially force Java to treat a variable as a number of another type by adding the name of this type in parentheses. The revised version of the above code that utilises variable casting is shown below:

```
int a = 7;
double b = 2;
double c = (double) a / b;
```

The use of (double) here ensures that a / b is treated as a double division, so the value stored in the variable c will be 3.5.

Variable casting can also help with converting a real number into an integer. The example below illustrates this idea:

```
double b = 3.5;
int c = (int) b;
```

Because of variable casting (int) we can lose the decimal point in b and store the value of 3 in the variable c.

6.8 Revised Chapter Problem: Aussie Postie

In order to illustrate the expressions with variables and practise the use of different Java operators let us consider a revised version of the chapter problem.

 To work on this problem in Clara's World please use the following URL: https://claraworld.net/link/C6P2.

Clara has returned back home to Australia after her holiday in the USA. She enjoyed working in mail delivery there, so she continues working as a "postie" in a small Australian village called "Claratown". Delivering mail is simpler back home. There are no flags on letterboxes to worry about. However, Clara must ride a motorcycle and her fuel allowance is limited. She must minimise petrol use and avoid unnecessary travel. The fact that she has a list of addresses of people requiring mail delivery helps her with this task. She can check this list and decide which houses can be skipped, so that her travel path can be optimised.

In Clara's World this problem would appear as shown in Figure 6.3, where Figure 6.3 a) illustrates the state of Clara's World before she commences mail delivery. Figure 6.3 b) shows the result of mail delivery.

Similar to the previous version of the chapter problem, Clara's town consists of 10 avenues, of which each finishes with a house at the end. Clara starts at the 10th avenue (bottom of the screen) and will keep moving north (towards the upper boundary of her world). She will only turn right and move all the way to the end of the avenue that she has marked as "for delivery" in her list and will otherwise drive past other houses. As shown in Figure 6.3 b), Clara had to deliver the mail to houses located on avenues 1, 2, 3, 5, 7, 9 and 10 and drove past other houses.

 You can see a video explanation of how to solve this problem step-by-step at https://claraworld.net/link/C6V2.

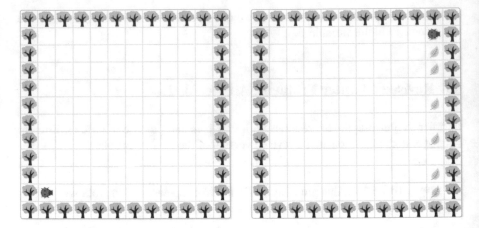

Fig. 6.3: a) Before Mail Delivery   b) After Mail Delivery.

Our task in solving this problem is twofold. Firstly, we have to find a good way of memorising the list of houses Clara must deliver mail to. Secondly, we must come up with a program that will ensure energy-efficient mail delivery to those houses present in the list.

The first part of the problem seems simple. We have exactly ten lanes in Clara's town and exactly ten houses. This number is not going to change any time soon. Your initial reaction to this information might have been to create ten variables for memorising whether each of the houses needs mail delivered or not. Since we only have two possible options (mail delivery required and mail delivery not required), it would have been reasonable to make these variables of type `boolean`. Below is an example of encoding the mail delivery configuration shown in Figure 6.3. In this code snippet a variable is set to true if mail delivery is required for the corresponding street and is set to false if delivery is not required.

```
boolean isDeliveryRequiredStreet1  =  true;
boolean isDeliveryRequiredStreet2  =  true;
boolean isDeliveryRequiredStreet3  =  true;
boolean isDeliveryRequiredStreet4  =  false;
boolean isDeliveryRequiredStreet5  =  true;
boolean isDeliveryRequiredStreet6  =  false;
boolean isDeliveryRequiredStreet7  =  true;
boolean isDeliveryRequiredStreet8  =  false;
boolean isDeliveryRequiredStreet9  =  true;
boolean isDeliveryRequiredStreet10 =  true;
```

This way of encoding mail delivery information, however, is associated with the following two problems:

1. We require a substantial amount of memory to allocate these variables (10 bytes), while a good programmer should always attempt to minimise the memory use of their programs.

2. Working with these variables is difficult. We would ideally want Clara to move in a loop rather than repeating the code for handling one street ten times. There is no simple way in Java to dynamically construct variable names and refer to a variable such as `isDeliveryRequiredStreet7` in the seventh iteration of the loop, so handling streets in a loop becomes problematic with this approach.

 Exercise: Try to come up with an alternative way of encoding mail delivery information while we continue with making Clara move around her town. This encoding should minimise the number of variables used and should make it possible to process them in a loop.

Let us postpone the decision on how to encode mail delivery information and focus on Clara moving around her town. When delivering mail she will move in a similar way to how she was moving in the USA version of the mail delivery problem with the exception that she will now be conserving energy and will not visit the houses that do not require mail delivery.

The first obvious thing we will need in our code is making Clara move until the end of the street (where a house is located). We can employ the familiar `moveToTree()` method for making this happen.

```
void moveToTree() {
    while (!treeFront()) {
        move();
    }
}
```

Next, let us create an empty `deliverMail()` method handling potential mail delivery and produce the code for the `run()` method that handles Clara's movement around her town.

```
public void run() {
    turnLeft();

    for (int i = 0; i < 9; i++) {
        deliverMail();
        move();
    }
}

void deliverMail () {
}
```

The first thing we want to do is making sure that Clara faces north (towards the upper boundary of her world). Then in the `run()` method we will make Clara move to the next street in the loop if there is no mail delivery required. The `deliverMail()` method will take care of the situation when mail delivery is needed, but so far this method is empty and mail delivery information has not been encoded yet. Therefore, the above code would simply result in Clara moving to the very top of her world.

Let us now consider how we handle the mail delivery situation. The mail delivery itself is quite straightforward. We simply need Clara to turn right, move until the end of the street, drop the leaf there and come back. We would, however, need to do this only when mail delivery is required (as per Clara's delivery list). Let us postpone the decision about how to encode the mail delivery information and add a `boolean` variable (`isMailDeliveryRequired`) that will receive a value of true if we need to execute mail delivery for the given street. We can already anticipate that since the loop repeats nine times we may have a potential OBOB (off by one bug) issue affecting mail delivery to the final street. To address this, we would need to repeat mail delivery one more time after the main loop if it is required. Thus, we can rewrite our code as follows:

```java
public void run() {
    turnLeft();

    boolean isMailDeliveryRequired;

    for (int i = 0; i < 9; i++) {
        if ( isMailDeliveryRequired )
            deliverMail();

        move();
    }

    // OBOB Fixing
    if ( isMailDeliveryRequired )
        deliverMail();
}

/*
 * Deliver mail to the street Clara is on
 * return after deliver and make sure that
 * Clara faces up
 */
void deliverMail() {
    turnRight();
    moveToTree();
    putLeaf();
    turnLeft();
    turnLeft();
    moveToTree();
    turnRight();
}
```

Hopefully by now you have had some time to think about how mail delivery can be encoded in a different way. Our solution would be to utilise one variable instead of ten and, therefore, would work perfectly well with a loop. What we propose is instead of treating each separate street as a `boolean` we will encode the entire town within an integer number (`mailToDeliver`) consisting of ten digits, where each digit represents one street. Since we only need to encode whether to deliver mail or not for each street, we would only require digits such as 0 and 1. Encoding the scenario shown in Figure 6.3 b) can then be done as `1110101011`. Deconstructing this number into individual digits would require our newly acquired knowledge of expressions and arithmetic operators.

Before continuing with the solution, let us analyse the situation Clara finds herself in. She has the mail delivery information encoded in a single integer number as shown above. Mail delivery is encoded in such a way that the last digit of the corresponding number represents mail delivery information for the first street and vice versa (the first digit corresponds to the last street). Thus, working with this number should start with the last digit and finish with the first digit. How can we extract the last digit? One way to do this is through division. If we divide the original number by `10` we would receive `111010101.1`. The digit after the decimal point would help us decide whether to deliver mail or not. If the digit after the decimal point is "0" then mail delivery is not required. Otherwise Clara would need to deliver mail (if this digit is "1"). You might have guessed by now that to inspect the last digit we require using the remainder operator. Remainders are useful for precisely this purpose, deciding whether there are numbers after the decimal point.

Instead of dividing our number by `10` we compute the remainder of division by ten (`mailToDeliver % 10`). If the result is `0` (no remainder) then we do not need to deliver mail, and if the result is 1 then we need to deliver mail. In the case of deciding whether to deliver mail to the first street the result is `1110101011 % 10 = 1`. This means that we must deliver mail to this street.

How do we decide about mail delivery to the next street? For this we would need to look at the second last digit. We could have computed `mailToDeliver % 100`, but there will be a remainder if the last digit is "1", so this is not a good approach. What we could do instead is performing a classical programming trick, which is to get rid of the data that is no longer required. In our case, after examining the last digit and delivering the mail if needed, we no longer require the information stored in the last digit. The practical meaning of this is that we could simply discard the last digit and make our number one digit shorter.

How can we remove the last digit from a number? The simplest way is to divide this number by `10`. In mathematics the result of `111010101 / 10 = 11101010.1`. However, in Java programming things are a little different, and this time the difference works in our favour. Both number we divide are integers, so the division will be treated as integer division, meaning that the result will also be an integer number. The same division in Java would produce the following result: `111010101 / 10 = 11101010`, which is exactly what we wanted (the number without the last digit). We are now ready to produce the final version of the `run()` method.

```
public void run() {
    turnLeft();
    boolean isMailDeliveryRequired;

    for (int i = 0; i < 9; i++) {
        // extract the last digit in the mail delivery list
        int remainder = mailToDeliver % 10;


        // decide on mail delivery
        if (remainder == 1)
            isMailDeliveryRequired = true;
        else
            isMailDeliveryRequired = false;

        // remove the last digit from the list
        mailToDeliver = mailToDeliver / 10;

        // perform mail delivery if necessary
        if ( isMailDeliveryRequired )
            deliverMail();

        move();
    }

    // OBOB Fixing
    if ( isMailDeliveryRequired )
        deliverMail();
}
```

In the above solution we inspect the last digit of mailToDeliver and depending on whether this digit is 0 or 1 we deliver mail to the corresponding street or not. After each iteration of the for loop inside the run() method we remove the last digit from mailToDeliver, so that the last digit of it will always contain information relevant to the street that Clara is currently on. Below is the complete solution of the revised chapter problem:

```
class MyClara extends Clara {
    int mailToDeliver = 1110101011;

    /*
     * Clara delivers mail to the streets
     * marked with 1 in mailToDeliver
     */
    public void run() {
        turnLeft();

        boolean isMailDeliveryRequired;

        for (int i = 0; i < 9; i++) {
            // extract the last digit in the mail delivery list
            int remainder = mailToDeliver % 10;
```

```
            // decide on mail delivery
            if (remainder == 1)
                isMailDeliveryRequired = true;
            else
                isMailDeliveryRequired = false;

            // remove the last digit from the list
            mailToDeliver = mailToDeliver / 10;

            // perform mail delivery if neccessary
            if ( isMailDeliveryRequired )
                deliverMail();

            // proceed to the next street
            move();
        }

        // OBOB Fixing
        if ( isMailDeliveryRequired )
            deliverMail();
    }

    /*
     * Deliver mail to the street Clara is on
     * return after deliver and make sure that
     * Clara faces up
     */
    void deliverMail() {
        turnRight();
        moveToTree();
        putLeaf();
        turnLeft();
        turnLeft();
        moveToTree();
        turnRight();
    }

    /*
     * Move until the end of the street
     * in the direction Clara is facing
     */
    void moveToTree() {
        while (!treeFront()) {
            move();
        }
    }
}
```

 To see the solution of this problem in Clara's World please use the following URL: https://claraworld.net/link/C6P2S.

6.9 More on Expressions

The coverage of expressions in Java would not be complete without touchinh upon the order of operations and operator precedence and providing an in-depth coverage of using the "+" operator for addition of numbers and concatenation of strings.

 Exercise: In the programming classes that we teach, there is usually a mid-semester test that takes place after covering the material presented in this chapter. This test often runs with hundreds of students located in the same room. In order to eliminate the temptation for students to identify people with similar questions and copy their answers, we have developed the following system. There is a limited number of different test paper versions. We do not want to reveal to students how many different test papers there are, so instead of printing a version number on each paper, we have programmed a script that prints all of our test papers and assigns a sequential number to each, such as: 1, 2, 3, 4, 5, 6, 7, ... 322, 323, etc. Here the version number is concealed behind the sequential number. If, for example, we have 7 different versions of the test, then version 1 of the test corresponds to sequential numbers 1, 8, 15, ...; version 2 corresponds to numbers 2, 9, 16, ..., etc. After collecting student submissions we have to automatically decode the sequential number into the version number (translate 15 back into 1 and 16 back into 2). As a mental exercise try to think about how this decoding can be achieved.

6.9.1 Operator Precedence

Mathematical expressions can be very complex. You may remember from high school that there is a set order in which arithmetic operations are carried out. For example, evaluating the following expression $6+3-4+6*3$ does not simply happen by performing one operator after another, moving from left to right. Evaluating it from left to right without respecting the correct order would look as follows:

$$6+3-4+6*3 = 9-4+6*3 = 5+6*3 = 11*3 = 33 \qquad (6.1)$$

What we know from algebra, however, is that multiplication has to be computed before addition and subtraction. In fact, there are more rules of this kind and levels of precedence present in algebra. These rules are also in place for Java programming. Table 6.2 outlines the order of operator precedence in Java.

The rules expressed in Table 6.2 are the same as those in mathematics. Unary negation has the highest priority, meaning that this is the operator that must be applied first. Multiplication, division and remainder are applied next, followed by addition and subtraction.

Table 6.2: Operator Precedence in Java

Priority	Operator	Associativity	Example	Result
1	- (unary negation)	Right to left	a = -5 + 3;	-2
2	* / %	Left to right	a = -2 + 4 % 3 * 12 + 2;	12
3	+ -	Left to right	a = 5 + 4 - 3 + 7 * 3;	27

These rules, however, can be modified with the use of parentheses. Both in mathematics and programming parentheses have the highest order of precedence. When parenthesis are used in an expression, the innermost parenthesis are processed first. If two sets of parenthesis are at the same level, they are processed left to right. The example shown below illustrates how expressions with parentheses are computed:

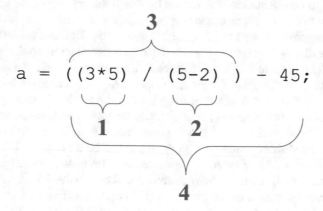

Here we start with the innermost sets of parentheses (1 and 2), evaluate those and compute the result of division as the result of (3). After evaluating 3 we then subtract 45 and obtain the result of -40.

6.9.2 The "+" Operator

The "+" operator can be used in two ways: as a concatenation operator and as an addition operator. If either side of the + operator is a string, the result will be a string.

Let us consider the following code to better understand how the "+" operator works in Java:

```
int value = 3;
System.out.print("Hello " + "World! ");
System.out.print("value 1 is: " + 5);
```

```
System.out.print(", value 2 is: " + value + 1);
System.out.print(", value 3 is: " + (value + 5));
```

The output of this code will be

```
Hello World! value 1 is: 5, value 2 is: 31, value 3 is: 8
```

What is important to remember about the "+" operator is that having a `String` value on one side of it is sufficient for the operation to be considerate to be concatenation rather than addition. The first two lines of the above example are easy to understand. Because the left-hand side of the "=" is the string there, concatenation is performed. The first line in this example simply concatenates two strings "Hello" and "World". The second line converts the string literal (5) into text and also performs concatenation.

The last two lines may be a little more difficult to understand. In both of them we have used the "+" operator twice. In the first case all occurrences of this operator were treated as concatenation. The reason for this is that by default we apply operators from left two right. When evaluating `", value 2 is: " + value + 1` Java first computes `", value 2 is: " + value`. Because the left-hand side is a `String`, the "+" operator is considered to be concatenation, so the result of applying it will be ", value 2 is: 3". The second "+" operator would have to be applied to this resulting `String` and the integer value 1. Again, because the left-hand side is the `String`, it is treated as a concatenation and the result is " value 2 is: 31".

The last line in our code snippet is different from the rest because of the use of parenthesis. Here `(value + 5)` will be evaluated first. Both the left-hand side and the right-hand side are numbers, so the result will be $3 + 5 = 8$. The remaining "+" operator would be treated as concatenation because of the `String` value on the left-hand side, and this is why the result will be ", value 3 is: 8".

Notice how the output of the above code is combined into a single line rather than having the output of each line of code appear on the new line. This is because we used `System.out.print()` instead of `System.out.println()`.

Another important use of the concatenation operator is combining long strings. Java commands that have string literals must be treated with care. A string literal value cannot span over multiple lines in Java code. The example code below would result in a compilation error due to spanning over multiple lines.

```
System.out.println("This line is too long and now
it has spanned more than one line, which will
cause a syntax error to be generated by the compiler. ");
```

The `String` concatenation operator can be used to fix this problem.

```
System.out.println( "These lines are " +
                    "now OK and will not " +
                    "cause an error as before.");
```

This updated code will compile without problems because multiple lines of text are connected with the concatenation operator and each `String` appears on one line.

6.9.3 Combined Assignment Operators

It is common in code that deals with variables to have assignment of the following kind:

```
sum = sum + 1;
value = value + 5;
```

For statements similar to those shown above, where the name of a variable appears on both sides of the assignment operator, Java language provides a set of combined operators (also known as shorthands). You already saw one such shorthand that is expressed as `i++`. Table 6.3 below shows the most popular combined operators and explains what they mean.

Table 6.3: Java Shorthands

combined operator	example	meaning
++	a++;	a = a + 1;
--	a--;	a = a - 1;
+=	a+=5;	a = a + 5;
-=	a-=7;	a = a - 7;
*=	a*=7;	a = a * 7;
/=	a/=7;	a = a / 7;
%=	a%=7;	a = a % 7;

Combined operators are convenient and frequently used, because they save programmers unnecessary typing. With the use of these shorthands programmers can avoid typing the same variables name twice, which is particularly convenient with longer variable names.

6.9.4 Relational Operators

In addition to arithmetic operators (+, -, *, /, %) Java offers a set of so-called relational operators that are used for working with boolean variables and expressions. These operators can be used for computing a value of a boolean variable or for calculating whether a certain expression contained within a conditional statement is `true` or `false`. Table 6.4 presents the list of possible relational operators and explains their meaning.

Table 6.4: Java Shorthands

combined operator	example	meaning
>	a > b	is a greater than b?
<	a < b	is a smaller than b?
>=	a >= b	is a greater or equal to b?
<=	a <= b	is a smaller or equal to b?
==	a == b	is a equal to b?
!=	a != b	is a not equal to b?

Relational operators are often used inside `if`-statements. The code below illustrates typical use of some of these operators:

```
if (a > b)
   System.out.println("a is greater than b");
if(a == b)
   System.out.println("a is equal to b");
if(a != b)
   System.out.println("a is not equal to b");
```

6.9.5 Summary Example: Line in the Middle

Let us finish the chapter with a small example that nicely summarises some of the important issues related to expressions.

Clara trains to become a carpenter. One of the skills she must acquire is measuring. As a part of her carpenter training course she must learn drawing a line of the given length in the middle of her world. To make sure that Clara has fully learned how to do this, she will be tested in multiple worlds of different length. The length of the line that she must draw will also vary. Clara's task is to develop a general-purpose approach that will work with a world of any dimensions and for a line of any length.

 To work on this problem in Clara's World please use the following URL: https://claraworld.net/link/C6P3.

Figure 6.4 a) shows the initial configuration of Clara's World for this problem. Figure 6.4 b) depicts the result of drawing a line of leaves with the length "7" in the

middle of this world. Notice that the line of leaves is centred on the main street of Clara's World, meaning that the distances from each end of the line to the closest wall are the same. The fact that the leaf line is in the middle is evident from the fact that there are exactly three empty spaces on each side of this line.

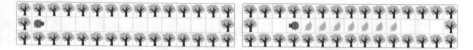

Fig. 6.4: a) Initial State   b) Final State.

 You can see a video explanation of how to solve this problem step-by-step at https://claraworld.net/link/C6V3.

We already have one important building block required for solving this problem. While working on the problem from Section 5.7, related to finding the middle of a street, we learned how to measure the length of a street. From Chapter 5 we also know how to request the length of the street using readInt and readDouble methods. Let us put this knowledge together and start producing our solution. The run() method below initialises two variables (lineLength and streetLength), requests the value of streetLength from keyboard and then makes Clara walk until the end of the main street in her world and count its length. After computing the length of the street Clara turns around and is ready to start drawing the line.

```
void run() {
    int lineLength = readInt("How long is the line?");
    int streetLength = 0;

    // measure the length of the street
    while ( !treeFront() ) {
        move();
        streetLength++;
    }

    turnAround();
    System.out.println("streetLength = " + streetLength);
}

void turnAround()
{
    turnRight();
    turnRight();
}
```

Let us run the above code and analyse the output. Figure 6.5 shows the result of executing our program. Clara will end up standing at the eastern end of the street (facing west). However, the resulting length of the street (12) is incorrect. The correct value for streetLength is 13.

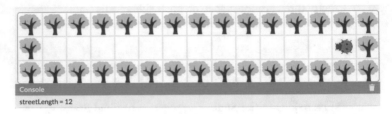

Fig. 6.5: The Result of Running our Partial Solution.

We have encountered a familiar problem that prevents us from correctly computing the length of the street. Since Clara occupies one of the cells in her world, the number of steps she will make before encountering the end of the street is equal to streetLength - 1. To account for this fact we could simply add the streetLength--; command before printing the value of the variable streetLength. There is, however, a better way, which is to change the initial value of streetLength from 0 to 1. Updating the initialisation of the streetLength variable to int streetLength = 1; would result in correctly printing streetLength = 13 on the screen.

Let us now think about how to draw the line and what drawing a line of leaves in the middle of the street actually means. Drawing the line is a simple task that we have already encountered before. It involves putting a leaf and moving the required number of times. But how can we make sure that this line is drawn in the middle? Try to stop reading, grab a piece of paper and a pen and think about this question for a couple of minutes before continuing to read this chapter.

Making sure that the line is drawn in the middle is not as difficult as it might originally sound. Let us rephrase the earlier question and ask: "How many steps must Clara make before starting to draw the line of leaves, so that this line appears in the middle of Clara's World"? This question is easier to answer. Let us look at Figure 6.6 that depicts how you might have solved problems of this kind in high school mathematics classes. We know the length of the line of leaves (y), and we know how long the street is (streetLength from the code above). If the line of leaves is in the middle of the street, the distances from each side (x) would be equal. Calculating the value of x would help us to solve the problem. It is sufficient for Clara to make x steps and then draw the line of length (y) to make sure that the line of leaves she draws appears in the middle. But how can we compute the value of x? We encourage you to again grab a piece of paper and a pen and think about this question for a couple of minutes before continuing to read further.

We can start computing the value of x with the help of the following expressions:

$$streetLength = x+y+x \Rightarrow streetLength - y = 2x \Rightarrow x = \frac{streetLength - y}{2} \quad (6.2)$$

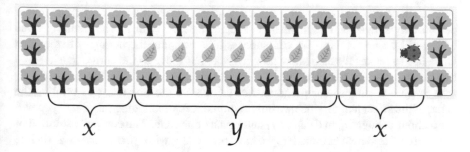

Fig. 6.6: Computing the Starting Position.

How do we translate the resulting expression into Java code and make Clara move x steps? Given that y in the above expression corresponds to the `lineLength` variable in the code that we produced earlier, your initial attempt to converting this into Java may look as follows:

```java
// calculate how many steps to move so that line is in the middle
int x = streetLength - lineLength / 2.0;

// now make Clara move x steps
for (int i = 0; i < x; i++) {
   move();
}
```

The above code is incorrect. In the situation shown in Figure 6.6 Clara must make 3 steps. If we substitute variables with the corresponding values, we would obtain the following equation: $x = 13 - 7/2.0 = 13 - 3.5 = 9.5$. Evidently, Clara would have to make 9.5 steps after these calculations, which is impossible to do (because she is unable to make a fraction of a step). This number also does not match our expectations of Clara having to make three steps. What went wrong with our calculations?

The first obvious error that was deliberately introduced is the use of 2.0 instead of 2. Having 2.0 in the above expression makes Java treat the division operator as a division of two real numbers. In our case, however, it would have been more useful for Java to treat this as integer division, so that the number of steps Clara has to make is an integer number. The second problem is the order of operators. Earlier in this chapter it was mentioned that division has a higher priority than addition or subtraction. This is why we would first compute the value of `lineLength / 2.0` and only then perform the subtraction operator. What we want instead is to compute the subtraction first and only then divide the result by 2. We can enforce this by using parentheses. Let us rewrite the equation for computing x as follows:

```java
int x = (streetLength - lineLength) / 2;
```

The above expression would correctly compute the value of x. We will no longer perform division of real numbers due to replacing 2.0 with 2. The resulting value of x will be x = 3. Now we can successfully compute the number of steps that Clara has to make. We also know how to make her move to the correct position, so that she can start drawing the line.

It is time to finalise our program. Let us remove the line that was printing the value of the street length, since we only required it for debugging purposes (you will learn about debugging in Chapter 7) and update our code. The complete solution of this problem is shown below. Here we have replaced x with stepsToMove (in line with Java conventions) so that the variable name better reflects its purpose.

```
class MyClara extends Clara {

    void run() {
        // TODO: Write your code below

        int lineLength = readInt("How long is the line?");
        int streetLength = 1;

        // measure the length of the street
        while ( !treeFront() ) {
            move();
            streetLength++;
        }

        turnAround();

        // computing steps to move
        int stepsToMove = (streetLength - lineLength) / 2;

        // move to the starting position
        for ( int i = 0; i < stepsToMove; i++) {
            move();
        }

        // draw the line
        for ( int i = 0; i < lineLength; i++) {
            putLeaf();
            move();
        }
    }

    void turnAround()
    {
        turnRight();
        turnRight();
    }
}
```

After running this code Clara will correctly produce a result that should look similar to what is shown in Figure 6.4 b). This solution is generic and would correctly work with all supplied example worlds. Due to the use of integer division in `int stepsToMove = (streetLength - lineLength) / 2;` Clara is able to correctly operate with worlds of both odd and even length.

 To see the solution of this problem in Clara's World please use the following URL: `https://claraworld.net/link/C6P3S`.

6.10 Summary

In this chapter we have learned about using boolean variables for memorising whether a certain event has or has not happened and illustrated this idea on the example of letterboxes with flags. It is important to remember that the values of these boolean values must be set by the programmer (you). They will not be magically flipping between `true` and `false` by themselves.

The most important part of this chapter covered arithmetic operators and expressions. You should have understood how operators are used in Java, what is operator precedence and how the order of operations is enforced. The revised example of the mail delivery problem extensively used operators with a particular focus on the remainder.

At the end of the chapter we talked more about the "+" operator and discussed how it can represent both addition and concatenation. We then further illustrated the use of variables and expressions on an example of drawing a line in the middle of Clara's World.

6.11 Exercises

 Exercises that target your understanding of the concepts covered in this chapter are available at `https://claraworld.net/link/C6Ex`.

Chapter 7
Debugging and Random Numbers

Now that you have a good understanding of variables and expressions and are starting to write more complex code, it becomes important to utilise debugging tools. Debugging helps to better understand complex code and quickly fix errors in it. In this chapter we will cover the key approaches to debugging that exist in programming with a particular focus on debugging tools that are available in Clara's World.

Another important topic that will be covered in this chapter is "random numbers". Random numbers are used for simulating unpredictability. Games, simulations and even design tools require random numbers. Clara's World supports random number generation and provides easy-to-use methods for working with random numbers.

The final objective of this chapter is to cover additional topics related to conditional statements and working with variables and expressions. Three chapter problems will help with explaining this diverse material.

Image features the "Pac-Man" 3D model by Gianmarco available under Creative Commons CC BY 4.0.

© Springer Nature Switzerland AG 2021
A. Bogdanovych, T. Trescak, *Learning Java Programming in Clara's World*,
https://doi.org/10.1007/978-3-030-75542-3_7

7.1 Chapter Story: Pac-man

Pac-man is one of the most popular video games of the 20th century. It is a maze arcade developed and released by Namco in 1980. In this game players control a simplistic yellow-coloured character called Pac-man, who must eat golden dots inside an enclosed maze while avoiding four coloured ghosts. Eating large flashing dots called "energisers" causes the ghosts to turn blue, allowing Pac-man to eat them for bonus points [13].

One of the most interesting aspects of the game are the ghosts. They are programmed in a very simplistic way, but appear very intelligent. Some players even assume a kind of super intelligence that drives the ghosts in this game. Here is a comment from one of the players describing the experience of being chased by intelligent ghosts: "the four of them are programmed to set a trap with Blinky leading the player into an ambush where the other three wait".

The reality of the Pac-man game is that the ghosts simply perform what is called a "random walk". The simplest way to describe the particular kind of random walk that happens in the game is to imagine that at every intersection a ghost would "toss a coin". If the coin falls on "heads", the ghost would move in the direction of the player, otherwise the ghost would pick a random direction. After leaving the intersection the ghost will stick to the chosen direction until it either gets stuck or reaches the next intersection. In both of these situations tossing a coin is repeated.

7.2 Chapter Problem 1: Ghosts Performing Random Walk

Clara learns to play Pac-man with her friends. One of the tasks she is currently training for is how to impersonate ghosts. After reading an article about Pac-man Clara found out that ghosts simply perform a random walk. Random walk involves making a number of steps and then changing direction at random. To make the task of learning how to perform random walk a bit more interesting Clara asks one of her friends to hide a leaf in her world. Her objective is to find this leaf via random walk.

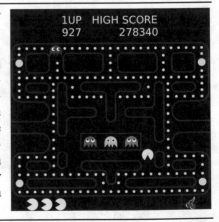

 To work on this problem in Clara's World please use the following URL: https://claraworld.net/link/C7P1.

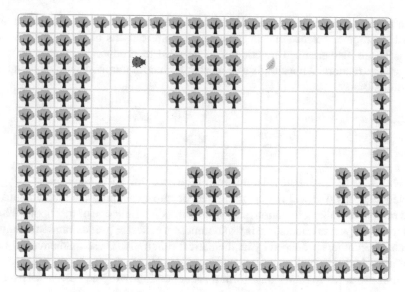

Fig. 7.1: Searching for a Leaf via Random Walk.

Figure 7.1 illustrates Clara's task in her world. She must get to the leaf while avoiding all obstacles along the way. The assumption is that Clara can be positioned anywhere in her world and the leaf can be placed in any empty cell. Clara must find the leaf by continuing to make a random number of steps followed by a random turn.

Solving this problem would require working with random numbers. Let us see what random numbers are and how to use them in Clara's World.

7.3 Random Numbers

There are types of software (such as games) that would lose their appeal without offering the element of surprise. Imagine a game where every single non-player character appears from the very same place and behaves in exactly the same way every time you play the game. This game will appear scripted, robotic and lacking intelligence and will not be fun to play. A popular approach to make a game appear less scripted and more unpredictable (and fun to play) is utilising random numbers. Random numbers are not only used in games, but are also widely used in cryptography, statistical sampling, simulation and design.

The simplest way to add variation and unpredictability with random numbers is to add many options and select one of them at random. This is precisely the technique the ghosts use in the chapter story and is the approach employed by many other video games.

In reality, computers are incapable of randomness. What we call random numbers in computer science and in programming are outputs of mathematical functions. These mathematical functions can be used to produce sequences of values that appear random. An example of generating random numbers with mathematical functions is shown below [14]:

$$x_{n+1} = a * x_n + b \pmod{m}$$
$$y_{n+1} = a * y_n + f(x_n) \pmod{m}$$
$$R_n = (x_n + m * y_n)/m^2$$

Here R_n is the n-th random number in sequence that will be generated using the above equations. We will not be going deeper into explaining the mathematics behind random number generation, since this is outside the scope of this book. What is important for you to understand is that computers generate pseudo random numbers, which are numbers produced by mathematical functions. These mathematical functions are selected in such a way that their values appear to form a random distribution within a given range rather than form a sequence following an easily discoverable pattern.

In Clara's World random numbers can be generated as follows:

```
int rnd = Clara.getRandomNumber(x);
```

This statement generates a random number in the range [0..x) and assigns this number as the value of the variable rnd.

Here is an example of generating a random number in the range [0..10).

```
int k = Clara.getRandomNumber(10);
```

The resulting value of the variable k will be a number between 0 and 9. Please note that when a range is defined in mathematics a square bracket "[" means that the value next to it is included, while a parenthesis ")" means that the value is excluded. In our case the value of "10" in the example above will never be generated, while the value "0" could be generated as a result of calling the Clara.getRandomNumber(10) method.

It is rarely the case that you would need a random number to be generated only once. More common is generating random numbers in a loop and calling the Clara.getRandomNumber(x) method multiple times. In this situation we will obtain a sequence of numbers between 0 and x. Generated numbers will appear to be randomly distributed within the [0...x) range.

7.3.1 Solving the Chapter Problem: Finding the Leaf via Random Walk

Let us put random numbers to the test and see how we can make Clara perform random walk. There will be a separate exercise for you to experiment with ghosts and make them perform the random walk Pac-man style. We do not want to spoil the fun of solving this by yourself, so here we will illustrate a much simple type of random walk.

In the following exercise our aim will be to help Clara find a leaf in a world full of obstacles. Instead of supplying Clara with information about the location of the leaf and then developing a clever obstacle avoidance solution, we will employ a much simpler strategy for finding the leaf. Clara will be repeating the process of randomly turning left or right and then making a number of steps forward. If there is an obstacle preventing her from moving, Clara will skip a turn hoping that the next random turn will make her go around the obstacle. Following this simple strategy we are hoping that after some time Clara will eventually get to the leaf and will celebrate all the hard work that went into finding it by eating the leaf.

Fig. 7.2: Making a Random Choice Simulates Unpredictability.

 You can see a video explanation of how to solve this problem step-by-step at https://claraworld.net/link/C7V1.

An important part of random walk is making a decision for which way to turn on the next iteration of the program execution (as shown in Figure 7.2). Instead of employing an intelligent navigation solution we are hoping that making a random decision will eventually result in Clara reaching the target location.

Let us apply this thinking to Clara's World shown in Figure 7.1. Clara is located in the world with some obstacles in it and must find her way to the leaf by performing a random walk. The essential part of random walk is making a random turn. Below is the code of the `randomTurn` method that can successfully perform a random turn with the help of random numbers:

```
void randomTurn() {
    boolean b = (getRandomNumber(2) == 1);

    if (b == true)
        turnRight();
    else
        turnLeft();
}
```

Turning at random is achieved by generating a random boolean variable with the following line of code:

```
boolean b = (getRandomNumber(2) == 1);
```

The above expression represents a compact way of generating a random number with the value of either "0" or "1" and then depending on the generated value to assign the boolean variable b with the value of `true` (if the generated number is 1) or `false` (if the generated value is anything else, which in our case can only be "0"). After generating a random boolean, Clara would then turn left or right depending on what this value is.

Now that we know how to make Clara turn at random, it is time to teach her how to make a random number of steps in the direction she is facing. This can be achieved by generating another random number in the range [0... 10). This number would then represent how many steps Clara has to make. Making Clara move that many steps can be done with the help of a `for` loop that repeats as many times as the value of the generated random number. Below is the code of the `randomMove()` method that utilises the variable `randomStepNr` for storing a random number that determines how many steps Clara needs to make:

```
void randomMove() {
    // generates a random number in the range [0..10)
    int randomStepNr = Clara.getRandomNumber(10);

    // move random number of steps
    for (int i = 0; i < randomStepNr && !onLeaf(); i++) {
        secureMove();
    }
}
```

It is important to focus your attention on the testing condition of the `for` loop, which is `i < randomStepNr && !onLeaf()`. This condition combines repeating the number of steps represented by the generated random number together with terminating the loop if Clara encounters a leaf prior to finishing the desired number of repetitions. It is important to have this combined condition to increase the likelihood of finding the leaf. If you remove the `!onLeaf()` part and change this condition to `i < randomStepNr`, you will notice that it would take Clara much longer to find the leaf and would see her passing over the leaf multiple times before she stops.

The final part of the solution that requires explanation is the use of secureMove. While performing a random number of steps we have to make sure that Clara does not run into a tree. To prevent her from doing this (and crashing the program) we utilise the familiar secureMove method shown below:

```
void secureMove()
{
    if (!treeFront())
        move();
}
```

With the two key building blocks (randomTurn and randomMove) in place, we can produce the complete solution for the random walk problem. What is required to solve the problem is placing these two commands inside a while loop that will continue repeating the new commands until Clara finds the leaf. It is important to understand that generating two random numbers and using those for making a random turn and a random number of steps will happen at every iteration of the while(!onLeaf()) loop. At each iteration of this loop these numbers will be generated again and are likely going to be different from those generated at the previous iteration. Below is the code of the random walk solution:

```
class MyClara extends Clara {
    /*
     * Random walk in search for a leaf
     */
    public void run()
    {
        while (!onLeaf())
        {
            randomTurn();
            randomMove();
        }

        removeLeaf();
    }

    /*
     * Make Clara perform a random turn
     */
    void randomTurn() {
        // flip a coin
        boolean b = (getRandomNumber(2) == 1);

        if (b == true)
            turnRight();
        else
            turnLeft();
    }
```

```
/*
 * Make Clara move for a random number of steps (up to 10)
 */
void randomMove() {
    // generates a random number in the range [0..10]
    int randomStepNr = Clara.getRandomNumber(10);

    // move random number of steps
    for (int i = 0; i < randomStepNr && !onLeaf(); i++) {
        secureMove();
    }
}

/*
 * Make Clara move, but don't let her run into trees
 */
void secureMove()
{
    if (!treeFront())
        move();
}
}
```

Try running the above code. It is recommended to substantially increase Clara's speed so that you are not required to wait for a very long time until she reaches the leaf. After running the code you would see Clara turning and moving around, acting in response to the generated random numbers.

 To see the solution of this problem in Clara's World please use the following URL: `https://claraworld.net/link/C7P1S`.

One last thing we would like you to think about is assigning a probability to the generated random number. In the chapter story ghosts would flip a coin at an intersection, meaning that with a probability of 50% they would chase the player. In the actual Pac-man game this probability increases over time with the goal of gradually making the game more difficult to play. Let us do something similar, but instead of chasing the player we will be increasing the likelihood of Clara turning right. At the moment, the probability of turning right is around 50% because we are alternating between two options (1 and 0) and converting them into a boolean value (`true` and `false`). How could we make Clara do a *random* turn, while increasing the likelihood of turning right?

Assigning a probability to a random action is actually quite simple. We can utilise the following updated code instead of what we previously had for making random turns:

```
void randomTurn() {
    // this variable determines the probability of turning
       right
    int desiredProbabilityForTurningRight = 75;

    // let the random number be in the range [0...100)
    int rnd = getRandomNumber(100);

    // assume that we are turning left by default
    boolean b = false;

    // if the generated number is within (0...75) -> turn right
    if (rnd < desiredProbabilityForTurningRight)
        b = true;

    if (b == true)
        turnRight();
    else
        turnLeft();
}
```

The trick we use here is to generate a random number within the [0...100) range and then give more prominence to the first 75% of this range [0...75). We will make Clara turn right if the generated number falls within this range and will make her turn left if it is outside of this range [75... 100). Most random number generators would produce a sequence of numbers that are evenly distributed within the given range. By associating 75% of all the possible values of the generated random numbers to turning right and reducing the range of numbers responsible for turning left to 25% we are ensuring that the likelihood of turning right is 75%.

If you use the above code instead of what we previously had for making Clara do a random turn and run it, you will notice that Clara will still occasionally turn left, but the right turn will happen much more frequently.

Now you are fully equiped with the necessary knowledge about random numbers and are ready to use it for solving the Pac-man exercise.

Exercise: Create a complete implementation of the Pac-man game by making Clara react to keyboard input and moving around her world. The second part of the exercise is coding ghosts to perform random walk and chase Clara. See the problem description at https://claraworld. net/link/C7ExPacman and try completing it step-by-step as per the description. This exercise is complex and time-consuming. We suggest working on it as you continue reading the book. Some steps will require concepts covered in Chapters 8 – 10.

7.4 Debugging

As your code gets more complex, it becomes more difficult to understand it and find errors. A popular solution to dealing with this complexity is to use various debugging techniques. The three most popular debugging techniques in programming are:

1. Desk-checking
2. Console output
3. Embedded debugger tools

Let us have a look at each of these techniques, but before doing this let us introduce the second chapter problem.

7.4.1 Chapter Problem 2: Repairing Clara's World after an Earthquake

Clara's World has experienced a high-magnitude earthquake. Many buildings have been destroyed and some have sustained significant damage. Figure 7.3 a) shows an example of a building with supporting columns. All columns have significant cracks in them (represented by leaves missing in the vertical leaf lines). To avoid any further damage Clara must quickly repair the damaged columns by patching them with leaves. The result of Clara's repair work should look similar to what is shown in Figure 7.3 b).

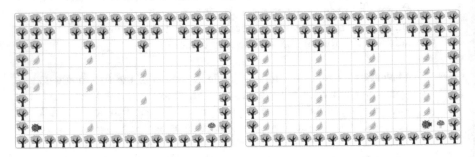

Fig. 7.3: a) Clara and Broken Columns   b) Columns after Repairs.

 You can see a video explanation of how to correctly solve this problem using a combination of the aforementioned debugging techniques at
https://claraworld.net/link/C7V2.

Unlike chapter problems that you saw earlier (which you had to solve from scratch) this problem also comes with a partial solution. The code below is the actual assignment submission from one of our students. This code, however, contains errors (bugs) that prevent it from correctly solving the problem. The student who produced it has spent a number of hours unsuccessfully trying to find and fix the bugs before contacting us.

```
class MyClara extends Clara {
    /** This program is buggy!
     * Clara doesn't stop in front of the mushroom.
     */
    void run() {
        turnLeft();

        while ( !mushroomFront() ) {
            fixingColumn();
            faceRight();
            fixingColumn();
            faceLeft();
        }
    }

    void fixingColumn() {
        for ( int i = 0; i < 5; i++ ) {
            if ( !onLeaf() )
                putLeaf();

            move();
        }

        if ( !onLeaf() )
            putLeaf();
    }

    void moveBetween() {
        for ( int i = 0; i < 4; i++ ) {
            if ( !mushroomFront() )
                move();
        }
    }

    void faceRight() {
        turnRight();
        moveBetween();
        turnRight();
    }

    void faceLeft() {
        turnLeft();
        moveBetween();
        turnLeft();
    }
}
```

To work on this problem in Clara's World please use the following URL: `https://claraworld.net/link/C7P2`.

We encourage you to run the above code and see what the outcome of its execution is before continuing with the chapter. However, please do not rush to fix or even understand this code. Instead, please read on and follow our instructions on how to work with this problem.

7.4.2 Desk-Checking

One possible approach to finding errors in the aforementioned chapter problem is desk-checking. Desk-checking is the simplest technique, but is also the least efficient one. The idea behind desk-checking is to trace program execution line-by-line. This can be done as a mental exercise, through dragging objects on the screen or by drawing on a piece of paper. In Clara's World desk-checking can be performed by going through a piece of code and using your mouse to move or rotate Clara in response to each command that you encounter. Moving is achieved by positioning your mouse cursor on top of Clara, clicking and holding the left mouse button and then dragging Clara (that will become attached to the mouse cursor) to a position of your choice. To make Clara turn, you can simply click on top of her with your mouse a number of times until she faces the direction of your choice.

For example, if you want to apply desk-checking to the `moveBetween` method in the above code, you should mentally execute the enclosed `for` loop. This would involve tracking the value of the loop counter in your head and moving Clara four times, while also testing for a tree in front of her.

Often the objective of desk-checking is to see how variables change their values and how objects in the environment (and the environment itself) are updated in response to executing the next line of code. The example below illustrates how desk-checking can be used for understanding the console output and for tracking the values of variables:

```
for (int i = 0; i < 10; i++) {
    System.out.print(i + " ");
}
```

Applying the desk-checking technique to the above code snipped is similar to emulating how Clara's World would execute your code. If the objective is to understand what will be printed on the screen after the `for` loop finishes execution then desk-checking would involve running the code in your head line-by-line and writing down its output on a piece of paper. The expected output for this exercises should be: 0 1 2 3 4 5 6 7 8 9.

In a similar way you could apply desk-checking to any program. It is a good practice to apply desk-checking as you write your code. This allows you to make sure that the program does what you expect it to, reduces the amount of time it takes to get a program working and helps to minimise the number of errors in your code.

Of course, the downside of desk-checking is that it is not suitable for understanding large programs. It is not uncommon for programming projects to span over millions of lines of code. It is not feasible to apply desk-checking to all this code. It is also impossible for a single person to have full comprehension of such a large program. The good news is that full comprehension is not required. What is needed instead is understanding important code fragments that are relevant to the task that the programmer is currently focusing on. Very often this task involves finding an error (a bug) in the code. While desk-checking is a technique that could certainly help with this task, it is not the most efficient one. The two debugging techniques presented below are much more suitable for working with large programs.

7.4.3 Console Output

Using console output for testing code execution is a very popular approach. Debugging with the help of the console output in Java is achieved by printing special messages or variable values with the help of the `System.out.println()` method. With the help of this command you can track the order of execution of your code or display the value of the variables in your code. Printing some text to console can help developers to narrow down their search in a large piece of code so that they can quickly identify the part of the code that is responsible for the error they are trying to fix. Once the problematic part of the code has been identified the developer can then apply desk-checking or other techniques to help understand and fix the error.

Let us now consider the aforementioned chapter problem 2. For effective debugging a complete understanding of the above code is not required. The objective behind debugging is actually to spend the least possible amount of time on understanding the code.

Let us try running this code first. The result would look similar to what is shown in Figure 7.4. Here Clara would successfully fix the columns, but would also crash into a tree after this. What the student who sent this code was specifically puzzled about was why would Clara not stop at a mushroom and why she would end up going all the way up after facing it.

The answers to these questions could be obtained after careful desk-checking of the code, however, this is not the most efficient way. Moreover, desk-checking is not an easy technique. The student who wrote this code has obviously tried it with little success. When debugging your code the key task you have is identifying the portion of the code responsible for the error in the fastest possible way. Narrowing down your search can be achieved through console output as shown below:

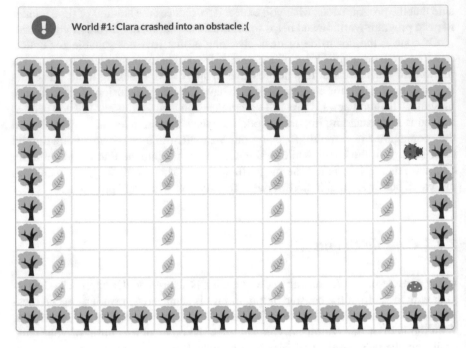

Fig. 7.4: The Result of Running our "Buggy" Code.

```
void run() {
    turnLeft();

    while ( !mushroomFront() ) {
        fixingColumn();
        System.out.println("1");
        faceRight();
        System.out.println("2");
        fixingColumn();
        System.out.println("3");
        faceLeft();
        System.out.println("4");
    }
}
```

The essence of this console output exercise is to simply print different numbers in front of every line inside the run() method and then to run your code
and see which numbers will be printed before and after the error. In this way
you will be able to quickly understand which of the methods present inside the
run() are responsible for the error. In our case number "3" would be printed
after Clara finishes fixing columns and she will then turn away from the mushroom (instead of stopping) and will continue going up. Evidently, our problematic
code is going to be the line located between System.out.println("3") and

`System.out.println("4")`. With this simple trick we were able to make a lot of progress in our understanding of the code. Now we know that we have to pay close attention to `faceLeft()` and that something inside this method makes Clara turn away from the mushroom instead of stopping. The `faceLeft()` method features only three lines of code. We can now easily understand what happens: Clara turns left and goes up instead of stopping. We do not yet understand why. The reason why is hidden somewhere in the three lines of code. It is important to notice that with this approach we have not developed much understanding of the entire solution. As mentioned earlier, understanding the entire program is not the objective of debugging. We are interested in fixing the problem and understanding why it occurs rather than in understanding every single aspect of the solution. Let us now take a closer look at the `faceLeft()` method.

```
void faceLeft() {
    turnLeft();
    moveBetween();
    turnLeft();
  }
}
```

What we wanted to happen is for this method to simply do nothing in the situation when there is a mushroom in front of Clara. Some readers might even wonder why this method would execute at all. Why would Clara not stop immediately when there is a mushroom in front of her as per the condition of the `while (!mushroomFront())` that is present in the `run()` method? The answer to these questions is that this is not how loops work in Java. The loop does not immediately terminate as soon as the associated condition becomes false (a mushroom appears in front of Clara). What happens instead is that the loop condition is only being tested once every iteration after executing the last line inside the loop's body. In our example the condition becomes false before `faceLeft()` is executed, but then the very first line inside `faceLeft()` makes Clara turn away from the mushroom. This means that by the time the loop condition is tested (after executing `faceLeft()`) Clara is no longer facing the mushroom and, therefore, the loop will not stop. Now that we understand why the loop does not stop it is time to remove the extra lines that we created for debugging and test another debugging technique, the embedded debugger.

7.4.4 Embedded Debugger

The embedded debugger is automatically activated in Clara's World after you set a break point next to a valid line of code in your program. Figure 7.5 shows a break point (solid red dot) next to the `faceLeft()` command.

You can create as many break points as you like by clicking with your mouse in the field immediately to the left of the line numbers in your program. If you put a break point next to an empty line or a line that only has comments, you will not

```
1  // source
2  class MyClara extends Clara {
3      /**
4       * This program is buggy!
5       * Clara doesn't stop in front of the mushroom.
6       */
7      void run()
8      {
9          turnLeft();
10
11         while ( !mushroomFront() )
12         {
13             fixingColumn();
14             faceRight();
15             fixingColumn();
16             faceLeft();
17         }
18     }
19
```

Fig. 7.5: Adding a break point.

be able to use the debugger. The debugger can be activated by running your code while having a break point that is placed next to a valid line of code. Once your program execution reaches the stage where the command located next to a break point is about to be performed, your program execution will pause and the debugger window appears. Figure 7.6 shows the result of stopping the program execution just before running the faceLeft() command in the last iteration of our loop.

The debugger window features two buttons ("Step" and "Continue"). These buttons allow you to continue running your code after stopping at a break point. Pressing the "Continue" button (two white arrows on green background) would result in executing the code until the next break point is encountered. Pressing the "Step" button (a single white arrow on orange background) would result in running the code line-by-line. The blue highlight shows the line that is to be executed next. In a situation when the next line is a method that is declared inside your program, this highlight would move to the first line of this method and the code window would automatically scroll to make it visible on the screen.

In our example we would need to use the "Step" button to understand how our code should be corrected. After pressing it a couple of times we would see Clara turning towards the mushroom (as the result of running the turnLeft() command inside faceLeft()). Then we will see no action in response to running moveBetween(), because moving within this method only happens in the situation when there is no tree in front of Clara. The last command inside faceLeft() is turnLeft(). After running this command you would be able to see that it is exactly the source of the problem. Clara would turn away from the mushroom and, therefore, the loop would not terminate. Now that we know what causes our problem

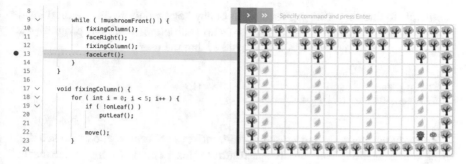

Fig. 7.6: Debugging Our Code.

we can easily prevent Clara from turning away from the mushroom by modifying the faceLeft() method as follows:

```
void faceLeft() {
   turnLeft();
   moveBetween();

   if ( !mushroomFront() )
      turnLeft();
}
```

With the help of the embedded debugger we were able to quickly correct our code without having to fully understand it. As you gain programming experience and start writing more complex code you should turn to the debugger frequently for correcting occasional errors.

7.5 Advanced Keyboard Input

In Chapter 6 we discussed how to receive input from the user with readInt, readDouble and readString commands. In addition to these commands, it is also possible for Clara to directly react to individual keyboard buttons being pressed.

The following method can be used for accessing the last key that the user has pressed on the keyboard:

```
Keyboard.getKey();
```

This method returns a String variable that contains the name of the key that was pressed last. In Clara's World each keyboard key has a corresponding String representation. For keys representing alphanumeric characters this String would represent the letter that corresponds to the key. For other keys (e.g. arrow keys) the String representation would feature words describing the key, such as "up", "down", "left" or "right". With the help of the Keyboard.getKey() method it

is possible to find the string representation of any key by putting this method inside
`act()` or a loop within `run()`. Below is an example of a simple program that
prints the `String` representation of every key that the user presses:

```
void act() {
   String keyPressed = Keyboard.getKey();
   System.out.println( keyPressed );
}
```

Try running this code and pressing different keys on your keyboard to see their
string representation. You can always return to this example to obtain the correct
string values for the keys that you want to use in your program.

Another method that is available to you is `Keyboard.isKeyDown`. With the
help of this method you can test whether a particular key has been pressed or not.
Let us illustrate the use of this method by creating a simple program that turns Clara
left or right in response to pressing the corresponding arrow keys on the keyboard.

```
public void act() {
    if ( Keyboard.isKeyDown("left") )
       turnLeft();

    if ( Keyboard.isKeyDown("right") )
       turnRight();
}
```

7.6 Creating Constants

Sometimes there are situations when what you require is not a variable, but a constant (a value that does not change over the course of running your program). While
variables can be used for such situations, for clarity and better readability of your
code it is recommended to use constants for all values that do not change. Constants
keep the program organised and easier to maintain. Constants in Java are declared
using the keyword "`final`".

A good example of a constant is the mathematical constant π. The precision of
your computations that use π would depend on how many numbers after the decimal
point in the *pi* constant would be used. Naturally, instead of remembering the value
of π and then typing this value everywhere where it is required, it is better to define it
once as the constant and use the name of this constant instead. Below is an example
of defining the π constant in Java:

```
final double PI = 3.141592653589793238;
```

Once a constant is defined, its value cannot change within your program. This
is helpful for preventing someone (or even yourself) accidentally redefining it by
typing something like `PI = 3.14` within one of the methods.

As per Java naming conventions, all constants must be named using upper-case letters and underscore characters "_" in-bctween words (instead of combining words as per camel case notation). Below are some examples of constant definitions:

```java
final double NSW_SALES_TAX = 0.725;
final double AUD_EXCHANGE_RATE = 0.72777;
```

In the next section we will show how constants can become very useful for improving the readability of your code. This example will also provide some further practice with variables and expressions.

7.7 The switch-case Construct

Sometimes in programming we encounter situations when many different decisions must be made depending on a value of a certain variable. Such situations can be handled with multiple if-statements. Java language, however, also offers the switch statement that is more compact and easier to work with.

In order to illustrate the usefulness of the switch statement let us imagine a situation when you have a certain variable in your code called testVariable and depending on the value of this variable your program would need to execute one of the four possible code snippets. One way to solve this is by using a number of if-statements. Below is an example of how your solution might look:

```java
if ( testVariable == 1) {
    command1();
    command2();
    command3();
}
else
if ( testVariable == 2) {
    command4();
    command5();
}
else
if ( testVariable == 3) {
    command6();
    command7();
}
else
if ( testVariable == 4) {
    command8();
    command9();
}
else
{
    command10();
    command11();
}
```

With the help of the `switch` statement you can rewrite the same code in a more compact and readable way.

```
switch (testVariable) {
    case 1:
    command1();
    command2();
    command3();
    break;

    case 2:
    command4();
    command5();
    break;

    case 3:
    command6();
    command7();
    command8();
    break;

    case 4:
    command9();
    command10();
    break;

    default:
    command11();
    command12();
}
```

The above code is equivalent to the previous code fragment that featured a number of `if` statements. The use of the `switch` statement starts with the `switch` keyword followed by either a variable name or an expression inside parentheses. This is followed by the body of the `switch` statement enclosed within a pair of curly brackets. Inside the curly brackets you can have a number of code blocks each starting with the Java reserved keyword `case`. The keyword `case` is followed by a possible value of the variable or expression that was provided inside the parentheses in the header of the `switch` statement. After the `case` statement you can have a number of commands that should end with the keyword `break`. The `break` keyword specifies the end of the corresponding `case` block. The body of a `switch` statement can have as many `case` blocks as you need.

The expression within the `switch` statement is limited to the following types: `byte`, `short`, `int`, `long` or `char`. If there is an associated `case` statement that matches the value of this expression, program execution will be transferred to that `case` statement. The use of the `break` statement is not compulsory. However, it is strongly recommended to end every `case` block with a `break` statement to improve readability of your code. If there is no `break` statement at the end of a `case` block, the execution would continue with the next case block even if its value does not match the expression inside `switch`.

It is possible to include the default section in addition to case blocks. This section is activated when the value of the switch expression does not match any of the case sections.

Let us illustrate the use of the switch statement on a less abstract example. Imagine that Clara is positioned somewhere in her world and currently faces east. You want to make Clara turn west, north or south depending on a value of a variable called direction. Below is a code snippet that illustrates how the switch statement can be used for performing this task:

```
final int WEST = 4;
final int EAST = 2;
final int NORTH = 1;
final int SOUTH = 3;

switch (direction) {
    case WEST:
    turnLeft();
    turnLeft();
    break;

    case NORTH:
    turnLeft();
    break;

    case SOUTH:
    turnRight();
    break;

    default:
    move();
    turnAround();
    move();
    turnAround();
}
```

Here we first define a number of integer constants that associate numeric values with names representing possible directions for Clara to turn. The direction of turning is determined by the value of direction variable that is declared and defined elsewhere. The process of turning is defined within the switch statement. Each direction is assigned with the corresponding case block that contains one or more commands for changing Clara's orientation. In the default block (that would also catch the value of EAST, we make Clara step forward and then return to her original position and face east. In the following section we will be returning to a modified version of this code.

7.8 Obstacle Avoidance Bug Style

We would like to dedicate the remainder of this chapter to further practising with `switch-case` statements, constants, variables and expressions. It is always best to practise by solving an interesting problem. Let us introduce you to the concept of *obstacle avoidance* and show you how we can significantly improve the performance (the number of moves and turns required) in the leaf search solution for chapter problem 1.

Obstacle avoidance is a technique used in video games, robotics and other disciplines for computing an obstacle-free path between two points. Modern video games predominantly rely on algorithms such as A* [15] or Artificial Potential Fields [16]. Such algorithms typically assume super-perception (complete knowledge of the game map) and are rather complex to explain in this book. One simple and elegant algorithm that is often overlooked is the "bug algorithm" [17]. This algorithm emulates the simplicity of insect navigation behaviour and assumes no knowledge of the environment (no super-perception). The key idea behind the bug algorithm is illustrated in Figure 7.7 a). The essence of it is to start by turning towards the finish point and then to keep moving towards this point on a straight line. If the bug encounters an obstacle it should turn left and then move along the obstacle while it is there. Once the obstacle is no longer present, the bug should turn towards its desired destination again and walk towards the finish point on a straight line. The algorithm repeats until the bug reaches the destination.

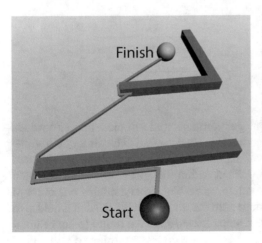
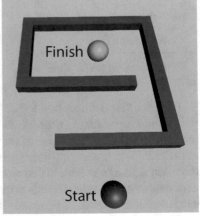

Fig. 7.7: a) Bug Algorithm   b) Bug Zapper.

7.8.1 Chapter Problem 3: Bug Navigation

Clara appears in a world full of obstacles similar to the one shown in Figure 7.8. Her task is to get to the leaf as quickly is possible. In the past we have employed random walk for this task, however, using random walk resulted in too many unnecessary moves and turns and a long waiting time. Clara's objective now is to learn proper obstacle avoidance using the aforementioned bug algorithm. She must get to the leaf following the algorithm shown below.

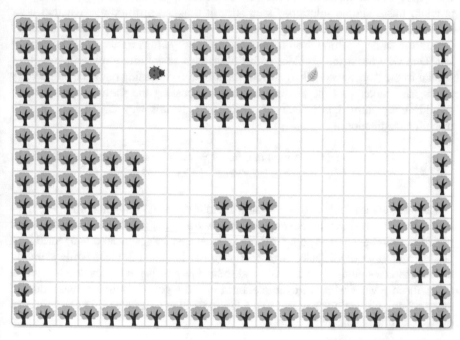

Fig. 7.8: Obstacle Avoidance in Clara's World.

A pseudocode version of the Bug Algorithm is as follows:

```
1. Turn towards destination
2. Walk towards destination
3. If obstacle in front: turn left
4. Follow obstacle until it is no longer present on the right
5. Repeat until at destination
```

Figure 7.7 a) illustrates how this algorithm can be applied. The virtual bug would start at the starting point (represented by a red sphere) and would walk on a straight line towards the desired destination (green sphere) labelled "Finish". The yellow line represents the trajectory of further movement. The virtual bug would turn left at a collision with an obstacle and would closely follow the obstacle (making sure it can be sensed on the right-hand side) until it can continue walking towards the de-sired destination again. The algorithm would repeat until the bug reaches its desired destination.

This algorithm has a known problem. In some circumstances the bug will become stuck in an infinite loop and will never reach the destination. Figure 7.7 b) illustrates the well-known "bug zapper" scenario for which this algorithm would not work correctly. If you trace the movement of a virtual bug with your finger, you will realise that it would keep moving towards the destination, would encounter obstacles and would attempt to avoid those by turning left and following the obstacle, but it would never enter the section of the environment that contains the destination. This problem has a simple solution. Essentially, it makes no difference whether after colliding with an obstacle the bug turns left or right. The main thing is to consistently turn in the same direction. You may choose to always turn right instead of turning left. One way to fix the problem with falling into an infinite loop with structures similar to the "bug zapper" is to switch the direction of turning once the bug detects that it has walked past the starting point. After passing the starting point the bug should always turn right instead of turning left. In this way it will very quickly reach the destination.

 To work on this problem in Clara's World please use the following URL: https://claraworld.net/link/C7P3.

Let us now turn Clara into an obstacle avoiding bug and implement the bug algo-rithm. Figure 7.8 shows an example of the starting configuration of Clara's World that our implementation is going to work with. Here Clara is located in a world con-taining a number of obstacles (trees). Her aim is to get to the leaf while avoiding all the obstacles along the way. As usual, our objective is not to develop a solution that will only work with one example, but to have a generic solution that works in any environment and for any leaf and Clara position (as long as it is not within an obstacle and is reachable by Clara).

 You can see a video explanation of how to solve this problem step-by-step at https://claraworld.net/link/C7V3.

In solving this problem we will be relying on the following set of additional methods:

- `getX(); // Returns the X coordinate of Clara`
- `getY(); // Returns the Y coordinate of Clara`
- `getLeafX(); // Returns the X coordinate of the leaf`
- `getLeafY(); // Returns the Y coordinate of the leaf`

These methods will help us to work with Clara's World as with a coordinate system, where the top left corner of Clara's World represents the origin (0, 0). The above methods will help us to receive Clara's coordinates and the coordinate of the leaf in this system. Knowing these coordinates is necessary for us to be able to instruct Clara to move towards the leaf.

As per the algorithm, Clara must move towards the leaf until she encounters an obstacle and then she must follow the obstacle while it is there and repeat until the destination is reached. Let us try to translate this into Java code. Reaching the destination means being on a leaf, so we can encode the `run()` method as follows:

```java
public void run() {
    while ( !onLeaf() ) {
        getToNextDesiredPos();
    }
}
```

Here both moving towards the leaf and following the obstacle are integrated into `getToNextDesiredPos()`, which Clara would continue executing until she finds herself on top of the leaf.

Let us now think about how `getToNextDesiredPos()` could be implemented. One way to do it is inspecting all surrounding cells and them making Clara move into the cell that is closest to the leaf. If this cell happens to be an obstacle, Clara should start avoiding it. In Figure 7.8 there are four possibilities for Clara's next step given her current position. She could go to the cell on the east, the cell on the west, the cell to the north or the cell to the south. It is obvious from the figure that the cell to the east is the closest one to the leaf (of those four possible options), so this is where Clara should be sent as the result of running `getToNextDesiredPos()`.

How could we possibly select the cell that is closest to the leaf? Let us turn to high school geometry. If we have two points $p_1 = (x_1, y_1)$ and $p_2 = (x_2, y_2)$, we can compute the distance between these two points (known as Euclidean distance) using the following equation (where d is the Euclidean distance between p_1 and p_2):

$$d^2 = (x_2 - x_1)^2 + (y_2 - y_1)^2. \tag{7.1}$$

In order to find the cell that is closest to the leaf we can compute the Euclidean distances between each of these cells and the leaf and select the one that is smallest. The above equation computes the distance squared, but since we only need this for comparison purposes it is sufficient for us to compare d^2 instead of comparing d for every cell (which could be obtained by computing the square root of d^2). Let us now translate this into code. It is going to be a good practice with expressions in Java.

At the moment we do not know how to use the power function to compute something like $(x_2 - x_1)^2$. However, we do not actually require the power function for this task, because we could represent $(x_2 - x_1)^2$ as $(x_2 - x_1) * (x_2 - x_1)$. How could we translate these equations into Java code and what would be the values of (x_1, y_1) and (x_2, y_2)? Let us consider the following code for `goToNextDesiredPos()`:

```
public void getToNextDesiredPos() {
    int claraX = getX();
    int claraY = getY();
    int leafX = getLeafX();
    int leafY = getLeafY();
}
```

Here we have the coordinates of two points (claraX, claraY) and (leafX, leafY). If we want to compute the Euclidean distance (squared) between these points we would use the following code:

```
int dSquared = (claraX - leafX)*(claraX - leafX) +
               (claraY - leafY)*(claraY - leafY);
```

Let us now think about how to obtain the coordinates of the four surrounding cells. The coordinate of the leaf would not change. What would be different for each of the four cells is the coordinate of the cell itself. The cell to the east of Clara (distEast) would have the same *y* coordinate as Clara, and the *x* coordinate could be expressed as claraX + 1. Similarly, the cell to the west of Clara (distWest) would have the same *y* coordinate as Clara and the *x* coordinate could be expressed as claraX - 1. The cell to the north of Clara (distNorth) would have the same *x* coordinate as Clara, and the *y* coordinate could be expressed as claraY - 1. Finally, the cell to the south of Clara (distSouth) would have the same *x* coordinate as Clara, and the *y* coordinate could be expressed as claraY + 1. We can now compute distances to the corresponding cells around Clara as follows:

```
int distEast = (claraX+1 - leafX)*(claraX+1 - leafX) + (claraY -
    leafY)*(claraY - leafY);
int distWest = ( (claraX-1) - leafX)*( (claraX-1) - leafX) +
    (claraY - leafY)*(claraY - leafY);
int distSouth = (claraX - leafX)*(claraX - leafX) + (claraY + 1
    - leafY)*(claraY + 1 - leafY);
int distNorth = (claraX - leafX)*(claraX - leafX) + (claraY - 1
    - leafY)*(claraY - 1 - leafY);
```

How do we now make Clara go in the direction we want? Let us do the following mental exercise and agree that we have a set of numbers (1, 2, 3, 4), where every number corresponds to a certain direction (e.g. 1 = east, 2 = west, etc.). We can then ask Clara to go east, west, north or south depending on which of the distances is the smallest. Let us imagine that there is a method called goGivenDirection that is capable of making Clara move one step in the direction represented by an integer number (1, 2, 3 or 4). We can then assign a variable (e.g. movementDirection) with a numeric value representing where Clara should go and call the goGivenDirection(movementDirection) method to make Clara actually go there. The value of movementDirection would be assigned depending on the distances computed. Here we will again use a method (goGivenDirection) that receives input from us. We will cover such methods in Chapter 8. For now it is important to understand that this method can receive input similar to the readInt and System.out.println methods.

Operating with numbers representing a direction can be quite difficult. Luckily, Java has constants that can help make this much more intuitive. A good way of simplifying your code is creating constants that represent these directions, and instead of operating with numbers we could then operate with intuitive names. These constants could be defined as follows:

```
final int WEST = 4;
final int EAST = 2;
final int NORTH = 1;
final int SOUTH = 3;
```

The final part of the getToNextDesiredPos() method that is left for us to implement is comparing the distances so that we know which way to send Clara. The code below shows the completed getToNextDesiredPos() method:

```
public void getToNextDesiredPos() {
    // Get Clara's coordinates
    int claraX = getX();
    int claraY = getY();

    // Get coordinates of the leaf
    int leafX = getLeafX();
    int leafY = getLeafY();

    // Compute all distances
    int distEast = (claraX+1 - leafX)*(claraX+1 - leafX) +
        (claraY - leafY)*(claraY - leafY);
    int distWest = ( (claraX-1) - leafX)*( (claraX-1) - leafX)
        + (claraY - leafY)*(claraY - leafY);
    int distSouth = (claraX - leafX)*(claraX - leafX) +
        (claraY + 1 - leafY)*(claraY + 1 - leafY);
    int distNorth = (claraX - leafX)*(claraX - leafX) +
        (claraY - 1 - leafY)*(claraY - 1 - leafY);

    int movementDirection = WEST;

    if ( distEast <= distWest && distEast <= distNorth &&
        distEast <= distSouth )
      movementDirection = EAST;

    if ( distNorth <= distWest && distNorth <= distEast &&
        distNorth <= distSouth )
      movementDirection = NORTH;

    if ( distSouth <= distWest && distSouth <= distEast &&
        distSouth <= distNorth )
      movementDirection = SOUTH;

    // send Clara in the direction closest to the leaf
    goGivenDirection(movementDirection);
}
```

Notice how after computing the distances we have a set of three if-statements for deciding which of the distances is the smallest. In order to make this decision we must compare each distance with every other distance. The movementDirection variable would be used for memorising which direction Clara should go to. Assigning it with some initial value (in our case WEST) helps to eliminate one extra comparison. We could have had another if-statement that would compare distWest with every other distance, but it is not required because in the situation when neither of the cells to the east, to the south or to the north represents the smallest distance, the value of the movementDirection variable would remain WEST. Thus, Clara will be going west by default and we do not have to create another if-statement.

Now it is time to see how the missing goGivenDirection method could be implemented. Our solution is shown below:

```
void goGivenDirection(int movementDirection) {
    switch (movementDirection) {
        // if we want to go to the cell to the east
        // we simply need to move forward
        case EAST:
        secureMoveAdvanced();
        break;

        // if we need to go to the west - then turn around
        // and move, as Clara initially faces east
        case WEST:
        turnAround();
        secureMoveAdvanced();
        turnAround();
        break;

        // if we need to go north - then we need to turn left
        // and then move, as Clara initially faces east
        case NORTH:
        turnLeft();
        secureMoveAdvanced();
        turnRight();
        break;

        // if we need to go to the south - then turn right
        // and then move, as Clara initially faces east
        case SOUTH:
        turnRight();
        secureMoveAdvanced();
        turnLeft();
        break;
    }
}
```

This method receives the direction where Clara should go as a numeric value that is stored in an internal variable movementDirection. We then rely on the method orientEast() that makes sure that Clara always starts by facing east at the start of this method. This helps us to keep track of her orientation and to make sure that she is indeed going in the direction where she is expected to go. Depending on the direction where Clara must go we would then make sure that Clara correctly turns so that she faces this direction, makes a step towards this direction (secureMoveAdvanced) and then faces east again after she is finished making the step. Because we are making the decision about which direction to go to based on a variable that has multiple possible discrete values, it is appropriate for this method to use the switch statement.

Another missing method present here is secureMoveAdvanced(). This method will either make Clara move one step in the direction she faces or would make her avoid an obstacle if the cell in front of Clara contains one.

Below is the complete solution of the bug algorithm with comments to help you understand the code a little better. We start by declaring the constants and creating two variables. The isTurningLeft variable defines which way Clara should turn when she encounters an obstacle (left or right). The orientation variable acts as a memory that contains Clara's current orientation. This variable helps Clara make sure that she can correctly orient east at the start of the goGivenDirection method and will be used to further track all orientation changes. You will see how this variable is used inside orientEast method to help Clara face east. Another method that uses this variable extensively is turnAway. It is called when Clara encounters an obstacle and has to avoid it by turning left or right. The orientation variable is updated as she turns. Finally, secureMoveAdvanced will either make Clara move if there is no tree blocking her way or follow an obstacle (avoidWall) if there is a tree in front.

```
/**
 * Clara does basic obstacle avoidance bug style.
 */
class MyClara extends Clara {
    // Declaring constants here.
    // Notice that those will be visible inside all methods.
    // Also notice how much more sense it makes to use names
    // like NORTH or SOUTH instead of numbers 3 and 4
    // and how using constants instead of numbers
    // helps to understand the code better
    final int WEST = 4;
    final int EAST = 2;
    final int NORTH = 1;
    final int SOUTH = 3;

    // determines the direction of turning at an obstacle
    boolean isTurningLeft = true;

    // remembers Clara's orientation
    int orientation = EAST;
```

```
/**
 * Bug obstacle avoidance algorithm.
 * Run the program, place the leaf in a new position, repeat.
 */
public void run() {
    while ( !onLeaf() ) {
        getToNextDesiredPos();
    }
}


/**
 * Make sure that Clara is facing east
 * Pre-condition: Clara is facing any direction
 * Post-condition: Clara faces east
 */
void orientEast() {
    while (orientation != EAST) {
        if (orientation == 1) {
            turnRight();
            orientation = EAST;
        }
        else
        if (orientation < 4) {
            orientation--;
            turnLeft();
        }
    }
}


/**
 * The method that makes Clara turn away from an obstacle.
 * Clara always turns left, until she realises that turning
 * left is not getting her anywhere (she is stuck in a loop)
 * then she will change the direction of turning.
 */
void turnAway() {
    if (isTurningLeft) {
        if (orientation > 1)
            orientation--;
        else
            orientation = 4;

        turnLeft();
    }
    else {
        if (orientation < 4)
            orientation++;
        else
            orientation = 1;

        turnRight();
    }
}
```

```
/**
 * Send Clara in the direction determined by the input.
 * Pre-condition: Clara is facing east
 * Post-condition: Clara made a step in the desired direction
 * She would face east when this method finishes.
 */
void goGivenDirection(int movementDirection) {
   orientEast();

   switch (movementDirection) {
      // if we want to go to the cell to the east
      // we simply need to move forward
      case EAST:
      secureMoveAdvanced();
      break;

      // if we need to go to the west - then turn around
      // and move, as Clara initially faces east
      case WEST:
      turnAround();
      secureMoveAdvanced();
      turnAround();
      break;

      // if we need to go north - then we need to turn left
      // and then move, as Clara initially faces east
      case NORTH:
      turnLeft();
      secureMoveAdvanced();
      turnRight();
      break;

      // if we need to go to the south - then turn right
      // and then move, as Clara initially faces east
      case SOUTH:
      turnRight();
      secureMoveAdvanced();
      turnLeft();
      break;
   }
}

// Move forward or avoid the wall and then move forward
void secureMoveAdvanced() {
   if ( !treeFront() )
      move();
   else {
      // Tracking wall collisions here!
      avoidWall();
   }
}
```

```java
/**
 * A method to avoid an obstacle/wall
 * by going around it on the right-hand side
 * in the similar way as maze navigation
 */
void avoidWall() {
    // Then we start turning and moving
    // so the orientation may change in an unpredictable way
    turnAway();

    while ( ( isTurningLeft && treeRight() ) || (
          !isTurningLeft && treeLeft() ) ) {
        // double-check that Clara is not turning in circles
        // and falls in an infinite loop. So we stop after
        // Clara turns 4 times = 360 degrees.
        // Notice the advanced use of && in the loop condition
        for (int i = 0; treeFront() && i < 4; i++ ) {
            turnAway();
        }
        move();
    }
}


// Standard method for turning 180 degrees
void turnAround() {
    turnAway();
    turnAway();
}

/**
 * Calculates which of the surrounding cells will bring Clara
 * closer to her goal (leaf) and makes her move to this cell.
 * If the cell contains an obstacle - Clara will avoid it
 * following the right hand rule principle
 */
public void getToNextDesiredPos() {
    // Get Clara's coordinates
    int claraX = getX();
    int claraY = getY();

    // Get coordinates of the leaf
    int leafX = getLeafX();
    int leafY = getLeafY();

    // Compute distances to the leaf from all surrounding cells
    // It's enough to compute distance squared for comparison
    // d2 = (x2 - x1)*(x2 - x1) + (y2 - y1)*(y2 - y1);

    int distEast = (claraX+1 - leafX)*(claraX+1 - leafX) +
        (claraY - leafY)*(claraY - leafY);
    int distWest = ( (claraX-1) - leafX)*( (claraX-1) - leafX)
        + (claraY - leafY)*(claraY - leafY);
```

```
    int distSouth = (claraX - leafX)*(claraX - leafX) +
        (claraY + 1 - leafY)*(claraY + 1 - leafY);
    int distNorth = (claraX - leafX)*(claraX - leafX) +
        (claraY - 1 - leafY)*(claraY - 1 - leafY);

    int movementDirection = WEST;

    if ( distEast <= distWest && distEast <= distNorth &&
        distEast <= distSouth )
      movementDirection = EAST;

    if ( distNorth <= distWest && distNorth <= distEast &&
        distNorth <= distSouth )
      movementDirection = NORTH;

    if ( distSouth <= distWest && distSouth <= distEast &&
        distSouth <= distNorth )
      movementDirection = SOUTH;

    goGivenDirection(movementDirection);
  }
}
```

 To see the solution of this problem in Clara's World please use the following URL: `https://claraworld.net/link/C7P3S`.

The above code solves Clara's navigation, but it is incomplete. Try running this code and move Clara and the leaf to different locations in the world and see whether Clara manages to get to the leaf. You should soon realise that on some occasions Clara will become stuck in an infinite loop and will not be able to get to the leaf. The reason for this lack of navigation intelligence is that Clara always turns the same direction (left) when she encounters an obstacle and does not track whether she is stuck in a loop or not. We discussed this problem when the bug zapper structure was presented. In Chapter 10 we will show a complete solution of this problem that correctly finds a way to the leaf in all possible scenarios. Before looking at the solution we recommend you treat fixing this code as an exercise and encourage you to attempt solving this part of the problem yourself.

 Exercise: As a good programming exercise we recommend you to try fixing the incomplete bug algorithm by making sure that you detect the situations where Clara starts going in circles and then change her direction of turning to the opposite one (if Clara was turning left at an obstacle before then you need to make sure that she starts turning right at an obstacle once going in circles has been detected).

Hint: A simple strategy you can use for detecting that Clara is going in circles is to memorise the coordinates of the the last two obstacle collisions. For the small world that we have it should be sufficient to check whether the coordinates of an obstacle that Clara encounters are the same as the one of those coordinates from the previous two obstacle encounters. Try creating the corresponding variables in your code and check those every time Clara finds herself in front of an obstacle.

7.9 Summary

In this chapter we showed how Clara can use random numbers and perform a random walk. Random numbers are useful for simulating unpredictability. We also looked into different debugging techniques and showed how to work with the embedded debugger tool. As your code becomes larger, it also becomes more difficult to understand and find errors (bugs) in this code. With the help of the debugger you will be able to quickly identify errors in your code and understand what is causing those. Finally, we have gained more experience with using variables, constants and expressions through turning Clara into a smart navigating insect. Clara is now able to successfully find her way to a leaf in her world and avoid all the obstacles along the way. The solution we produced is incomplete. A good programming exercise for you is to finish it by testing whether Clara is going in circles and then reverse the direction of turning at an obstacle as she does. Our example world for this problem is small, and it is sufficient to track the coordinates of Clara's last two obstacle encounters in order to check whether she is going in circles. For larger worlds you would require a better strategy (e.g. memorising all obstacle encounters). In Chapter 9 we will discuss the concept of arrays that helps you to create collections of variables. Using arrays for storing the coordinates of all obstacle encounters should be the next step towards improving this solution.

7.10 Exercises

 Exercises that target your understanding of the concepts covered in this chapter are available at `https://claraworld.net/link/C7Ex`.

Chapter 8
Methods

In Chapter 4 we discussed decomposition, which is breaking a larger problem into smaller logical sub-problems and coding these sub-problems as Java methods. The methods we have created until now received no input and returned no output. In this chapter we will have a more detailed look into methods with a particular focus on creating methods that receive input and return output. We will discuss how Java executes such methods, will have an in-depth look into the use of variables within methods and will present the concept of information hiding.

Image features the "Super Mario 3D" 3D model by TeoProductions available under Creative Commons CC BY 4.0.

© Springer Nature Switzerland AG 2021
A. Bogdanovych, T. Trescak, *Learning Java Programming in Clara's World*,
https://doi.org/10.1007/978-3-030-75542-3_8

8.1 Chapter Story: Simulating Projectile Motion in Video Games

In many video games, especially in popular platform games[1] such as Super Mario Bros. [18], it is required for the player character to jump in response to pressing the corresponding control button.

For jumps to be believable it is essential that the jumping character follows a parabolic trajectory as observed in projectile motion. Projectile motion is the motion of an object thrown or projected into the air, subject to only the acceleration of gravity [19]. The object is called a projectile, and its path is called its trajectory. Where accurate physics simulation is required, game developers typically have to solve physics equations similar to those shown below [19].

$$x = x_0 + V_{0x} * t \tag{8.1}$$

$$y = y_0 + V_{0y} * t - \frac{1}{2} g(t)^2 \tag{8.2}$$

Here (x, y) is the position of the jumping character at a time t, (x_0, y_0) is the initial position of the character, $V_{0}x$ and $V_{0}y$ are horizontal and vertical components of the jump velocity at the moment when the jump was initiated and g is gravity (9.80665 m/s^2). With the help of these equations we can calculate the updated position of the player (x, y) and update it for every new frame of the game that is drawn on the screen.

8.1.1 Simplified Projectile Motion Simulation

Many early video games did not require high accuracy in visualising jumps. What was required instead is for the jump to look believable and to be performed fast enough on the slow and limited computers that were available at the time. For such cases a simpler and less computationally demanding approach was used. One easy simplification, for example is to work with an approximate value of gravity: 9.80665 $m/s^2 \approx 10 m/s^2$. However, even this approximation was not enough to achieve high performance on limited hardware. An even more radical simplification that we will consider here is assuming that the unit of time is not one second, but the time required to draw one frame on the screen and then making the following substitution:

$$\frac{1}{2} g(t)^2 \approx 1 \tag{8.3}$$

After applying the above approximation we can turn the computation of updated position into adding two vectors (velocity and gravity). Figure 8.1 illustrates an example of such a simplified version of jump simulation.

---

[1] A game in which the player controlled character has to frequently jump on top of platforms similar to what is shown in the figure above.

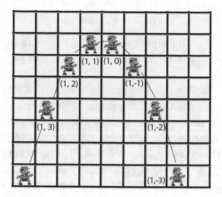

Fig. 8.1: Jumping in Platform Games.

In this example we assume that at the moment when the jump starts Clara has the initial velocity $(1,3)$. Here 1 is the horizontal displacement in a unit of time, meaning that Clara would move 1 virtual metre along the horizontal axis in a unit of time. And 3 is the vertical displacement, meaning that Clara would move 3 virtual metres in a unit of time. While in physics the unit of time is usually selected as 1 second, for our purposes it is more practical to consider one unit of time being the time needed to update the picture on the screen (time required for drawing the next frame on the screen). In simple terms, the velocity $(1,3)$ would result in a displacement of the character by 1 metre horizontally and 3 metres vertically in the next frame (in relation to its position in the previous frame). The forces that act upon the character are this initial velocity and gravity.

Gravity acts upon the character in the direction that is opposite to the positive direction of the Y axis and (after applying the aforementioned approximation) can be represented as $(0,-1)$. There is no impact of gravity along the horizontal axis, hence the value is 0, and -1 is the impact along the vertical axis. We can now rewrite the simplified equations as follows. Here gravity is expressed as $(g_x = 0, g_y = -1)$, V_{Xprev} and V_{Yprev} are the horizontal and vertical components of the character velocity in the previous frame, while V_{Xnew} and V_{Ynew} are the updated velocity components for the new frame. Finally, x_{prev} and y_{prev} are the coordinates of the character in the previous frame and x_{new} and y_{new} are the updated coordinates of the character in the new frame.

$$x_{new} = x_{prev} + V_{Xnew} \tag{8.4}$$

$$y_{new} = y_{prev} + V_{Ynew} \tag{8.5}$$

$$V_{Xnew} = V_{Xprev} + g_x \tag{8.6}$$

$$V_{Ynew} = V_{Yprev} + g_y \tag{8.7}$$

With the help of the above equations we can compute how the position of the player character (x_{new}, y_{new}) will change over time, so that we can correctly simulate projectile motion.

Let us now see how applying these equations would result in the behaviour shown in Figure 8.1. Let us assume that at the moment when the jump starts the character is located at coordinate $(0,0)$ and starts the jump with the velocity of $(1,3)$. In the next frame the x coordinate of the new position would be $(x_{new} = 0 + 1 = 1)$ and the y coordinate would be $(y_{new} = 0 + 3 = 3)$. The x component of the updated velocity would be $(V_{Xnew} = 1 + 0 = 1)$, and the y component of the updated velocity would be $(V_{Ynew} = 3 + (-1) = 2)$. As we can see, the x component of velocity would remain unchanged since there is no force that affects the horizontal movement of the character. Only the vertical component of character velocity would be changing in response to gravity. Thus, in the next frame the character would move to the coordinate $(1,3)$, as shown in Figure 8.1, and the velocity would change to $(1,2)$. Following the same approach, we could compute the updated positions of the character in the following frames, and these would be the positions shown in Figure 8.1. The vertical component of the velocity will decrease all the way down to -3 when the character would land on the ground and the jump would finish. With this knowledge at hand let us now start thinking about how to turn Clara into a jumping super flea.

8.2 Chapter Problem: Jumping Like a Flea

Clara continues her development into a super powerful insect, and the new skill she is practising to acquire is jumping like a flea. Clara was told that she would become the main character in the new video game called "Super Clara Sisters" if she learns how to jump properly. Clara's jump must look believable, so her task is to simulate projectile motion shown in the picture in response to the "up" arrow key pressed by the user.

To work on this problem in Clara's World please use the following URL:
https://claraworld.net/link/C8P1.

Let us have a detailed look at solving this problem in Clara's World. Clara starts in an empty world shown in Figure 8.2 a). What we want to achieve is to make her jump in response to the user pressing the "up" arrow key on the keyboard. The trajectory of the jump should be marked with leaves. Clara should also be able to perform multiple jumps, where the next jump would start from the position where she has landed after performing the previous jump as shown in Figure 8.2 b).

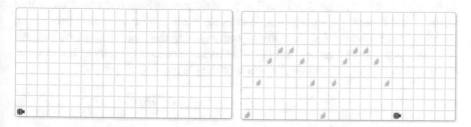

Fig. 8.2: a) Clara before Jumping   b) Clara after Jumping.

 You can see a video explanation of how to solve this problem step-by-step at https://claraworld.net/link/C8V1.

For solving this problem you would need to rely on the new method that was specifically created for it (changePosition). This new method receives input from the user in the form changePosition(startXPos, deltaX, deltaY), where startPos is the starting position of Clara along the X axis, deltaX is the displacement of Clara along the X axis in relation to deltaX and deltaY is the displacement of Clara along the Y axis. The result of calling this method is positioning Clara at the new position as per startXPos, deltaX and deltaY.

In the remainder of this chapter we will finally reveal how methods can receive input and return output. Thus, let us look at the new material before solving this problem.

8.3 Methods

By now you have had a lot of practical experience with using methods in Java. A method is a block of code that contains some distinct pattern of behaviour and defines a distinct name for it. Using methods helps to break a complex problem down into smaller manageable pieces. In this way methods can simplify programs. Using methods is also helpful if a certain task must be performed in multiple places within a program. Expressing such repetitive pieces as methods and using a method name instead of duplicating the code is known as *code reuse*.

Methods is an abstraction that you can apply to just about anything in the world. For example, you can see a video game console (similar to the one shown in Figure 8.3) as a method. Game consoles have the distinct functionality of loading a particular video game and playing it on the screen. However, in contrast to many methods we have encountered so far, game consoles can also receive input (a cartridge) and can produce output (image on the screen). The input in this case would determine the output. If we put a cartridge with the Pac-man game, the output would be images of coins and ghosts. Inserting a cartridge with Super Mario Bros. would result in a different output. The game console itself can be seen as a processing device that contains the functionality of transforming the input into the output. An important property of a game console is that it can be used with many different types of input (cartridges) without modification of the player.

Fig. 8.3: Video Game Console as a Method.

In many programming languages methods are called *functions*. This is due to the mathematical origins of programming. Java is a relatively modern programming language and has adopted a new terminology, and Java programmers are encouraged to use the term "methods". However, you will see many programmers (especially those whose first programming language was not Java) use the term "functions". You can use whichever of these two terms that you are most comfortable with.

Mathematical functions represent another good metaphor for methods that receive input and return output. For example, the following expression looks very similar to how methods are used in programming:

$$y = cos(x) \tag{8.8}$$

This function (*cos*) receives *x* as the input and returns *y* as the output. The input here is translated into the output via the function.

8.3.1 The `void` Returning Methods

So far we have created methods that return nothing (`void`). The `moveToTree()` method below is an example of a method that returns no value. This method simply executes the given task of moving without reporting anything back.

```
void moveToTree() {
  while ( !treeFront() ) {
    move();
  }
}
```

Formally speaking, this method contains two parts: the method header and the method body. The *method header*, which appears at the beginning of its definition (`void moveToTree()`) specifies the method name, its output type (`void`) and can also define the expected input (none in this case). The *body* of the method is the collection of statements contained within the curly brackets. These statements will be executed line-by-line when the method is called. Another term for calling a method is *invoking*.

Apart from the return type, name and input the method header can also determine the method's visibility. For, example the same `moveToTree()` method could have been defined as follows:

```
public void moveToTree() {
  while ( !treeFront() ) {
    move();
  }
}
```

The difference here is the use of the keyword `public`. This Java reserved keyword determines the visibility of the method outside of its defining class (`MyClara`). The use of the keyword `public` makes the method accessible from external classes, while the use of the keyword `private` (or having no `private` or `public` present) would make a method only accessible from within its class. We will return to this topic in Chapter 10, where classes and objects are discussed.

8.3.2 *Methods Returning a Value*

In some situations it is not only required to perform a certain operation (e.g. move to
the closest tree) but also to do some computation (e.g. counting the number of leaves
that Clara encounters while moving). For such situations Java language provides the
possibility of returning a value within a method. We have already used methods that
return values in Chapter 6. Here is an example of such a method:

```
int n1 = readInt("Enter n1: ");
```

The `readInt` method in the above example receives keyboard input from the
user and returns it as an integer variable. In order to define a method that returns a
value you must first change the returning type from `void` to a type that you want to
return. A method can only return a variable, so the return type you provide should
be the expected type of this variable. In addition, you must also use the special
command `return`. This command will terminate the method and will return the
resulting variable back to the code that called this method.

Below is an example of a method that makes Clara walk until the next tree and
then returns the number of leaves Clara encounters on the street:

```
int moveToTreeAndCountLeaves() {
    int retVal = 0;

    while (!treeFront()) {
        if (onLeaf())
            retVal++;

        move();
    }

    // OBOB fixing
    if (onLeaf())
        retVal++;

    return retVal;
}
```

 To work on this problem in Clara's World please use the following URL:
`https://claraworld.net/link/C8P2`.

The definition of the `moveToTreeAndCountLeaves()` method, unlike most
methods we have created so far, starts with the keyword `int` instead of `void`.
This is because the number of leaves that Clara encounters will be returned in an
integer variable as the result of running this method. To make this happen a local
integer variable called `retVal` was created and then its value was updated within
the `while` loop. Finally, the `return` command terminates the method and returns
the value of `retVal` outside.

Correctly counting the leaves and producing the desired output can be accomplished by calling the `moveToTreeAndCountLeaves()` method from within `run()` as shown below:

```
void run() {
    int leaves = moveToTreeAndCountLeaves();
    System.out.println("Leaves found = " + leaves);
}
```

Figure 8.4 shows an example of the starting configuration of Clara's World and the desired output "Leaves found = 5".

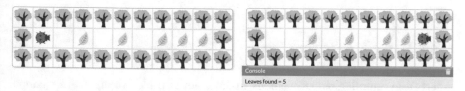

Fig. 8.4: a) Starting Configuration   b) Result of Counting Leaves.

Within the `run()` method we create the `leaves` variable and use it for storing the value that is returned after executing the `moveToTreeAndCountLeaves()` method. The value of this variable is then printed on the screen.

 To see the solution of this problem in Clara's World please use the following URL: `https://claraworld.net/link/C8P2S`.

8.3.3 Using `return` with `void` Methods

For methods that are defined as void it is not necessary to use the `return` command. Such methods are not expected to return anything, and this is why the `return` command is usually omitted. However, the use of `return` is acceptable in `void` returning methods. Let us have a look at the below code example. This example would make Clara move to the first leaf in her world. You should consider Figure 8.4 as a reference for analysing this code.

```
void moveToLeaf() {
    while (!treeFront() ) {
        if ( onLeaf() )
            return;
        move();
    }
}
```

In the above code `return` was used to terminate the `moveToLeaf()` method as soon as the leaf is encountered. The use of return is in a way similar to the use of the `break` command within loops. The key difference, however, is that the `break` command only terminates the innermost loop and the method continues executing if there are additional commands after the loop or if there is an outer loop containing the one that was terminated. In contrast, the `return` command will terminate the method entirely. No further commands that appear below `return` within this method would execute.

While using `return` is acceptable in such context it is not recommended and is considered to represent bad coding style. A much better way of solving this problem would have been to change the loop condition to `while(!onLeaf())`.

8.3.4 Methods Receiving Input

Apart from returning output methods in Java can also receive input. An example of an input receiving method that you would have been using for quite some time is `System.out.println`. This method receives a parameter of type `String` representing the value to be printed. For example, the following code would pass the "Hello" value to the method, and this is what will be printed on the screen:

```
System.out.println("Hello");
```

The values passed to a method are called *parameters* or *arguments*. Methods can receive input in the form of variables. When declaring methods that receive input you should list data types and internal names of all variables within parenthesis as follows:

```
retType methodName(inType1 var1, inType2 var2, ..., inTypeN varN)
```

In this general method definition the `retType` is the data type (such as `int` or `void`) of the method's return. The `inType1`, `inType2`, ..., `inTypeN` are the data types (such as `int`, `double`, `boolean`, etc.) of each of the input parameters. The names of the input parameters (`var1`, `var2`, ..., `varN`) have similar limitations as Java variable names. Within these limitations parameter names can be anything you want. The input parameters can be used inside the body of the method in a similar way as any local variable (defined within the method's body). Let us have a look at an example of a method that has input parameters.

```
void run() {
   printValue(3);
}

public void printValue(int num) {
   System.out.println("The value is " + num);
}
```

Here the `printValue(int)` method receives only one parameter of type `int`. This parameter would be known inside the method's body as num and can be treated as any other variable, because it is implemented as a variable.

Calling (or *invoking*) the `printValue(int)` method is shown within the `run()` method above. Here we pass the value of 3 inside parenthesis. This is the value that would be assigned to the parameter num and then the value that would be printed on the screen.

When you pass an argument to a method, it is important to make sure that the argument's data type is compatible with the parameter's data type. For example, both `printValue` calls below would result in an error because the methods expects the input of type `int` and not `double` or `String`.

```
void run() {
   String s = "Hello";
   printValue(3.5);
   printValue(s);
}
```

Methods can receive as many input parameters as necessary. Below is an example of a method that receives two integer numbers and returns the result of their multiplication:

```
public int mult(int num1, int num2) {
   int result;
   result = num1 * num2;
   return result;
}
```

It is important to mention that the method parameters will be assigned in the same order as the order in which they appear within the method's definition. For example, executing the code below would result in the value of 1 being assigned to the parameter num1 and the value of 2 being assigned to the parameter num2. This happens because of the order in the `mult(x,2)` call. Please also note that it is perfectly acceptable in Java to use a value returning method as an input parameter for another method. In our case the `mult(int)` method would be used in an expression forming the input for the `System.out.println(String)` method.

```
void run() {
   int x = 1;

   System.out.println( "The value is + " + mult(x, 2) );
}
```

In the above example of the `mult` we have created the `result` variable that was used for computing the value to be returned. In some situations a method may be performing a simple function of analysing the input and returning a verdict about it in some form. For such methods it is not necessarily useful to create additional variables. Below is an example of a method that analyses the input and returns `true` if the input is an even number and `false` if the input is an odd number.

```
private boolean isEven(int x)
{
   return ( (x % 2) == 0 );
}
```

Here it was decided not to use an additional variable that will be returned by the method. The method returns an expression directly in the return line. Within this expression we first compute the remainder of division of the input parameter by 2. Naturally, if the remainder is 0, this means that the input is an even number and if it is 1, then it is an odd number. This is exactly what the remainder of the expression is about. Comparing the remainder with 0 would return `true` if the remainder is 0 and `false` otherwise. Thus, the `isEven(int)` method would return `true` if the input parameters is an even number and `false` otherwise.

8.4 Information Hiding

Another topic we would like to discuss is *information hiding*. Information hiding is the practice of defining your method in such a way that the person who ends up using this method is not required to know anything about how this method is implemented. Specifying a good name for the method itself and for all input parameters, providing comments explaining what this method does and what it returns is what makes information hiding possible. Let us illustrate this idea on another metaphor for a method. A method can be seen as a coffee machine as shown in Figure 8.5.

The coffee machine has a number of inputs (water, buttons for selecting the type of coffee and coffee pods). Calling or invoking the coffee machine method is achieved by pressing the corresponding "start" button. The output of this method is a cup of coffee. The important characteristic of a coffee machine that relates to information hiding is the fact that it hides all the particulars of the internal process of delivering a cup of coffee, has various input parameters and works with any type of coffee pods that fit inside. The user of the coffee machine is not required to understand how it transforms water and coffee pods into coffee. All that is required for the user to know is where to insert the coffee pod and which button to press.

Information hiding similar to what was explained above about the coffee machine is what you should aim for when creating your methods. Your should always attempt for the methods to be self-contained and self-explanatory. In this way you will facilitate code reuse (copying some of the relevant methods into other projects), and it will be easier for other programmers to work with you on large projects.

Another powerful characteristic of information hiding is that you can change the implementation of your method at any time without having to notify the users of your method. If we apply the coffee machine metaphor to this idea, this means that if your install a more powerful or more technologically advanced coffee brewing

Fig. 8.5: Coffee Machine as a Method.

element while repairing a coffee machine, the user would not even notice the change (unless you change the interface for interacting with it).

8.5 Solving the Jumping Clara Problem

Now that we have sufficient understanding of methods that receive input and return output, it is time to tackle the chapter problem. Figure 8.6 a) illustrates the initial state of Clara's World and shows the resulting state after pressing the up arrow key on the keyboard twice in Figure 8.6 b). Drawing the leaves and moving Clara to a particular position in her world is achieved via the changePosition(int, int, int) method. This method receives the starting position on the X axis, X displacement and Y displacement as input parameters. For solving this problem we would be relying on the act() method rather than run() method. This is required for the changePosition method to work correctly.

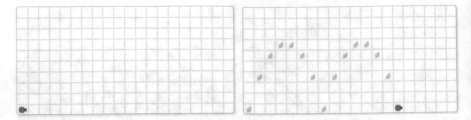

Fig. 8.6: a) Clara before Jumping   b) Clara after Jumping.

Solving this problem follows the same simplified pattern of simulating projectile motion as shown in Section 8.1. Let us first define some of the values that influence Clara's jump as follows:

```
class MyClara extends Clara
{
    final int JUMP_VELOCITY_X = 1;
    final int JUMP_VELOCITY_Y = 3;
    final int GRAVITY_X = 0;
    final int GRAVITY_Y = -1;

    public void act() {
        // TODO: Write your code below
    }
}
```

Here we have created constants for the horizontal and vertical components of the starting velocity of the jump and gravity. The reason we declare those as constants is that these values are not going to change. The principles of good coding style dictate that all such values are declared as constants.

What we essentially want is for Clara to perform the jump cycle every time the user presses the "up" arrow key. If we assume that the jumping behaviour is encoded within the jump() method we can rewrite the act() method as follows:

```
public void act() {
    if ( Keyboard.isKeyDown("up") ) {
        jump();
    }

    if ( Keyboard.isKeyDown("down") ) {
        stop();
    }
}
```

To avoid having Clara stuck in an infinite loop we have also created the possibility for the program to terminate if the user presses the "down" arrow key.

Let us now think about how the jump() method could be implemented. What we are required to do for visualising the jump is to update the position of Clara multiple times using the changePosition method, so that these positions correspond to the leaves shown in Figure 8.6 b). Having to move Clara to multiple positions should trigger the thought in your head that we would probably be using some kind of a loop. This thought would be absolutely correct. You may look at Figure 8.6 b) and count that each jump is represented by exactly 8 leaves. Knowing this might make you decide that a `for` loop would be suitable for solving this problem. However, this would only be true if our jump velocity is always $(1, 3)$. For other velocities this would not always be the case. While it has never been mentioned that your program should correctly work with other velocities, you should always attempt to come up with the most generic solution possible. What if after testing you decide that the jump is not believable enough and decide to increase the velocity? If your program is written in a generic way then all that is required to make it happen is to change the values of the corresponding constants. Thus, let us attempt to produce a generic jumping solution, which means that we would be using a `while` loop instead of `for`. Inside this loop you would be updating Clara's position and velocity using the equations from Section 8.1. Let us see how applying these equations works.

```
void jump() {
    int posY = 0;
    int posX = 0;

    while (posY > 0) {
        posX = posX + JUMP_VELOCITY_X;
        posY = posY + JUMP_VELOCITY_Y;

        changePosition(0, posX, posY);

        inVelocityX = JUMP_VELOCITY_X + GRAVITY_X;
        inVelocityY = JUMP_VELOCITY_Y + GRAVITY_Y;
    }
}
```

In the above code snippet we created two variables `posX` and `posY`. These variables are used for calculating the updated position of Clara for every frame and memorise the resulting Clara's position. The code above for updating `posX`, `posY`, `inVelocityX` and `inVelocityY` comes directly from the equations shown in Section 8.1. This code, however, has a significant problem, which is the condition of the `while` loop. We wanted to express the fact that updating Clara's position should stop as soon as Clara lands on the ground, which corresponds to the value of `posY` becoming 0. This logic is correct, but the problem we have is that at the very start of the jump Clara would be located on the ground and her `posY` would be 0 at the very start, which means that the `while` loop with this condition would terminate immediately. If only there was a way to execute our loop body for the first time (when Clara is on the ground), update her position and then continue repeating until she is on the ground again. All of this is possible in Java with the use of the `do-while` loop. This loop allows you to execute the first iteration of the loop first and only check the condition after every line in the loop's body has been executed. Let us rewrite the `jump()` method so that it employs the `do-while` loop.

```
void jump() {
    int posY = 0;
    int posX = 0;

    do {
        posX = posX + JUMP_VELOCITY_X;
        posY = posY + JUMP_VELOCITY_Y;

        changePosition(0, posX, posY);

        inVelocityX = JUMP_VELOCITY_X + GRAVITY_X;
        inVelocityY = JUMP_VELOCITY_Y + GRAVITY_Y;
    }
    while (posY > 0);
    }
}
```

This method would make Clara correctly jump and simulate the projectile motion trajectory. There are, however two problems with this method. The first problem is that the method relies on external constants. While this is allowed, it is usually considered to be a bad thing due to problems with method reuse. As a programmer you should make every effort to follow the principle of information hiding and make your methods self-contained. A self-contained method could be easily copied into another program that requires the same functionality. In our case, we would not only need to copy the method but also the corresponding constants for velocity and gravity. One way to avoid this is to pass gravity and velocity as input parameters.

The second problem is even more serious. Our current jump method always assumes that Clara's starting position on the X axis is 0. If we attempt to press the "up" arrow key after Clara has performed the first jump, we would see Clara moving back to the beginning of the street and copying the same trajectory as the one she followed for her first jump. In order to fix this problem we must somehow memorise the resulting X coordinate of where Clara lands and then instead of calling `changePosition(0, posX, posY)` for her next jump we would replace 0 with the correct x coordinate. This coordinate is already being computed for us as `posX`. Once the `while` loop terminates, the `posX` variable will contain the resulting displacement along the X axis that would reflect the starting position for Clara's next jump. We could create an external variable and modify it within the `jump()` method, but this would violate the principle of trying to have every method being self-contained and easy to copy into another program. Thus, the best way to pass this value to the act method is to use the `return` statement.

Below is the complete program for Clara's jumping that addresses the two aforementioned problems. Now our `jump()` method is self-contained. It has five input parameters and returns the horizontal coordinate where Clara lands after the jump. Storing this coordinate in a `currentX` variable and passing this very variable as the value of `inOriginalX` for every jump ensures that every jump will begin from the same position where Clara lands after the previous jump.

Exercise: The code below makes Clara jump from left to right after pressing the "up" arrow key. In most video games it is possible to jump in the opposite direction (from right to left) as well. Try extending the code so that Clara jumps from right to left in response to the "left" arrow key. Also change Clara's behaviour so that she jumps from left to right after the user presses the "right" arrow key.

```
class MyClara extends Clara {
    final int JUMP_VELOCITY_X = 1;
    final int JUMP_VELOCITY_Y = 3;
    final int GRAVITY_X = 0;
    final int GRAVITY_Y = -1;

    int currentX = 0;

    public void act() {
        if (Keyboard.isKeyDown("up")) {
            currentX = jump(currentX, JUMP_VELOCITY_X,
                JUMP_VELOCITY_Y, GRAVITY_X, GRAVITY_Y);
        }
    }

    int jump(int inOriginalX, int inVelocityX, int inVelocityY,
        int inGravityX, int inGravityY) {
        int posY = 0;
        int posX = 0;

        do {
            posX = posX + inVelocityX;
            posY = posY + inVelocityY;

            changePosition(currentX, posX, posY);

            inVelocityX = inVelocityX + inGravityX;
            inVelocityY = inVelocityY + inGravityY;
        }
        while (posY > 0);

        return inOriginalX + posX;
    }
}
```

To see the solution of this problem in Clara's World please use the following URL: `https://claraworld.net/link/C8P1S`.

8.6 Passing Parameters by Value

In Java, all method parameters of primitive data types are passed by value. This means that only a copy of an argument's value is passed into a parameter variable and modifying the parameter's value within a method does not affect the original variable. Let us illustrate this idea on an example.

```java
public void run() {
    int x = 3;
    addSeven(x);
    System.out.println("x = " + x);
}

void addSeven(int inNumber) {
    inNumber = inNumber + 7;
}
```

Here we have created a method called `addSeven(int)`. This method receives an integer number as an input parameter and increases the value of this parameter by 7. Inside the `run` method we then create a variable called x, set the value of this variable to 3 and pass x as the input for `addSeven(int)`. What do you think will be the value that is printed on the screen as the result of running the above code?

Before revealing the answer let us recall what was mentioned in the beginning of this section. The variables of primitive data types are passed by value. Passing something by value means that we copy the value and store it in a local variable. Primitive data types are those that are directly embedded into Java language as known keywords. Examples of primitive data types include `int`, `double`, `char`, `boolean`, `short` and `float`. Our `addSeven(int)` method's input parameter is of type `int`, which is a primitive data type. This means that when we call `addSeven(x)` inside the `run()` method the value of x will be extracted and then stored within `inNumber` when the `addSeven` method is executed. Whatever manipulations we do with `inNumber` will not affect our x, as these are two separate variables. Therefore, what will be printed on the screen is the original value of x (the value that x had before calling `addSeven(x)`), which is 3.

The above explanation might seem like common sense to some readers, so let us make the code a little more complicated by renaming `inNumber` to x.

```java
public void run() {
    int x = 3;
    addSeven(x);
    System.out.println("x = " + x);
}

void addSeven(int x) {
    x = x + 7;
}
```

Now that we are using x everywhere, calling `addSeven(x)` should certainly result in 10 being printed on the screen, right? The reality of Java is that renaming inNumber to x made absolutely no difference and the same value (3) would be printed as the result of running the above code. The reason for this is variable visibility, which was discussed in Chapter 5. Each variable is only known inside the pair of curly brackets where it was created. In case of a method or a for loop the variable would be visible to the entire method or loop's body correspondingly. The variable x that was defined within the run() method and the variable x that was defined within addSeven(int) are two different variables that have nothing in common apart from their name. When we call addSeven(x) inside run() we are passing this variable by value, which means the value of x (3) would be passed to the addSeven method and the x variable within addSeven would be set to 3 and then would be incremented by 7 to become 10. At the same time, the variable x in the run() method would remain unaffected by these manipulations. It is a different variable (with the same name) that has the value of 3. And this is the value that would be printed on the screen as the result of running the code.

How could we correct our program so that x is correctly incremented? We can achieve this by returning the result of x from addSeven and memorising it. The code below would correctly print 10 on the screen:

```java
public void run() {
    int x = 3;
    x = addSeven(x);
    System.out.println("x = " + x);
}

int addSeven(int x) {
    x = x + 7;
    return x;
}
```

The above explanation may sound overly complicated to some readers. You may question the usefulness of having an example where two methods share the same variable name. This practice, however, is quite common in programming. When coding their solutions programmers have to work efficiently and having to come up with a unique name for every single variable in a program with thousands or even millions of lines of code is a rather unpleasant and brain energy consuming exercise. Luckily, due to Java's variable visibility restrictions we are able to recycle the same name in many places without having to spend additional brain energy on coming up with many unique names and memorising the names that have been already used. You have probably already noticed that almost every for loop that is featured in this book uses the same variable as the counter (i). This is possible due to the fact that the loop counter will only be known inside a particular loop and will cease to exist outside of this loop.

8.7 Passing Parameters by Reference

Complex data types such as arrays (covered in Chapter 9) and objects (covered in Chapter 10) are not passed by value in methods. Such variables are passed by reference. This means that modifying the value of a method's input parameter inside the body of the method will result in changes of the value of the original variable that was passed to this method. This happens because variables of non-primitive data types may potentially use a significant amount of memory. Creating a copy of such a variable for every method call is inefficient. In Section 9.4 we will show an example of passing arrays to methods and will further discuss the issues associated with passing variables of non-primitive data types by reference rather than by value.

8.8 Summary

In this chapter we learned about methods that receive input and return output. Using such methods helps to promote information hiding in your code, which means creating methods that are self-contained and are independent from external variables or other code. Such methods can be easily copy-pasted into a new project without having to worry about their dependencies. Methods that return input are very similar to mathematical functions, and many programmers use the term "function" when they refer to a method. Methods that return output are useful for various kinds of calculations.

8.9 Exercises

 Exercises that target your understanding of the concepts covered in this chapter are available at https://claraworld.net/link/C8Ex.

Chapter 9
Arrays

Starting from Chapter 5 we have been using variables for solving programming problems. Variables give Clara memory. They are useful for memorising particular events or for performing computations. Computers are much better than humans when it comes to operating with large amounts of data. In most cases this data is stored within variables. You may have heard the term "big data" that relates to computers processing terabytes of information. Most variables we have used so far hold one to eight bytes of data. Imagine how many variables would be required to store 1 terabyte (1,024,000,000,000 bytes) and how many lines of code would be needed to define these variables. Luckily, most programming languages (including Java) offer the array concept. Arrays allow for storing a collection of data of the same type within a single variable. In this chapter we introduce this concept and discuss how arrays can be used for solving different types of programming problems.

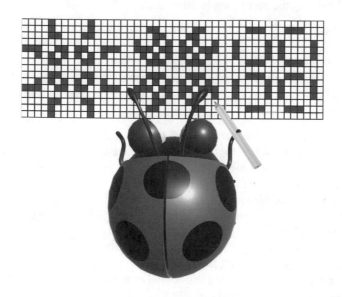

© Springer Nature Switzerland AG 2021
A. Bogdanovych, T. Trescak, *Learning Java Programming in Clara's World*,
https://doi.org/10.1007/978-3-030-75542-3_9

9.1 Chapter Story: Game of Life

In his attempt to come up with a simulation of a living system, a British mathematician, John Horton Conway, developed the concept of the Game of Life [20]. In this game checker-like objects replicate themselves and form patterns on a grid similar to the one shown in Figure 9.1.

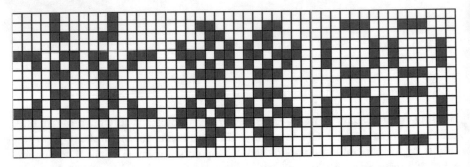

Fig. 9.1: A Game of Life Example: Three Iterations of Pulsar.

Figure 9.1 represents a game space composed of the combination of white and dark squares. A dark square simulates a live cell, and a white square is a dead cell. One of the most interesting aspects of this game is to see how the entire population of live cells would change over time.

In his work [20] Conway developed a set of simple rules that would determine how the game state should evolve. Live cells would die, remain alive or produce offspring following the set of simple rules below:

1. Any live cell with fewer than two live neighbours dies, as if caused by under-population.
2. Any live cell with two or three live neighbours lives on to the next generation.
3. Any live cell with more than three live neighbours dies, as if by overcrowding.
4. Any dead cell with exactly three live neighbours becomes a live cell, as if by reproduction.

Figure 9.1 features three iterations of the game for a pattern called "pulsar". Pulsar is a shape that is know for its interesting property of appearing as a pulsating flower. As the above rules are applied over time, the pulsar shape will continuously go through the three iterations shown in the figure.

While the Game of Life is an interesting puzzle in itself, its key practical contribution is that it has inspired many interesting computational algorithms (known under the umbrella term "cellular automata") that help solving problems in the areas of art, music and video games and are used for developing various simulations and graphical effects. Simulating fire flames and fire spread, automatic modelling of realistic terrain, generating art and music and cryptography are some examples of areas where cellular automation is widely applicable.

9.2 Chapter Problem 1: Game of Life in Clara's World

Clara is progressing with her intellectual and computational abilities. She has learned the rules of the Game of Life and has created a few interesting leaf patterns in her world (as shown in the picture). She now wants to apply those rules and see the leaf patterns change over time as the result of applying these rules. To make this happen she must analyse every cell in her world and apply the rules to this cell.

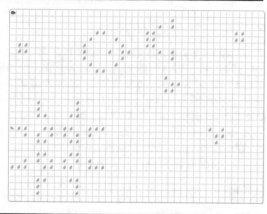

This chapter problem seems too difficult. How could Clara analyse every single cell? Would she be required to move through the entire world to do this? How would she check all the neighbours of every cell? How to make sure that changing one of the cells does not lead to incorrect results because the new value would affect the neighbouring cells? Let us cover some new material and see how to answer all these questions.

9.3 Arrays

Arrays are collections of elements of the same type. While primitive variables are designed to contain only one value at a time, arrays allow us to hold as many values of this type as your computer's memory can allocate.

Array elements are ordered, meaning that every array element is assigned with a number representing its index in the collection. All elements of an array must be of the same type (e.g. `int` or `String`).

9.3.1 Creating an Array

Arrays are collections of variables and are declared in a very similar way to standard variables. When declaring an array you must use a pair of square brackets `[]`. Below is an example of creating an array that holds integer numbers:

```
int[] array;
```

Once an array has been created you must decide on the number of elements the array will contain. This number has to be explicitly stated in your code. Below is an example of how to declare an array that contains six elements of type integer:

```
array = new int[6];
```

Here we use the `array` variable that was declared above, create a new collection of type `int` with six elements and assign this collection to this variable. The right-hand side of this expression is in charge of allocating six array elements using the Java reserved keyword `new`. The number inside the square brackets determines the number of elements that would be allocated for this array. This number must be non-negative. Once an array is created, its size cannot be changed.

Similar to traditional variables we could declare and assign the value to an array on the same line as shown below:

```
int[] array = new int[6];
```

Once an array has been created its elements would be allocated in computer's memory and assigned with the default value for the corresponding element type. The default value for the type `int` that was used in the above code is 0. Figure 9.2 illustrates the result of executing the above code. Six array elements would be created, and each element would be assigned with the value of 0.

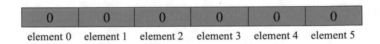

element 0   element 1   element 2   element 3   element 4   element 5

Fig. 9.2: Creating an Array with Six Elements.

All arrays are ordered, and each element will have the corresponding index by which it can be accessed. In programming we usually start counting from zero, and array indexes are no exception. The very first element of an array would have the index 0, and the sixth element would have the index 5.

Array elements can be of any type. Here are some examples of declaring arrays that hold elements of types `float`, `char`, `long` and `double`.

```
float[] marks = new float[500];
char[] symbols = new char[120];
long[] stats = new long[30];
double[] payments = new double[100];
```

The array name that appears on the left-hand side of the above expressions is not any different from a traditional variable. In the case of arrays this name represents a reference to the address of the start of the element collection in computer's memory.

9.3.2 Working with Array Elements

Once an array is created and its elements are allocated we can access the elements by their indexes. For example, changing the element with the index 1 in the array called `array` from the earlier example we could use the following code:

```
array[1] = 7;
```

In the code above the index of the element we want to change has been specified in square brackets. Figure 9.3 demonstrates how each of the elements of our `array` collection of integer numbers can be accessed. As the result of running the above code, the updated value of the second element (with index 1) will become 7, while all other elements will remain set to the default value (0).

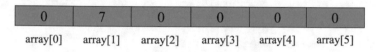

| 0 | 7 | 0 | 0 | 0 | 0 |
| array[0] | array[1] | array[2] | array[3] | array[4] | array[5] |

Fig. 9.3: Accessing Array Elements.

Once we access an array element by its index we obtain a variable that is no different from variables that we have encountered earlier in this book. Everything we could do with variables before, we can also do with array elements.

Array element indexes have to be integer numbers. When specifying an element index you are not limited to using integer literals. Instead of providing an integer literal it is possible to use variable names, expressions and method calls (such as `readInt`). Below are some examples of possible ways of accessing array elements by index in Java:

```
double[] hoursWorkedLastWeek = new double[7];
final int WEDNESDAY = 3;

hoursWorkedLastWeek[0] = readInt("Enter value: ");
hoursWorkedLastWeek[1] = 7.5;
hoursWorkedLastWeek[WEDNESDAY - 1] = 7.5;
hoursWorkedLastWeek[readInt("Enter day: ")] = readInt("Enter
    hours:");
```

This example demonstrates creating an array (`hoursWorkedLastWeek`) that stores how many hours a person worked last week. Each array element stores the hours worked in the corresponding day (represented by the index). As you can see from the code above, we can perform similar operations with array indexes and values assigned to these as operations we could perform with variables from Chapter 6. For assigning the values of elements with indexes 0 and 1 we employ integer literals. One of the indexes is computed as the result of an expression (`WEDNESDAY - 1`). Judging by having all upper-case letters in the name `WEDNESDAY`, we are subtracting one from a constant that was defined elsewhere. Finally, the last line of code in the above snippet dynamically obtains the array index by asking the user to enter it from keyboard and then asks the user to type the value of the corresponding array element.

9.3.3 Processing Arrays

As you can see, arrays allow you to work with large collections without having to create many individual variables for each element. Very often it is required to parse the collection in search for an element or to perform some operation on each element. For such situations it is useful to employ `for` loops. Below is an example of printing all elements of an array:

```
int[] exampleArray = new int[10];

for (int i = 0; i < 10; i++) {
   System.out.print( exampleArray[i] + " " );
}
```

The output of this code is: 0 0 0 0 0 0 0 0 0 0.

You should always keep in mind that the very first element of an array has the index 0 and the last element will have the index equal to array length − 1. A typical beginner programmer mistake would be to write the code of the above `for` loop as follows:

```
for (int i = 1; i <= 10; i++) {
   System.out.print( exampleArray[i] + " " );
}
```

This loop would also repeat 10 times, but would not print the first element (with index 0) and would attempt to print the element with index 10. Since the element with index 10 does not exist (because 9 is the index of the last element), the above code would produce a runtime error.

9.3.4 Alternative Array Declaration

Java makes it possible to declare arrays in two different ways. We have already showed declaring an array as follows:

```
int[] array;
```

It is, however, also possible to declare an array by putting the square brackets after the array name (rather than after the name of the data type of its elements). Below is an example of an alternative array declaration that is equivalent to the above code.

```
int array[];
```

Which of the two notations to chose is your personal choice. The key difference between them lies in declaring multiple arrays on one line. Similar to traditional variables it is possible in Java to declare multiple arrays of the same type as follows:

```
int[] numbers, marks, payments;
```

This code would create three arrays of type int. In contrast, the code below would work slightly differently:

```
int numbers[], marks, payments;
```

Here only numbers is an array, while marks and payments are integer variables (not arrays).

9.3.5 Array Length

A convenient feature of arrays is that each array carries its length with it. The length (or size) of an array can be obtained using the length variable. The code example below illustrates how this variable can be used:

```
int exampleArray[] = new int[10];

for (int i = 1; i <= exampleArray.length; i++) {
   System.out.print( exampleArray[i] + " " );
}
```

In this code we are using exampleArray.length instead of 10. In Chapter 10 you will learn about objects and classes and will understand that arrays in Java are implemented as objects and that length is a class variable. Until then you should simply know that the length of an array can be obtained as arrayName.length, where arrayName is the name of an array that you want to obtain the length of.

Being able to access the length of an array might not look like a particularly useful feature to you. You may wonder why it should ever be used given that typing "10" is quicker than typing "exampleArray.length". However, being able to access the length variable makes your code easier to read and, more importantly, easier to modify. Let us consider the code fragment below for better understanding of the usefulness of the length variable:

```
int hoursWorked[] = new int[7];
int hourlyRate = 50;
int totalHours = 0;

for (int i = 1; i <= hoursWorked.length; i++) {
   hoursWorked[i] = readInt("hours worked in day " + (i+1));
}
```

```
for (int i = 1; i <= hoursWorked.length; i++) {
  totalHours += hoursWorked[i];
}

System.out.println("Money earned = " + totalHours * hourlyRate);
```

Here we are letting the user enter a number of hours that he or she worked each day of last week. After entering these values and storing them in an array we compute the total number of hours the user worked last week. We then multiply this number by the pay rate to obtain the total amount of money earned. Imagine now that we were asked to modify this code and compute the amount of money earned last fortnight. Had we not used the `length` variable, we would not only be required to change the size of the array to 14, but would also need to change the header of each `for`-loop (by replacing 7 with 14). However, because we used `hoursWorked.length` inside both loops, we would only need to change the size of the array and would not need to modify the loop headers. This feature becomes particularly useful if the code for computing total hours and entering array elements is located in separate methods. The use of the `length` variable allows developers to follow the principle of information hiding when employing arrays inside methods. Methods that rely on `length` (instead of externally declared constants or literals representing the size of an array) can be easily copy-pasted into another project without having to search for dependencies.

9.3.6 Array Initialisation

For situations when an array only contains a small number of elements it may be useful to initialise an array within code. One way to do this is illustrated by the code fragment below:

```
String [] weekDays = new String[7];
weekDays[0] = "Monday";
weekDays[1] = "Tuesday";
weekDays[2] = "Wednesday";
weekDays[3] = "Thursday";
weekDays[4] = "Friday";
weekDays[5] = "Saturday";
weekDays[6] = "Sunday";
```

With the help of this code we could make entering the number of hours that the user has worked each day much more user-friendly. Instead of requesting to enter "hours worked in day 1" we could be requesting "hours worked on Monday" by replacing the following code:

```
for (int i = 1; i <= hoursWorked.length; i++) {
  hoursWorked[i] = readInt("hours worked in day " + (i+1));
}
```

with the version that uses our new `weekDays` array:

```
for (int i = 1; i <= hoursWorked.length; i++) {
    hoursWorked[i] = readInt("hours worked in day " + weekDays[i]);
}
```

In addition to initialising individual array elements Java language provides an alternative (more compact) way of initialising arrays by listing all array elements within curly brackets. The code fragment below shows how our `weekDays` array could have been initialised differently:

```
String[] weekDays = {"Monday", "Tuesday", "Wednesday",
        "Thursday", "Friday", "Saturday", "Sunday"};
```

This code would have the same effect as the previous initialisation, but is significantly shorter. Here we are not required to explicitly allocate seven elements. By providing a list of comma-separated elements within curly brackets we are also communicating the number of elements that our array must contain. As the result of running this code Java would count how many elements we are passing, would allocate an array of seven elements (`new String[7]`) and would assign their values as per what was passed within curly brackets.

9.4 Passing Arrays to Methods

Complex data types such as arrays and objects (which will be discussed in Chapter 10) are not passed by value in methods. Such variables are passed by reference, which means that modifying the method's input parameter would result in changes of the original outside variable that was passed to this method. This is mainly because non-primitive variables may use a substantial amount of memory and creating a copy for every method call would be inefficient. Imagine a situation when you are passing an array with ten million elements to a method. In this case creating a copy of this array every time a method is called would require allocating a significant amount of memory and would also slow down the execution of your program (because allocating so many elements and copying them requires a lot of processing). This is why when working with arrays or objects as method parameters Java automatically passes them by reference rather than by value.

Let us illustrate how passing by reference works on using the friendship algorithm example from Chapter 5.

```
public void run() {
    String[] userLikes = {"", "", "", "", ""};
    arrayFromKeyboard(userLikes, "Enter your interest: ");
    System.out.println(userLikes);
}
```

```
void arrayFromKeyboard(String[] inArray, String inMessage) {
    for (int i = 0; i < inArray.length; i++) {
        inArray[i] = readString(inMessage + " #" + (i + 1) + ": ");
    }
}
```

Here we use the `arrayFromKeyboard` method to populate the `userLikes` array with text that the user enters from keyboard. The `userLikes` variable is passed to the `arrayFromKeyboard` method and becomes the `inArray` variable inside. This variable is then modified inside the method and is not returned back. The result of running this code will not be an array of five empty strings being printed on the screen (as it would have been in the situation of passing the parameter by value). What will be printed instead are the five text values that the user enters from keyboard. This outcome is possible because the `userLikes` array is passed by reference and modifying its internal counterpart (`inArray`) results in modifying the original variable.

In a similar way to receiving an array as input to a method we could also return an array as method output. Consider a modified version of the `arrayFromKeyboard` method below:

```
String[] arrayFromKeyboard(String inMessage) {
    String[] retVal = new String[5];

    for (int i = 0; i < retVal.length; i++) {
        retVal[i] = readString(inMessage + " #" + (i + 1) + ":
            ");
    }

    return retVal;
}
```

Here instead of receiving an already declared and allocated array we create a new array with ten elements, populate it from keyboard and return it as the output of the method.

Let us further expand on this example and present it as chapter problem 2. In the version of the friendship algorithm problem that was presented in Chapter 5 Sheldon only had one interest (physics). Having only one interest is quite limiting. The use of arrays creates new and exciting opportunities. Now we do not have to be limited by a single interest and can have as many interests as we want. The following section presents an updated version of the friendship algorithm problem that allows Sheldon to have many interests.

9.5 Chapter Problem 2: Friendship Algorithm with Arrays

Clara wants to become friends with all other creatures in her world. She decides to create a program for Sheldon's friendship algorithm presented in Chapter 5. Clara has multiple interests and wants to store these in an array. Clara already knows how to find the least objectionable activity. Now she must create a program that allows her to input two arrays from keyboard and then find a common interest in these two arrays. The first array must represent the interests of the user (potential friend), and the second array has to store Clara's interests (where Clara is assuming the role of Sheldon Cooper).

To work on this problem in Clara's World please use the following URL: https://claraworld.net/link/C9P2.

9.5.1 Sequential Search Algorithm

The problem of finding a particular element in an array is known as "sequential search". The key idea behind sequential search is to go through all elements of a collection (in our case an array) and to compare each element with the search value. Our situation is a little more complicated, as we have to search for a common element in two collections. However, the sequential search principle would still apply to this problem. Our version of the sequential search algorithm would involve extracting an element from the first collection and then performing search for a similar element in the second collection. If the match is found, we would stop our search or otherwise we would extract the next element from the first collection and conduct another round of sequential search.

Below is the pseudocode of the modified sequential search algorithm that can be used for finding a common element in two arrays:

```
Initialise array1 and array2
Repeat until the end of array1 is encountered
Select an element from array1 and treat is as search value
Sequentially step through array2
Compare each element of array1 with the search value
Stop when the value is found
Otherwise assign the next element of array1 as search value
```

Let us illustrate how this algorithm works in Java on an example. Below is a declaration of two arrays with one common element "physics":

```
String[] yourLikes = {"trains", "monkeys", "physics", "flags"};
String[] userLikes = {"programming", "physics", "basketball"};
```

Applying the sequential search algorithm to these two arrays would go as follows. We start our search by nominating the first element of the first array (yourLikes) as the search value. We then compare this element ("trains") with every element of the second array (userLikes). Since there is no match, we then nominate the second element of the first array ("monkeys") as the search value and compare it with every element of the second array. There is again no match. The search would finally finish after we nominate the third element of the first array ("physics") and find the match by comparing it with the second element of the second array.

9.5.2 Solving Chapter Problem 2: Finding the Common Interest

Now that we have a good understanding of how sequential search works, let us implement the relevant portion of the friendship algorithm. We would need to perform two high-level operations: populating an array with data by typing text from keyboard and searching for a common element in two arrays. Let us implement each of these operations as a separate Java method.

 You can see a video explanation of how to solve this problem step-by-step at https://claraworld.net/link/C9V1.

Populating an array from keyboard works by calling the readString method in a loop and assigning the corresponding array element within the same loop. Below is the code for this method:

```
void populateArrayFromKeyboard(String[] inArray,
                               String inMessage) {
    for (int i = 0; i < inArray.length; i++) {
        inArray[i] = readString(inMessage + " #" + (i+1) + ": ");
    }
}
```

Passing arrays as method parameters is different from passing variables of primitive data types (such as int, double or char). Variables of primitive data types are passed by value, meaning that a local copy of the variable is created within a method and is then destroyed when the method is finished executing. In contrast, arrays are passed by reference. This means that modifying an array within the method would result in changing the original array. In our code we pass inArray as an input parameter to the populateArrayFromKeyboard method. The variable behind this parameter would then be used for populating inArray with data. Any modification we perform with inArray would impact the original array that was passed as a parameter to this method from within run or somewhere else. Another important aspect of the above code is printing the message in the text entry dialog that would appear on the screen prompting the user to enter interests from keyboard. In the solution we presented in Chapter 5 it was sufficient to print "Tell me an interest of yours" in this dialog. This, however, was not very user-friendly. While creating your code you should always think about user experience and try to make it more pleasant. In our case, we would be asking to enter a number of interests. For the person entering those to have a perception of progress, it is best to also display the number of the interest that is currently being entered. In our code this is achieved by printing the value of the loop counter (i). Since loop counters in programming normally start with 0, we print i + 1 instead of i, because "Please enter interest #0" would make much less sense to the user than "Please enter interest #1".

The final thing left for us to do is finding a common element in two arrays. This task involves having two nested for-loops, where the outer loop sequentially nominates one of the elements of the first array as the search value and the inner loop is in charge of comparing all elements of the second array with the search value. The code of this method is shown below:

```
String findCommonInterest(String[] array1, String[] array2) {
    String retVal = "nothing";

    for (int i = 0; i < array1.length; i++) {
        for (int k = 0; k < array2.length; k++) {
            if (array1[i] == array2[k]) {
                retVal = array1[i];
                return retVal;
            }
        }
    }
    return retVal;
}
```

Notice that this method returns a value. Its value will either be the first matching element (if such an element exists) or "nothing". We would find the matching element if the nominated search value from the first array (array1[i]) is the same as one of the elements of the second array (array2[k]). The matching element itself is either array1[i] or array2[k]. It does not matter which one of those two values we pick, since both of them would be identical, so in our code we select array1[i] that is then returned by the method.

Now that we have implemented the methods for populating arrays with data and for finding the common element, we can produce the solution of the friendship algorithm problem. The resulting code is shown below:

```
class MyClara extends Clara {

/**
 * That's where our class starts executing.
 * Notice that we need an instance of MyClara present
 * or otherwise nothing will happen.
 */
void run() {
    String[] yourLikes;
    String[] userLikes;
```

```
    // dynamically allocating our arrays
    int arraySize = readInt("How many interests do you have?");
    yourLikes = new String[arraySize];
    arraySize = readInt("How many interests does user have?");
    userLikes = new String[arraySize];

    populateArrayFromKeyboard(yourLikes, "Enter your interest");
    populateArrayFromKeyboard(userLikes, "Enter user interest");
    String activity = findCommonInterest(yourLikes, userLikes);
    System.out.println("Let's do " + activity + " together!");
}


/**
 * Allows to initialise a String array from keyboard
 * Input: inArray, number of elements in this array,
 * inDialogBoxMessage is what will be shown in the dialog
 */
void populateArrayFromKeyboard(String[] inArray,
                               String inMessage) {
    for (int i = 0; i < inArray.length; i++) {
        inArray[i] = readString(inMessage + " #" + (i+1) + ": ");
    }
}


/**
 * Finds a common interest (element) in two arrays by testing
 * whether any of the two elements are identical.
 */
String findCommonInterest(String[] array1, String[] array2) {
    String retVal = "nothing";

    for (int i = 0; i < array1.length; i++) {
        for (int k = 0; k < array2.length; k++) {
            if (array1[i] == array2[k]) {
                retVal = array1[i];
                return retVal;
            }
        }
    }
    return retVal;
}

}
```

The run method of the above code declares two arrays and initialises them by calling the populateArrayFromKeyboard method. After initialising both arrays we call the findCommonInterest method to identify the common element. Both arrays are passed as input to this method. An important thing for you to notice in the run method is that our arrays are allocated at runtime. With the help of the readInt method we ask the user to specify the size of each array and allocate them after obtaining the size from the user. This size would then determine how many interests would be entered in the `for`-loop of the `populateArrayFromKeyboard` method. This again shows the usefulness of the `length` variable. With its help we are able to create a method for working with an array the size of which is not known at compilation time.

 To see the solution of this problem in Clara's World please use the following URL: `https://claraworld.net/link/C9P2S`.

If we run the above code, pass 4 and 3 as the values for array sizes and then enter the elements of the first array as {`"trains"`, `"monkeys"`, `"physics"`, `"flags"`} and values of the second array as {`"programming"`, `"physics"`, `"basketball"`}, we would receive the output "Let's do physics together!".

We are almost ready for solving chapter problem 1 (Game of Life), but a few more aspects of working with arrays must be covered first.

9.6 Array Variables as References

It was already mentioned in the beginning of this chapter, that when we declare an array, its name becomes a reference (also known as pointer in other programming languages) to the starting location of the allocated array elements in memory (once these elements have been allocated). Running the code below would find the first available slot in memory to allocate six elements of type `int` and would associate the variable `array` with this address:

```
int[] array = new int[6];
```

After allocating the array in memory it is no longer possible to change its size. What is possible, however, is to allocate a new collection of elements and reassign the array variable.

```
array = new int[10];
```

The result of running the above code is allocating the new set of ten integer values and reassigning the address associated with the `array` variable to the address of the first element in this new collection. The previous six elements would be lost and destroyed by the so-called garbage collector. Let us consider the following code to illustrate this idea:

```
int[] array = new int[6];
array[1] = 7;
array = new int[10];
System.out.println(array[1]);
```

The output of this code will be "0" because after setting the value of `array[1]` to 7 we have allocated the new collection and reset the `array` variable so that it points to this new collection. The old collection will be destroyed, and the value of each element in the new collection would be set to the default value for the `int` type (0). This is why 0 is the output of this code.

9.6.1 Copying Arrays

Not fully understanding how references work in the case of array names may lead to unexpected effects. Consider the code below as an example:

```
int[] array1 = {1, 2, 3, 4, 5, 6, 7};
int[] array2 = array1;
array2[0] = 0;
System.out.println(array1);
System.out.println(array2);
```

You may think that when we call the `array2 = array1` command we are creating an independent copy of `array1` and that modifications we make in `array2` do not affect `array1`. This, however, is not the case because array names are nothing more than references to array elements. When we call `array2 = array1`, we are not allocating a new independent collection for `array2`, but are creating another synonymous name for the same collection. Therefore, changing an element in `array2` would also change the same element in `array1`. If we run the above code we would see the following output:

```
0,2,3,4,5,6,7
0,2,3,4,5,6,7
```

Once again, both arrays that were printed have the same elements because both `array1` and `array2` are references to the same collection. If you want to create an independent copy of an array, you would have to allocate it and reassign elements as shown in the example below:

```
int[] array1 = {1, 2, 3, 4, 5, 6, 7};
int[] array2 = new int[array1.length];

for (int i = 0; i < array1.length; i++)
    array2[i] = array1[i];

array2[0] = 0;
System.out.println(array1);
System.out.println(array2);
```

The output of this updated code is as follows:

```
1,2,3,4,5,6,7
0,2,3,4,5,6,7
```

9.6.2 Comparing Arrays

Because array variables are references to collections, comparing arrays may also pose problems for beginner programmers. The below code fragment illustrates where confusion may come from:

```
int array1[] = {1, 2, 3, 4, 5};
int array2[] = {1, 2, 3, 4, 5};

if (array1 == array2) // This does not work as expected
   System.out.println("The arrays are identical");
else
   System.out.println("The arrays are not identical");
```

Despite the fact that array1 and array2 have the same number of elements and these elements are identical, the output of this code will be "The arrays are not identical". Because array variables are treated as references, the if-statement would only return true if both array1 and array2 refer to the same address in memory. In our case array1 and array2 are two different collections that are located in different places in computer memory and, therefore, the code statement if (array1 == array2) would return false.

The code for correct comparison of two arrays for being identical would look similar to the example shown below:

```
int array1[] = {1, 2, 3, 4, 5};
int array2[] = {1, 2, 3, 4, 5};

void run() {
    if ( areArraysIdentical( array1, array2) )
       System.out.println("The arrays are identical");
    else
        System.out.println("The arrays are not identical");
}

boolean areArraysIdentical(int inArray1[], int inArray2[]) {
    // arrays of different size
    // cannot be identical
    if (inArray1.length != inArray2.length)
       return false;

    // compare all elements and
    // return false if at least one is different
    for (int i = 0; i < inArray1.length; i++) {
       if (inArray1[i] != inArray2[i])
          return false;
    }

    return true;
}
```

Here we had to first check whether both arrays have the same size and immediately assume that they are not identical if their sizes are different. In the situation when both arrays are of the same size we would need to compare all elements one-by-one and only assume that arrays are identical if we do not find any differences between array elements.

9.7 Multidimensional Arrays

So far we saw examples of arrays where elements are of either a primitive data type or of type `String`. Arrays, however, are not limited to those types. In Java it is also possible for an array element to be an object (see Chapter 10 for object coverage) and even an array. Arrays of arrays are called multidimensional arrays. Java allows you to have as many dimensions as you want. The most common multidimensional array type, however, is a two-dimensional array.

9.7.1 Two-Dimensional Arrays

A two-dimensional array is a concept that is similar to tables and matrixes [21] in mathematics. A two-dimensional array has elements sorted into rows and columns as shown in Figure 9.4.

	column 0	column 1	column 2	column 3
row 0	[0][0]	[0][1]	[0][2]	[0][3]
row 1	[1][0]	[1][1]	[1][2]	[1][3]
row 2	[2][0]	[2][1]	[2][2]	[2][3]
row 3	[3][0]	[3][1]	[3][2]	[3][3]

Fig. 9.4: An Example of a Two-Dimensional Array.

Declaring a two-dimensional array involves including two sets of square brackets as follows:

```
int[][] 2dArray = new int[3][4];
```

The first number in square brackets after the "new" keyword represents the number of rows the array would have, and the second number determines how many columns the allocated collection would have.

Elements of a two-dimensional array are accessed with the help of two square brackets and providing the row and column of the desired element as follows:

```
2dArray[3][1] = 7;
```

Figure 9.5 illustrates the outcome of the above assignment. The value of the element with `row` = 3 and `column` = 1 is changed to 7.

	column 0	column 1	column 2	column 3
row 0	0	0	0	0
row 1	0	0	0	0
row 2	0	0	0	0
row 3	0	7	0	0

Fig. 9.5: Accessing an Element of a Two-Dimensional Array.

9.7.2 Initialising Two-Dimensional Arrays

It is possible to initialise two-dimensional arrays directly in your code similar to how it is done for one-dimensional arrays. The key difference is that we have to use multiple sets of curly brackets. The example below initialises an array of three rows and four columns:

```
int[][] 2dArray = { {1, 2, 3, 4},
                    {5, 6, 7, 8},
                    {9, 10, 11, 12} };
```

Here every row is enclosed in its own pair of curly brackets, and the comma-separated rows are then enclosed in a pair of curly brackets as well. Similar to one-dimensional arrays, Java would automatically allocate the necessary number of rows (4) and columns (3) for the above code and would assign the elements accordingly.

9.7.3 Processing Two-Dimensional Arrays

Processing two-dimensional arrays usually involves having two nested loops. The example code below illustrates populating a two-dimensional array from keyboard:

```
void populateArrayFromKeyboard(int[][] inArray) {
    for (int row = 0; row < inArray.length; row++) {
        for (int col = 0; col < inArray[row].length; row++) {
            inArray[row][col] = readInt("enter value: ");
        }
    }
}
```

Here the outer loop is processing array rows and the inner loop processes columns. The use of the `length` variable requires an additional explanation. Two-dimensional arrays are, essentially, arrays of one-dimensional arrays. It is an array of multiple rows, where each row is an array itself. Because of this, `inArray.length` would not return the total number of elements in the above two-dimensional array, but would return the number of rows this array has. To obtain the number of columns we would have to extract an individual column and then use the `length` variable assigned with this column as follows: `inArray[2].length`.

9.7.4 Ragged Arrays

Multi-dimensional arrays are arrays of arrays. While it is more common for each of the dimensions to have the same number of elements, it is also perfectly valid in Java to have so-called "ragged arrays". Ragged arrays are arrays that allow for having different sizes between dimensions. In a two-dimensional case a ragged array would have rows of different lengths. Declaring a ragged array looks as follows:

```
int[][] raggedArray = new int[3][];

ragged[0] = new int [2];
ragged[1] = new int [3];
ragged[2] = new int [4];
```

In the above code we have initially allocated a two-dimensional array with three rows but no columns. In the code that follows each row is allocated individually as a one-dimensional array and each of these arrays is of different length.

Because it is possible to have ragged arrays, it is recommended that when you process a two-dimensional array you individually check the length of each row rather than assuming that all rows have the same length.

9.7.5 More than Two Dimensions

Java does not limit you regarding the number of dimensions an array could have. Many modern problems (e.g. machine learning) require working with multidimensional data. It is, however, difficult for most people to think in more than three dimensions. As a metaphor for a three-dimensional array consider the Rubik's Cube shown in Figure 9.6.

Fig. 9.6: Rubik's Cube: a Metaphor for a Three-Dimensional Array.

This cube has exactly six faces, and each face can be seen as a two-dimensional array (3 × 3). If we were to program the Rubik's Cube we could have used the following three-dimensional array:

```
int[][][] rubikCube = new int[6][3][3];
```

Here the first set of square brackets would refer to the face of the cube, the second set represents the row on this face and the third one determines the column. Accessing an individual piece and changing its colour would then look as follows:

```
rubikCube[3][2][1] = GREEN;
```

9.8 Solving Chapter Problem 1: Game of Life

Now that we have covered everything that you need to know about arrays, it is time to tackle chapter problem 1. In order to make it possible for us to implement the Game of Life program we have created three additional Clara commands:

- `boolean onLeaf(int row, int column)` – returns `true` if there is a leaf in Clara's world at the cell specified by its row and column.
- `void removeLeaf(int row, int column)` – removes a leaf from the cell specified by its row and column.

- void putLeaf(int row, int column) – puts a leaf at the cell specified by its row and column.

In our example Clara's World is of size 30 × 40. For processing the world we would require two two-dimensional arrays with the same dimensions. The first array (currentWorldState) would contain the information about the current state of Clara's world and the second array (nextWorldState) would pre-compute how the state would change after applying the Game of Life's rules.

Our program should only preform one iteration of Game of Life. For observing how the world evolves over time you would be required to run it multiple times. The initial configuration of Clara's World and the result of applying the Game of Life rules once are shown in Figure 9.7.

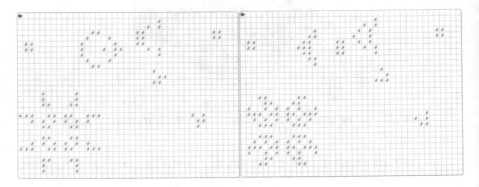

Fig. 9.7: Two Iterations of the Game of Life.

 You can see a video explanation of how to solve this problem step-by-step at https://claraworld.net/link/C9V2.

Let us start approaching this problem by producing a high-level algorithm in the form of pseudocode.

```
Translate the world into the currentWorldState array
Apply Game of Lives rules and store result in nextWorldState
Update the world in accordance with nextWorldState array
```

The above algorithm can be translated into the following code:

```
final int WORLD_HEIGHT = 30;
final int WORLD_WIDTH = 40;

// variables for tracking and updating the world state
boolean[][] currentWorldState;
boolean[][] nextWorldState;
```

```
/**
 * Apply the game of life rules once per program execution
 */
void run() {
   // translate the world state into an array
   currentWorldState = worldToArray();

   // play game of life if not running for the first time
   nextWorldState = applyGameOfLifeRules(currentWorldState);
   updateWorld(nextWorldState);
}
```

With the help of the new onLeaf method we can quickly scan through the entire world within the worldToArray method and determine whether there is a leaf at a particular cell. If there is a leaf, we would assign the corresponding element of the currentWorldState array with the value of true and would assign it with false otherwise. Once we have the world translated into an array, we can count each array element's neighbours and apply the Game of Life rules to this element within the applyGameOfLifeRules method. The result of running this method would be stored in the nextWorldState array. The final operation we need to perform is updating Clara's World to simulate the resulting state of the game. This is achieved within the updateWorld method with the help of the new putLeaf and removeLeaf methods. For every element in the nextWorldState array that is true we would have to put a leaf in the corresponding cell of Clara's World, and for every element that is false we have to make sure that the leaf is removed. Below we present the complete solution of this problem:

 Exercise: After experimenting with the solution below try to modify it in such a way that each of the cells is initialised at random. To make this process even more interesting, experiment with creating a constant in your code that determines the probability for the randomly assigned cell to be a live cell. For example, try setting the probability of having a live cell to 70%. This should result in roughly 70% of all cells in Clara's World being populated with leaves.

```
class MyClara extends Clara {
   // World dimensions constants
   final int WORLD_HEIGHT = 30;
   final int WORLD_WIDTH = 40;

   // variables for tracking and updating the world state
   boolean[][] currentWorldState;
   boolean[][] nextWorldState;
```

```
/**
 * Apply the game of life rules once per program execution
 */
void run() {
    // translate the world state into an array
    currentWorldState = worldToArray();

    // play game of life if not running for the first time
    nextWorldState = applyGameOfLifeRules(currentWorldState);
    updateWorld(nextWorldState);
}


/**
 * Scan the world for leaves and put true as the value of the
 * corresponding array element if a leaf is found
 */
boolean[][] worldToArray() {
    boolean[][] retVal = new boolean
        [WORLD_HEIGHT][WORLD_WIDTH];

    for (int i = 0; i < WORLD_HEIGHT; i++) {
        for (int k = 0; k < WORLD_WIDTH; k++) {
            if ( onLeaf(i,k) )
                retVal[i][k] = true;
            else
                retVal[i][k] = false;
        }
    }
    return retVal;
}


/**
 * Apply game of life rules to every element of inInitArray
 * Results will be stored in the array that this method returns
 */
boolean[][] applyGameOfLifeRules(boolean[][] inInitArray ) {
    boolean[][] resultingArray = new
        boolean[inInitArray.length][inInitArray[0].length];

    // go through all elements and count neighbours and
    // apply game of life rules to every cell using this number
    for (int i = 0; i < inInitArray.length; i++) {
        for (int k = 0; k < inInitArray[i].length; k++) {
            int neighbours = countNeighbours(inInitArray,i,k);

            // Any live cell with fewer than two live neighbours
            // dies, as if caused by under-population
            if (neighbours < 2)
                resultingArray[i][k] = false;

            // Any live cell with more than three live neighbours
            // dies, as if by overcrowding
            if (neighbours > 3)
                resultingArray[i][k] = false;
```

```java
            // Any live cell with two or three live neighbours
            // lives on to the next generation
            if ( (inInitArray[i][k] == true) && (neighbours == 2
                || neighbours == 3) )
                resultingArray[i][k] = true;

            // Any dead cell with exactly three live neighbours
            // becomes a live cell, as if by reproduction
            if (neighbours == 3 && inInitArray[i][k] == false)
                resultingArray[i][k] = true;
        }
    }
    return resultingArray;
}

/**
 * Remove all the leaves in Clara's world
 */
void cleanWorld() {
    for (int i = 0; i < WORLD_HEIGHT; i++) {
        for (int k = 0; k < WORLD_WIDTH; k++) {
            removeLeaf(i, k);
        }
    }
}

/**
 * Count the number of live neighbours for
 * a cell at position [x][y].
 */
int countNeighbours(boolean[][] inArray, int x, int y) {
    int retVal = 0;

    // we need to check all 8 surrounding cells
    // including those on the diagonal
    for ( int i = -1; i <= 1; i++ ) {
        for (int k = - 1; k <= 1; k++) {
            // do not count ourselves
            if (i == 0 && k == 0)
                continue;

            // don't try to assign values outside of array bounds
            if ((x + i < 0) || ( y + k < 0) || (x + i >=
                inArray.length) || ( y + k >= inArray[0].length))
                continue;

            // do the counting
            if ( inArray[x + i][y + k ] == true )
                retVal++;
        }
    }
    return retVal;
}
```

```
/**
 * Receives an array as input
 * and for every element that is true in this array puts a leaf
 * in Clara's world at the corresponding coordinate.
 */
void updateWorld(boolean[][] inArray) {
    cleanWorld();

    for (int i = 0; i < inArray.length; i++) {
        for (int k = 0; k < inArray[i].length; k++) {
            if (inArray[i][k] == true)
                putLeaf(i, k);
            else
                removeLeaf(i, k);
        }
    }
}
```

 To see the solution of this problem in Clara's World please use the following URL: `https://claraworld.net/link/C9P1S`. Try running the program multiple times to see how the world changes over time.

9.9 Summary

In this chapter we learned about arrays. Arrays allow programmers to work with collections of many variables without having to declare each individual variable separately. Array elements must all be of the same type and are accessed by their indexes. Arrays can be passed as input to methods, but they will be passed by reference rather than by value, meaning that modifying elements of an array using the local variable within a method will modify the original array that was passed to the method via this variable. To illustrate working with arrays we showed two chapter problems. In chapter problem 1 we demonstrated how Clara's World can be transformed into the Game of Life. In this game leaves represent living organisms. Executing our implementation of the Game of Life multiple times represents a simplistic simulation of how large populations of living organisms evolve over time. In chapter problem 2 we presented an updated version of the friendship algorithm from Chapter 5 that allows for allocating two arrays containing user interests and Sheldon's interests and finding a common interest in these arrays.

9.10 Exercises

 Exercises that target your understanding of the concepts covered in this chapter are available at `https://claraworld.net/link/C9Ex`.

Chapter 10
Classes and Objects

Many software developers often find themselves in a situation when a particular pattern of behaviour is required again and again in different parts of a large project or when a portion of code that was written for one project solves a substantial part of a problem in another project. Good programmers always try to increase the efficiency of their work, so instead of rewriting the code from scratch, such situations are best resolved through code reuse (using your old code for solving a new problem).

Up until now we were able to reuse code by either copy-pasting it or by placing a block of code into a method and then using the method name as an alias for the corresponding functionality. In this chapter we will introduce a new way of reusing code through classes. We will give a brief overview of classes and will talk about objects (class instances) and manipulations with those. We then show how with the help of classes we can borrow functionality from multiple chapter problems and how we can work with multiple Clara objects. We will illustrate the class and object concept on an example of ants searching for food.

Image features the "Ant" 3D model by martina.fabricci available under Creative Commons CC BY 4.0.

© Springer Nature Switzerland AG 2021
A. Bogdanovych, T. Trescak, *Learning Java Programming in Clara's World*,
https://doi.org/10.1007/978-3-030-75542-3_10

10.1 Chapter Story: The Amazing Ants

Ants are remarkable creatures that have been dominating our planet for millions of years. As a species they are amazingly successful. Their success is predominantly attributed to complex social organisation and particularly division of labour [22]. Ants live in large colonies, which possess complex social structures and engage in sophisticated group activities. These activities range from collecting food, building nests and nurturing their offspring to fighting wars with other colonies, farming (e.g. growing a particular type of fungus), enslaving ants from other colonies and "domesticating" other insect species (such as aphids). These complex activities require strict division of labour and coordination.

Division of labour is one of the most impressive features of ant colonies. Each ant plays a particular role with the majority of them continuously working or searching for work. The queen is the central figure of every ant colony. Her key task is reproduction. While she is working hard on delivering new colony members, other ants selflessly cater for her needs and protect her. In many ant species labour division is age-dependent with older ants often performing more dangerous duties. It is common for younger ants to remain in the nest and engage in domestic activities such as feeding the queen, tending eggs, construction or farming. In contrast, older ants are often involved in searching for food outside the nest, defending the colony from intruders, attacking other colonies and sometimes even conducting slave raids to increase the size of their labour and fighting forces.

Fig. 10.1: Communication of the Ants.

You may be curious to know how ants coordinate their efforts and whether these tiny insects are capable of some form of communication. They can, indeed, communicate, and their communication is quite rich and diverse. It ranges from communicating via sound (e.g. by scratching legs against their bodies), to dancing, touch and pheromone exchange [22]. Ant antennae play the key role in communication. Ants can directly touch each other with their antennae and directly transmit simple messages in this way, as shown in Figure 10.1. More important is the role of the antennae for smelling. Being able to smell is extremely vital for ants. They rely on their sense of smell much more substantially than many other living creatures, because one of their primary forms of communication happens to be exchange of chemicals (so-called pheromones).

With the help of pheromones ants can differentiate between ants from the same social group and strangers. Similar to dogs they can follow a pheromone trail until they reach a particular destination. Ants can release different types of pheromones and can spread these in various different ways. They can, for example, spray pheromones in the air to alert others of intruders in the nest or deposit them on the ground to mark a path to a food source [22].

Marking a path to food with pheromones is one of the most remarkable strategies. When a worker ant discovers a source of food, it collects a food sample and deposits a pheromone trail on its way back to the nest. On arrival back home the ant will wave her head when meeting other workers, touch them with her two antennae and offer a regurgitated food sample to them. After tasting her offering other ants run out along the trail to the newly discovered food source [22].

 A video featuring an experiment that confirms pheromone following is available at `https://claraworld.net/link/C10V1`.

Many interesting experiments have been conducted with ants to test their food searching strategies. Some of these experiments had a significant impact on computer science [23]. Let us have a look at some of these experiments and try to understand why they are relevant to computer scientists. Figure 10.2 features the basic experimental setup for experiment 1.

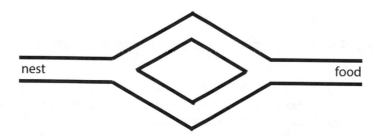

Fig. 10.2: Experiment 1: Symmetric Bridge. Modified from [24].

In this experiment researchers [24] created an artificial environment featuring an ant nest connected to a food source by two bridges. Both bridges are of equal length.

Now that you are familiar with the pheromone depositing strategy, we encourage you to engage in a simple mental exercise and try to imagine what would happen when many small ants are released from their nest in search of food. What do you think is the most likely pattern of ant behaviour that would emerge over time? Would ants spread out with some of them using the bridge shown in the upper part of Figure 10.2 and others using the bridge shown in the lower part of the figure? Alternatively, would most of them stick to one of the bridges and use it for travelling back and forth between the nest and the food source? You will find the answer to these questions on the next page. However, we kindly ask you not rush to discover the answer and try to challenge yourself by thinking about an even more interesting experiment.

Figure 10.3 illustrates the experimental setup for experiment 2. Similar to experiment 1 the nest is connected to the food source with two bridges. However, the bridges this time are of different length (with the bridge shown in the bottom part of the figure being substantially longer). Try asking yourself the same questions as before. What would happen to ants released from the nest over a long period of time? Will then evenly spread between both bridges or will they pick one bridge and congregate there? Try coming up with an explanation for your chosen answer.

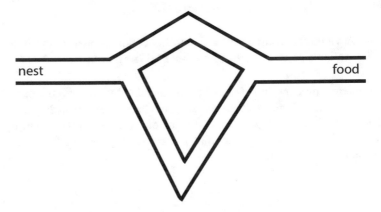

Fig. 10.3: Experiment 2: Asymmetric Bridge. Modified from [24].

Hopefully you have participated in our simple mental exercise and are keen to know the correct answer. Figure 10.4 shows a schematic illustration of what would happen over time in experiment 1. Here you can see that the majority of ants have congregated on one of the bridges. They will not necessarily choose this particular bridge. Since both bridges are of equal length, the choice of the bridge to congregate on will be driven by pure luck. The first group of ants would leave the nest and would randomly spread between the two bridges. On their return home the ants would start depositing pheromones. The bridge that would end up having more pheromone after the first group returns home would attract more ants, who will be guided by the pheromone smell in their search for food. These ants would no longer search at random, but would be closely following the pheromone trail produced by their colleagues. More and more pheromone would be deposited on the bridge that was initially chosen by the first group, and the pheromone on the other bridge would eventually evaporate. Over time most of the ants would congregate on the bridge that was originally selected by the first food explorers and would abandon the other bridge.

Fig. 10.4: Experiment 1 Result. Modified from [24].

 A video showing experiment 1 performed with actual ants is available at https://claraworld.net/link/C10V2.

You may rush to apply the same logic to experiment 2 and jump to the conclusion that one of the bridges would be chosen at random. This logic, however, does not quite apply in this experiment because the length of the bridges is different. While the ants at the start are likely to evenly spread between both bridges, the time it would take for the ants on the shorter bridge to reach the source of food would be shorter. As a result of this, the ants going through the shorter bridge would be moving between the food and the nest much quicker. Over time more pheromone would be depositing on the shorter bridge, while the pheromone on the longer bridge would continue to evaporate.

Figure 10.5 provides a schematic representation of the outcome of experiment 2. The ants would congregate on the bridge that represents the shortest path between the nest and the food source. Thus, the remarkable property of this simple food searching strategy is that ants will always find the shortest path between their nest and the source of food.

 A video showing experiment 2 performed with actual ants is available at https://claraworld.net/link/C10V3.

A class of computer science algorithms called "ant algorithms" (also known as "ant colony optimisation algorithms") have emerged as an alternative to traditional mathematical approaches to solving many complex problems. One of the key benefits of ant algorithms is that they can be easily applied to dynamic systems that

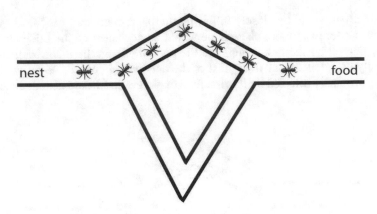

Fig. 10.5: Experiment 2 Result. Modified from [24].

continuously change their topology, such as the Internet. Not surprising is that ant algorithms are widely used in network routing, sequential ordering and constraint optimisations and often outperform traditional approaches. In particular, ant algorithms are often more robust, reliable and scalable compared with the conventional routing algorithms available in ad hoc networks [25]. It is remarkable that the algorithm developed by small insects that many would not consider intelligent can outperform algorithms developed by some of humanity's smartest mathematicians.

10.2 Chapter Problem: Clara Imitates Ant Behaviour

Clara has established a colony of ladybugs and attempts to rule its population following similar principles to those used by ants. All the insects in Clara's new colony have developed skills to search for food by depositing and smelling pheromones. They must now apply these skills to successfully search for food by creating pheromone trails from a food source to the nest once a food source is found by one of the insects.

Let us see how this problem looks in Clara's World. Figure 10.6 a) shows the initial configuration of Clara's World that is populated with obstacles, a single leaf (depicting the source of food) and Clara's nest (represented as a home icon). Figure 10.6 b) shows multiple insects crawling around and outlines a situation when one of the insects travels back to its original position and places pheromones (red dots) to mark the path from the source of food to the nest (initial position).

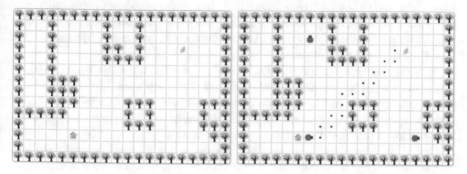

Fig. 10.6: a) Initial State   b) Final State After Finding Food.

 To work on this problem in Clara's World please use the following URL: https://claraworld.net/link/C10P1.

Let us learn how this scenario can be brought to life with the help of the "class" concept.

10.3 Introduction to Classes and Objects

Java is an object-oriented programming language, meaning that your program is designed as a set of classes that become objects during program execution. If you look into any of the code examples in this book, you would realise that all completed programs are typically enclosed within the following code:

```
public class MyClara extends Clara {
    ...
}
```

You will notice that this code explicitly mentions the word "class". This is because each Java program must be written inside a class, and in our case this class is called MyClara. This class can be seen as a container that encapsulates your program's data and behaviour, where variables that you create represent the data and methods are behaviours.

Every Java program must contain at least one class but can also feature multiple classes. The Clara's World framework does not permit creating any desired number of classes, but does allow you to work with more than one class. All additional classes in Clara's World must be defined in the Clara World's editor during the definition of a particular exercise.

A class can be seen as a code blueprint. To execute this blueprint you must create an instance of the class (an object). Each visual element in Clara's World (e.g. Clara, tree, leaf) has the corresponding class that defines the key functionality, and every visual element that you see during your program's execution is an object. You can create many objects (instances) of the same class, and each object would be executing the same code blueprint.

To better illustrate the idea of classes and objects let us discuss Figure 10.6. In this figure we can see that the following classes have been used: Tree, MyClara, Leaf, Pheromone and Home. You can see many objects, instances of the Tree and Pheromone class. There is only one instance of the Leaf class, one instance of the Home class and three instances of MyClara.

One of the powerful characteristics of classes is that they can be organised into hierarchies that feature parent classes and child classes (also known as subclasses). Figure 10.7 shows the hierarchy of classes used in the example shown in Figure 10.6.

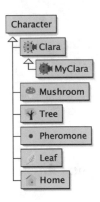

Fig. 10.7: Class Hierarchy in Clara's World.

The arrows in the above diagram represent a parent-child relationship between two classes, where a child class is the class the arrow originates from and a parent class is the one the arrow points at. You will notice that the MyClara class has the following two parent classes: Character and Clara. Every other class has only one parent class, Character. Each of the classes inherits behaviour and data from all its parent classes. In our case, the Character class defines basic behaviour that is common to all visual objects in Clara's World. This behaviour includes making objects appear and disappear and having objects update their location in Clara's world. The data (that is not directly available to you) includes the coordinates of the object and its visibility status. In our examples so far you only were able to edit the `MyClara` class. All other classes were hidden from your view and could only be accessed by the person who created the corresponding exercises. These classes, however, do exist behind the scenes.

When your program executes (as the result of pressing the "run" button) the Clara's World execution environment is continuously calling the `act` or `run` methods of each object of type `Character` and all of its subclasses. In situations where neither `act` nor `run` methods are present, the `Character` will be excluded from the list of objects that require code execution.

10.4 Creating Objects

The Clara's World framework automatically creates objects for each graphical element (e.g. leaf, Clara, tree) that exists inside the corresponding world. Using methods such as `putLeaf` results in creating new objects of the corresponding class (`Leaf`). In Java programs that do not use a visual framework similar to Clara's World, all objects must be created by the programmer manually by typing the corresponding code. It is useful for us to learn how objects can be created in Java. The code example below illustrates how a new instance of the `Leaf` class is created inside the `putLeaf` method behind the scenes:

```
Leaf theLeaf = new Leaf();
```

The result of executing the above line of code would be creating an object that is an instance of the `Leaf` class in your computer's memory. This object is assigned with the variable called `theLeaf`, and this variable name can be used for working with this object.

10.5 Creating a Class Example

Let us illustrate the key aspects of working with classes on an example of creating a class. As usual, the class that we will work with is the `MyClara` class, the class that would be in charge of turning Clara into a pheromone-guided insect capable of collaboratively searching for food with other colony members. At present the code for this class appears as follows:

```
class MyClara extends Clara {
    /**
     * Here we should not have a main loop to avoid freezing
        other bugs
     */
    public void act() {
    }
}
```

The very first line in this code means that we are editing the class called MyClara and that this class is the child class of the Clara class (that is evident from the use of the extends clause). The fact that we extend the Clara class means that we are able to borrow the functionality of the corresponding class such as placing and removing leaves, sensing trees, etc.

This class does not have a run method, but has an empty act method. Our task would be to populate the act method with code that will be executed by every instance of this class (every MyClara object) that is placed inside Clara's World. In addition to defining the act method we would also need to create additional data and behaviours for this class. The data means new variables defined at the class level (outside of methods), and behaviours are new methods of this class.

Let us first think of possible additional data that we require. Our MyClara would need to know the location of its nest, so that it knows where to return to after finding food. For simplicity let us assume that Clara's nest is represented by one cell in her environment. The position of this cell is then determined by the corresponding x and y coordinates of this cell. Let us create the corresponding variables for remembering the coordinates of the nest and call them _homeX and _homeY. Notice that we used the underscore "_" character in front of the variable names. This is in accordance with Java notation, where all instance variable names should start with the underscore character. **Instance variables** are variables that represent the data associated with the class. These variables are typically defined at the very top of the class code and must be declared outside any of the class methods. Similar to instance variables, methods of a class are often called **instance methods**.

Let us also create additional methods for receiving the values of these variables (getHomeX() and getHomeY()). After these modifications our updated code should look as follows:

```java
class MyClara extends Clara {
    private int _homeX = 0;
    private int _homeY = 0;

    public void act() {
    }

    public int getHomeX() {
      return _homeX;
    }

    public int getHomeY() {
      return _homeY;
    }
}
```

10.6 Access Specifiers `private` and `public`

An important point to discuss in relation to the above code is the use of the `private` and `public` keywords. Any variable or method can be declared with these keywords (also known as **access specifiers**) in front. Declaring a variable or method as `private` would mean that this variable or method are for internal use only (can only be accessed inside the corresponding class). The `public` keyword is used for declaring a variable or method that can be used by other classes. Methods or variables that are public can be accessed by any other class. For example, the `Leaf` class would be able to call the `getHomeX()` and `getHomeY()` methods, but will not be able to access the `_homeX` and `_homeY` variables.

Most of the time in this book we have not used access specifiers because these are not compulsory and it was difficult to explain their purpose before explaining what a class is. In prior chapters we would have declared the home coordinates as follows:

```
int homeX = 0;
int homeY = 0;
```

We would have, of course, not used the "_" prefix and would have omitted the `private` keyword. Declaring your instance variables in this way is very similar to declaring them as `private`. Such variables (or methods) will not be accessible by most other classes. However, declaring variables or methods without the `private` or `public` keyword is slightly less restrictive than `private`. Such variables would be accessible inside the subclasses of the class where they were declared.

Now that we know about classes it is best to explicitly specify whether a variable or method should be `public` or `private`. This decision of which of them to choose is up to you. Java guidelines, however, dictate that you should use the keyword `public` in exceptional circumstances only, when it is absolutely necessary to directly access the corresponding variable or method. It is also recommended to make all variables `private` and to provide access to variables that must be used in other classes via the corresponding methods such as `getHomeX()` and `getHomeY()`.

10.7 The `static` Keyword

Another important keyword that can be used with variables and methods is `static`. Declaring a variable or a method as `static` would result in only having a single copy of this variable or method that is shared across all instances of a particular class. Modifying a `static` variable in one of the objects would mean that all other objects would also be using this updated value.

The keyword `static` is useful for our purposes, since all ants should have the same values for the coordinates of their home. Therefore, we can declare our variables as follows:

```
private static int _homeX = 0;
private static int _homeY = 0;
```

Variables and methods declared with the keyword `static` are called the **class variables** and **class methods**. This refers to the fact that all instances of the class would be using the same instance of a class variable or method. For variables and methods that are not declared as `static` each class instance would be using its own copies of these variables and methods.

10.8 Inheritance

Probably the most powerful feature of classes is inheritance. **Inheritence** is the ability of classes to borrow data and behaviours from their parent classes. In Java it is possible for a class to have up to one parent class. A class that does not have a parent class is declared as follows:

```
public class NoParent {
   ...
}
```

A class that has a parent uses the keyword `extends` in its declaration (similar to how `MyClara` was declared with `Clara` as the parent class). A class that has a parent would borrow all variables and methods from its parent and can use these directly in its code. Java only permits a class to have one parent class, however, it is also permitted for a parent class to have a parent itself. Similar to other programming languages Java allows for establishing complex class hierarchies similar to the hierarchy shown in Figure 10.7. To illustrate this concept let us show how `MyClara` can use the functionality of its parent class `Clara` and its grandparent class `Character` inside the `act()` method. The `Character` class is the parent class for class `Clara`. The `Character` class has methods (`getX()` and `getY()`) for obtaining the X and Y coordinates of the corresponding cell. The code below shows how these methods can be directly used in the `MyClara` class:

```
class MyClara extends Clara {
    private static int _homeX = 0;
    private static int _homeY = 0;

    public void act() {
       if (_homeX == 0)
          _homeX = getX();

       if (_homeY == 0)
          _homeY = getY();
```

```
    if ( !treeFront() )
        move();
}


public int getHomeX() {
    return _homeX;
}

public int getHomeY() {
    return _homeY;
    }
}
```

The above code allows us to memorise the coordinates of where the corresponding MyClara object was placed inside Clara's World as _homeX and _homeY. These variables would be declared with the initial value set to 0, which is an impossible value because Clara would never be placed at this coordinate. The very first time the act() method is executed we would obtain the real coordinates of where the corresponding MyClara object was placed in Clara's World by calling the getX() and getY() methods of their grandparent class Character. The values of _homeY and _homeY are then updated to the actual coordinates and would remain unchanged even after we call the move() method of the parent class Clara, because we only reset these variables if their value is equal to zero.

The above code fragment shows how remarkably easy it is to use inheritance in Java. We were able to use the move() and treeFront() methods of the parent class Clara in the same way we would have used them inside the Clara class itself. Moreover, we were also able to use getX() and getY() methods of the grandparent class Character in the same simple way as if these methods were declared inside MyClara.

10.9 Overriding Methods

Another key feature of classes that goes hand-in-hand with inheritance is method overriding. Any subclass can override methods of any of its parent classes and give them a new meaning. Method overriding happens when a subclass declares a method with the same name and the same list of parameters as the parent class. In this case the newly declared method would change the behaviour of the method of the parent class. Below is an example of how MyClara can give a new meaning to the putLeaf() method of its parent class Clara:

```
class MyClara extends Clara {

    public void run() {
        putLeaf();
    }
```

```
public void putLeaf() {
  System.out.println("Putting a leaf");
}
}
```

In the above code we have actually overridden two methods putLeaf() and run(). We have replaced putting a leaf with printing a line of text on the screen and have also given a new meaning to the run() method that was empty in the parent class Clara.

Method overriding is a very powerful tool. To understand how powerful it is consider how our framework works. Similar to classical Java frameworks, the entry point of every program is the main() method of the Clara class. This method (as well as everything else in the Clara class) is not directly visible to you. The reason why placing your code inside act() or run() results in some action is that the main() method of the Clara class calls the empty run() and act() methods declared inside Clara. When you place your code inside MyClara (that is a subclass of Clara) you would override one of these empty methods, which results in running your code. The powerful feature is that you can create a class that calls an empty method in some strategic place and this empty method can be overridden by a subclass, so that the method of the subclass is then called in the strategic place instead of the empty method.

10.10 Accessing Methods and Variables

Now that we understand how to declare a class, how to create instance variables and methods and how to use inheritance, let us learn how to work with the corresponding objects. Once an object (instance of a class) has been created, it is possible to access its methods and variables using the "." symbol as follows:

```
MyClara theAnt = new MyClara();
int x = theAnt.getHomeX();
int y = theAnt.getHomeY();
```

The general form for accessing an instance variable is objectName.var. For accessing an instance method of an object you should use the following syntax: objectName.method(). Here, of course, var is a name of a variable that is declared in the corresponding class and method is the name of a method declared in this class.

10.11 Constructors

In the above code for creating an object we have used a special method called a constructor that is automatically created by Java for every class. This method has the same name as the name of the class (MyClara() in our case). The line new MyClara() results in calling the MyClara() method of the MyClara class if this method exists. If it does not exist, the Java compiler would automatically create a so-called **default constructor**. The default constructor is a constructor with no parameters such as MyClara().

Constructors can be explicitly present in your code. A constructor is usually a method that appears at the very top (after declarations of instance variables). Constructors are declared as methods that return no value (not even a void). Constructors are typically used for initialising some of the instance variables. Below is an example of initialising home coordinates in a constructor:

```
class MyClara extends Clara {
   private static int _homeX;
   private static int _homeY;

   public MyClara() {
     _homeX = 0;
     _homeY = 0;
   }
}
```

It is also possible to create a constructor that has input parameters as follows:

```
class MyClara extends Clara {
   public MyClara(int inX, int inY) {
     _homeX = inX;
     _homeY = inY;
   }
}
```

In this case an instance of the MyClara class has to be created differently, as per the example below:

```
MyClara theAnt = new MyClara(0,0);
```

In classical Java you can create multiple constructors in your classes and call any constructor you like for creating your objects. Our framework, however, uses a limited version of Java where having multiple constructors is not supported.

Another *limitation of our framework* that directly affects our chapter problem is related to creating instances of one class from within another class. In such situations you must use a constructor that receives an instance of the class that it was created in and explicitly call its initialise() method. The code fragment below illustrates creating an instance of MyClara class from within the Home class:

```
class Home extends Character {
   void run() {
      MyClara clara = new MyClara(this);
      clara.initialise();
   }
}
```

Here MyClara(this) refers to a constructor that receives an instance of the Character class. The keyword this returns a variable that represents the instance of the class (object) where the code calling this is executing at runtime. In the above case this would return an object in Clara's World that is in charge of the visual element that looks like a house in Figure 10.6. The behaviour of this graphical element is controlled by the Home class.

The above code would be calling the constructor of the parent class (Clara) that is shown below:

```
   void Clara(Character inCharacter) {
     ...
   }
}
```

Note that the input parameter of the above constructor must be an instance of the Character class. Why do we then pass the instance of the Home class instead? This is because Home is the subclass of Character. In Java you can pass any subclass instead of its parent class anywhere where a parent class is required.

10.12 Method Overloading

The concept of method overloading is not supported in our framework. However, it is important to mention this idea so that you have a basic understanding of classes in Java. Method overloading refers to creating multiple methods with the same name. Traditional Java (not the limited version of Java used in our framework) is able to determine which method you want to use depending on the input parameters that the method is called with. To illustrate this idea consider the following example:

```
public class Addition {
   public int add(int num1, int num2)
   {
      int sum = num1 + num2;
      return sum;
   }

   public float add(float num1, float num2)
   {
      float sum = num1 + num2;
      return sum;
   }
```

```
public String add(String str1, String str2)
{
   String combined = str1 + str2;
   return combined;
}
}
```

Here method overloading allows the developer not to invent new names for methods that compute the addition of variables of different types, but to reuse the same name multiple times. The choice of the method to execute will be made depending on the types of input parameters. For example, attempting to call the `add` method with two `float` arguments would result in calling the "`public float add(float num1, float num2)`" method. Calling the same method with one `int` and one `float` parameter would result in a compilation error, because a method with such parameter types does not exist.

Our framework, however, does not support method overloading. Having multiple methods with the same name in Clara's World would result in a compilation error: "Method overloading is not supported".

10.13 Passing Objects as Method Arguments

Similar to how we were able to pass variables of primitive data types and arrays as input to methods, it is also possible to pass objects to methods. Similar to arrays, objects are passed by reference, meaning that only the object address is passed to the method and modifying the input parameter would result in modifying the original object. The example below illustrates passing an object to a method:

```
public class ValuePrinter {
   void printCoordinates(MyClara inAnt) {
      System.out.println(inAnt.getHomeX() + ", " +
         inAnt.getHomeY());
   }
}
```

Here we pass a `MyClara` object to the `printCoordinates` method of the `ValuePrinter` class. This class then outputs the coordinates of the given object.

10.14 Chapter Problem Solution

Now that we have a basic understanding of classes and objects, let us use this new knowledge for solving the chapter problem.

You can see a video explanation of how to solve this problem step-by-step at https://claraworld.net/link/C10V4.

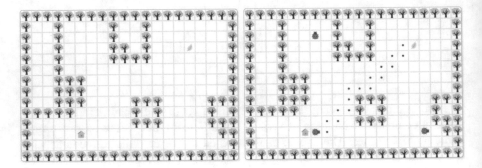

Fig. 10.8: a) Initial State   b) Final State.

Figure 10.8 a) shows the initial state of Clara's World before the program execution, where you see a Home object, obstacles (represented by trees) and a food source (leaf). Figure 10.8 b) illustrates the result of one of the insects finding the food source and returning back to its starting position (nest) while marking the way back with pheromones (red dots).

This problem appears substantially complex, and it is difficult to decide on how it could be approached. Let us recall that we have actually solved parts of this problem earlier in this book. The initial task for each Clara is to conduct a random walk in search for food. This very problem has already been solved in Section 7.3.1. After finding food Clara must navigate back to her nest. On the way back she must no longer perform a random walk, but should find a way back to her nest in an optimal way. Since Clara knows the coordinates of her nest, we can employ the bug algorithm that was covered in Section 7.8 for this task.

One way to continue with our solution could have been to identify all the relevant methods from our earlier solution of the random walk problem and from the solution of the bug algorithm problem, paste these into MyClara and then use the corresponding methods in Clara's act() method. There is, however, a better way of doing this with classes.

Let us start by slightly modifying our earlier bug algorithm solution. The solution shown in Section 7.8 was incomplete. In some situations Clara could get stuck and would keep walking in circles in an infinite loop. This problem was illustrated on a bug zapper example shown in Figure 7.7 b). We discussed that such infinite loops can be avoided by detecting that Clara is walking in circles and then changing the direction of turning after encountering an obstacle. The program below shows the complete solution of the bug algorithm that was modified to address the bug zapper problem. In the modified version we use two sets of variables (_lastCollisionX, _lastCollisionY and _preLastCollisionX, _preLastCollisionY) that are employed for memorising the coordinates of the last two obstacle collision points. Every time Clara encounters an obstacle she would compare her current coordinate with these variables to determine whether a collision at these coordinates has already happened in the past. The direction of turning (controlled by the _isTurningLeft variable) would be changed to the opposite one if Clara's current coordinate matches a perviously stored collision point. In order to simplify the code of NavigatingClara we have also moved the orientEast() method inside Clara class. This method was also modified to account for orientation randomness that will be introduced within RandomClara.

The updated code is shown below. The corresponding class was renamed from MyClara to NavigatingClara, so that we can easily reuse this code without copy-pasting all its methods and variables.

```
/**
 * Clara does basic obstacle avoidance bug style.
 */
class NavigatingClara extends Clara {
    // Declaring constants here.
    // Notice that those will be visible inside all methods.
    // Also notice how much more sense it makes to use names
    // like NORTH or SOUTH instead of numbers 3 and 4
    // and how using constants instead of numbers
    // helps to understand the code better
    final int WEST = 4;
    final int EAST = 2;
    final int NORTH = 1;
    final int SOUTH = 3;

    // determines the direction of turning at an obstacle
    boolean _isTurningLeft = true;

    // remembers Clara's orientation
    int _orientation = EAST;

    // variables that are used to remember the position of the
        last 2 wall collisions
    int    _lastCollisionX = 0;
    int    _lastCollisionY = 0;
    int    _preLastCollisionX = 0;
    int    _preLastCollisionY = 0;

    /**
     * Bug obstacle avoidance algorithm.
     */
    public void act() {
        getCloserTo(3, 5);
    }

    /**
     * A method to avoid an obstacle/wall
     * by going around it on the right-hand side
     * in the similar way as maze navigation
     */
    void avoidWall() {
        // Then we start turning and moving
        // so the orientation may change in an unpredictable way
        turnAway();
```

```
    while ( ( _isTurningLeft && treeRight() ) || (
        !_isTurningLeft && treeLeft() ) ) {
        // double-check that Clara is not turning in circles
        // and falls in an infinite loop. So we stop after
        // Clara turns 4 times = 360 degrees.
        // Notice the advanced use of && in the loop condition
        for (int i = 0; treeFront() && i < 4; i++ ) {
            turnAway();
        }
        move();
    }
}

/**
 * The method that makes Clara turn away from an obstacle.
 * Clara always turns left, until she realises that turning
 * left is not getting her anywhere (she is stuck in a loop)
 * then she will change the direction of turning.
 */
void turnAway() {
    if (_isTurningLeft) {
        if (_orientation > 1)
            _orientation--;
        else
            _orientation = 4;

        turnLeft();
    }
    else {
        if (_orientation < 4)
            _orientation++;
        else
            _orientation = 1;

        turnRight();
    }
}

/**
 * Send Clara in the direction determined by the input.
 * Pre-condition: Clara is facing east
 * Post-condition: Clara made a step in the desired direction
 * She would face east when this method finishes.
 */
void goGivenDirection(int movementDirection) {
    switch (movementDirection) {
        // if we need to go north - then we need to turn left
        // and then move, as Clara initially faces east
        case NORTH:
        turnLeft();
        secureMoveAdvanced();
        turnRight();
        break;
```

```
      // if we want to go to the cell to the east
      // we simply need to move forward
      case EAST:
      secureMoveAdvanced();
      break;

      // if we need to go to the west - then turn around
      // and move, as Clara initially faces east
      case WEST:
      turnAround();
      secureMoveAdvanced();
      turnAround();
      break;

      // if we need to go to the south - then turn right
      // and then move, as Clara initially faces east
      case SOUTH:
      turnRight();
      secureMoveAdvanced();
      turnLeft();
      break;
   }
}

/**
 * Standard function for turning 180 degrees
 */
void turnAround() {
   turnLeft();
   turnLeft();
}

/**
 * Move forward or avoid the wall and then move forward
 */
void secureMoveAdvanced() {
   if ( !treeFront() )
      move();
   else {
      // Tracking wall collisions here!
      // if the current collision position is the same
      // as the previous one then we are stuck
      // in an infinite loop and should try changing
      // the direction in which Clara turns to avoid obstacles
      if ((_lastCollisionX == getX() && _lastCollisionY ==
          getY()) ||
      (_preLastCollisionX == getX() && _preLastCollisionY ==
          getY())) {
        _isTurningLeft = !_isTurningLeft;

        // prepare debug string
        String turnSideString = "left";
```

```
        if (!_isTurningLeft)
            turnSideString = "right";
    }

    _preLastCollisionX = _lastCollisionX;
    _preLastCollisionY = _lastCollisionY;
    _lastCollisionX = getX();
    _lastCollisionY = getY();

    avoidWall();
    }
}

/**
 * Calculates which of the surrounding cells will bring Clara
 * closer to her goal (leaf) and makes her move to this cell.
 * If the cell contains an obstacle - Clara will avoid it
 * following the right hand rule principle
 */
public void getCloserTo(int x, int y) {
    // Get Clara's coordinates
    int claraX = getX();
    int claraY = getY();

    // Compute distances to the leaf from all surrounding cells
    // It's enough to compute distance squared for comparison
    // d2 = (x2 - x1)*(x2 - x1) + (y2 - y1)*(y2 - y1);
    int distWest = (x - (claraX - 1) )*( x - (claraX - 1) ) +
        (y - claraY)*(y - claraY);
    int distEast = (x - (claraX + 1) )*( x - (claraX + 1) ) +
        (y - claraY)*(y - claraY);
    int distNorth = (x - claraX)*( x - claraX) + ( y - (claraY
        - 1) )*( y - (claraY - 1) );
    int distSouth = (x - claraX)*( x - claraX) + ( y - (claraY
        + 1) )*( y - (claraY + 1) );

    int movementDirection = WEST;

    if ( distEast <= distWest && distEast <= distNorth &&
        distEast <= distSouth )
        movementDirection = EAST;

    if ( distNorth <= distWest && distNorth <= distEast &&
        distNorth <= distSouth )
        movementDirection = NORTH;

    if ( distSouth <= distWest && distSouth <= distEast &&
        distSouth <= distNorth )
        movementDirection = SOUTH;

    goGivenDirection(movementDirection);
    }
}
```

Let us next focus on the random walk problem. Our random walk solution requires little modification. The only two things we would need to change are: 1) renaming the `act()` method to `findFood()`, so that we have a method with a sensible name for performing a random walk, and 2) changing the name of the class from `MyClara` to `RandomClara`. Since we want to also use the bug algorithm functionality and to make it possible for Clara to use it, we should make the new class be a subclass of `NavigatingClara`. In this way the `RandomClara` class would have access to the `findFood()` method that is in charge of performing the random walk and would also contain a copy of the `getCloserTo` method that would navigate Clara to a desired coordinate (position of the nest in our case) using the bug algorithm. The resulting code is shown below:

```
/**
 * Clara explores her world using the random walk technique.
 * She stops if she finds a leaf.
 */
class RandomClara extends NavigatingClara {
    /**
     * Since we need multiple characters to call act()
     * we can't use loops here or other characters might freeze
     */
    public void act() {
        findFood();

        if ( onLeaf() ) {
            removeLeaf();
            stop();
        }
    }

    /**
     * Move one step in random direction
     */
    public void findFood() {
        randomTurn();
        secureMove();
    }

    /**
     * Turn left or right at random
     */
    public void randomTurn() {
        boolean isTurningLeft = getRandomBoolean();

        if (isTurningLeft)
            turnLeft();
        else
            turnRight();
    }
```

```
/**
 * Returns a random boolean variable.
 * The probability will be around 50%.
 */
boolean getRandomBoolean() {
    return Clara.getRandomNumber(100) < 50;
}

/**
 * Move and avoid all the trees along the way
 */
public void secureMove() {
    if ( !treeFront() )
        move();
}
}
```

After making the above modifications we would have created the following two classes: `NavigatingClara` (that implements the corrected version of the bug algorithm) and `RandomClara` (that contains the code for performing a random walk). Your template code for this chapter problem already features these classes. It now contains multiple tabs, where every tab corresponds to a separate class that you can modify as shown in Figure 10.9.

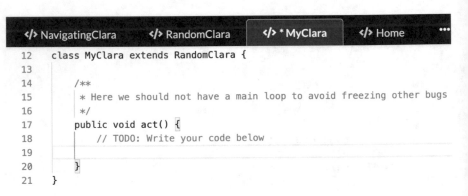

Fig. 10.9: Working with Multiple Classes in Clara's World.

These tabs are shown in the upper part of Figure 10.9. One of the tabs (for editing the `MyClara` class) is currently open and features the skeleton code for `MyClara`. Note that `MyClara` is declared as follows:

```
class MyClara extends RandomClara {
    ...
}
```

The fact that MyClara is a subclass of RandomClara allows it to use the functionality of all the corresponding parent classes. The hierarchy of all the relevant classes in our project is shown in Figure 10.10. As is evident from this figure, MyClara class is the subclass that borrows functionality from Character, Clara, NavigatingClara and RandomClara.

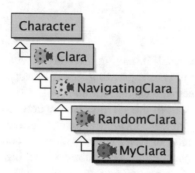

Fig. 10.10: The Hierarchy of the Key Classes.

Let us temporarily switch our attention to the Home class. This is where we must create instances of MyClara. At the moment no instances of MyClara are present in our project, which means that whatever code we put inside MyClara will not run. This is because the code inside a class will only run if a corresponding object (an instance of this class) is created at runtime. In our earlier projects instances of MyClara were created because the corresponding visual element (ladybug) was present in Clara's World. This time, however, we only have the home object and no ladybugs. Earlier in this chapter we showed the code for creating an instance of MyClara. This code looked as follows:

```
void run() {
    MyClara clara = new MyClara(this);
    clara.initialise();
}
```

Replacing the run() method of the Home class with this code would create a single instance of MyClara. For our solution, however, we require multiple bugs. How can we create multiple MyClara objects? The easiest way to create multiple objects is employing a for loop. A good practice for a situation like this is to create a dedicated constant that specifies how many insects would be spawned and then use this constant in the loop for creating the corresponding number of MyClara instances. Using a constant facilitates quick future modification of this code. Modifying the number of insects to be spawned would be as easy as changing the value of this constant. The complete implementation of the Home class that incorporates this idea is shown below:

```
class Home extends Character {
   final int INSECTS_LIVING_HERE = 3;

   void run() {
      for (int i = 0; i < INSECTS_LIVING_HERE; i++) {
         MyClara clara = new MyClara(this);
         clara.initialise();
      }
   }
}
```

Running this code would result in having three `MyClara` objects appearing at the same location as where the corresponding `Home` object was placed in Clara's World. Now that we can create the desired number of `MyClara` objects, it is time to make them move. At the start of this chapter we created some basic code for the `MyClara` class. Let us use this code as the foundation for our solution. This initial code memorises the coordinates of Clara's nest within the corresponding variables as shown below. The only change that is required is making sure that we extend `RandomClara`, so that `MyClara` has access to the random walk and bug algorithm functionality.

```
class MyClara extends RandomClara {
   private static int _homeX = 0;
   private static int _homeY = 0;

   /**
    * Here we should not have a main loop to avoid freezing
    *    other bugs
    */
   public void act() {
      if (_homeX == 0)
         _homeX = getX();

      if (_homeY == 0)
         _homeY = getY();
   }

   public int getHomeX() {
      return _homeX;
   }

   public int getHomeY() {
      return _homeY;
   }
}
```

It is now time to start utilising the random walk, so that Clara is able to search for food. The `RandomClara` class encapsulates this functionality inside the `findFood()` method. Calling this method inside `act()` would result in Clara continuously making a step in a random direction. Simply adding this method at the end of `act()` would make the random walk happen.

In our implementation we require Clara to operate in two modes. She would initially start in the mode where the source of food has not been detected. In this mode she is performing the random walk. Once the food source is found, Clara must switch into a different mode, in which she returns home using the bug algorithm and places pheromones along the way.

Detecting the food source is simple. We can utilise the `onLeaf()` method for this. In order to place pheromones at Clara's current position we have created the `putPheromone()` method inside the `Clara` class. In addition, there is also the `onPheromone()` method. This method returns `true` if Clara is located on top of a pheromone and returns `false` otherwise. With the help of these new methods we can now place and sense pheromones in Clara's World. In order to differentiate between the two aforementioned modes we will be adding two variables (`_foodX` and `_foodY`) that memorise the coordinates of the food source. Similar to the coordinates of Clara's home, these variables can be initialised with impossible values (0, 0) and would be reset to the actual coordinates of the food source once it has been detected. Below is the updated `act()` method and the corresponding additional methods that make Clara operate in two different modes. After finding the food source Clara would no longer perform the random walk but would execute the `getCloserTo` method for navigating back to her nest. The process of navigating back to Clara's nest is encoded within the dedicated `returnHome` method.

```java
public void act() {
    // Initialise home coordinates first time act is called
    if (_homeX == 0)
        _homeX = getX();

    if (_homeY == 0)
        _homeY = getY();

    // if we don't know where food is - find it using random
    //   walk
    if ( !isFoodFound() )
        findFood();

    // the food is found if Clara is on a leaf
    if ( onLeaf() && !isFoodFound() ) {
        _foodX = getX();
        _foodY = getY();
    }
    else if ( isFoodFound() )
        returnHome();
}

boolean isFoodFound() {
    return _foodX != 0 && _foodY != 0;
}
```

```
/**
 * After food has been found - make Clara return home.
 * For that she uses the functionality of NavigatingClara.
 */
public void returnHome() {
    // The navigation algorithm only works
    // if Clara is facing east.
    // Make sure she does.
    orientEast();

    if ( (getX() != _homeX) || (getY() != _homeY) ) {
        getCloserTo(_homeX, _homeY);
    }
    else {
        _foodY = 0;
        _foodX = 0;
    }
}
```

If you run the above code, you will realise that our solution is nearly complete. Each of the Clara instances would perform the random walk at the start and would return to the nest once the food source has been found.

It is not our objective to develop a complete implementation of the ant algorithm that would also include having other insects following the pheromone trails, making pheromones evaporate and increasing the amount of pheromone every time an insect returns via the corresponding cell again. We encourage you to treat this as an advanced programming exercise and implement it yourself.

Our objective with this example is to illustrate how working with multiple classes makes code reuse more effective. With this educational goal in mind we will consider a limited implementation of the ant algorithm, which would terminate after the first insect finds food and successfully returns home. To make this happen we must have a mechanism for stopping the program. What makes the stopping task complicated is that now we have multiple Claras, where each Clara acts independently. How could we make all of them stop at the same time?

One good way to synchronise multiple objects of the same class is to use static variables. A static variable represents a single address in memory shared by all instances of a particular class. Stopping all Claras can be achieved by creating a static boolean variable _isFinished that is set to true once the first insect reaches the nest. All other insects can routinely check this variable to determine whether their act() method should be terminated. Stopping all Claras, therefore, can be achieved by placing the following code inside the act() method of MyClara:

```
if (_isFinished)
    stop();
```

The final task that must be accomplished is placing pheromones in every cell that Clara traverses on her way back to the nest after finding food. Your initial reaction could be to insert putPheromone() inside the returnHome() method.

If you attempt doing this, however, you will see that pheromone would be missing from some cells. This is because the getCloserTo method (that is used inside returnHome) would on some occasions make Clara move multiple times. Multiple moves would be performed when Clara must avoid obstacles. Your next idea could involve modifying the code of NavigatingClara in such a way that every Clara's move is followed by placing pheromone. This approach, however, is not ideal. As a programmer you should make every attempt not to modify the classes you have borrowed from solving other problems. One of the reasons for this is that at some later stage you may require the original implementation of the bug algorithm (without placing pheromone). In this case you would need to revise your code again and remove the functionality of placing pheromone before making a move. Having to adapt your classes to every problem is not optimal. It is better to leave the NavigatingClara in its original form and try to place pheromone inside MyClara instead.

The most elegant way of making sure that pheromone is placed before every Clara's move is to override the move method that was defined in the parent class Clara. Overriding a method is as simple as creating a method with the same name and the same input and output inside the relevant subclass. Adding the following code inside MyClara would result in Clara placing pheromones at every cell where Clara moves if she operates in the mode where the position of the food source is known:

```
public void move() {
    if ( isFoodFound() )
        putPheromone();

    super.move();
}
```

An important thing to notice is that after testing whether the food source has been found and putting pheromone accordingly, Clara must also move. We do not actually know how moving is achieved within the code of Clara, because it is hidden from us. This knowledge, however, is not required. What we can do to make Clara move is call the original version of the move() method. This can be achieved with the help of the super keyword. In the above context using this keyword helps us to execute the move() method of the parent class (RandomClara). The RandomClara class does not have the move() method and neither does its parent class NavigatingClara. In such situations Java will continue searching for the corresponding method in all parent classes until it is found inside the Clara class. Calling the super.move() method would then correspond to calling the move() method of Clara class.

The complete implementation of the MyClara class is shown below:

 To see the solution of this problem in Clara's World please use the following URL: https://claraworld.net/link/C10P1S.

```
/**
 * A partial implementation of the ant algorithm.
 * Clara would start at her home and will initially perform
 * random walk searching for food (leaf). When the food is
 * found - she would use the functionality of NavigatingClara
 * to find her way back home while avoiding obstacles.
 * On the way back home she will deposit pheromones.
 */
class MyClara extends RandomClara {
    int _homeX = 0;
    int _homeY = 0;
    int _foodX = 0;
    int _foodY = 0;

    static boolean _isFinished = false;

    /**
     * Avoid having a main loop or it will freeze other bugs
     */
    public void act() {
        // Initialise home coordinates.
        // when act() is called for the first time
        if (_homeX == 0)
            _homeX = getX();
        if (_homeY == 0)
            _homeY = getY();

        // if we don't know where food is, find it with random walk
        if ( !isFoodFound() )
            findFood();

        // the food is found if Clara is on a leaf
        if ( onLeaf() && !isFoodFound() ) {
            _foodX = getX();
            _foodY = getY();
        }
        else if ( isFoodFound() )
            returnHome();

        if (_isFinished)
            stop();
    }

    /**
     * We override the standard move() method
     * (that was defined inside Clara class)
     * to put pheromone when Clara is going back home
     */
    public void move() {
        if ( isFoodFound() )
            putPheromone();

        super.move();
    }
```

```java
/**
 * After food has been found - make Clara return home.
 * For that she uses the functionality of NavigatingClara.
 */
public void returnHome() {
    // The navigation algorithm only works if Clara faces
    // east, so make sure she does when we start
    orientEast();

    if ( (getX() != _homeX) || (getY() != _homeY) ) {
        getCloserTo(_homeX, _homeY);
    }
    else {
        _foodY = 0;
        _foodX = 0;

        _isFinished = true;
    }
}

boolean isFoodFound() {
    return _foodX != 0 && _foodY != 0;
}
}
```

As the result of running this code all Clara insects would start randomly searching for food. As soon as one of the insects finds food, it will return to its nest and would deposit pheromones along the way. Once one of the insects successfully arrives back to its nest, the program would terminate and all other insects would stop their food search.

 Exercise: Try extending this program so that each insect conducts multiple rounds (e.g. 3) of food delivery before terminating the program. To help them get there quicker you should incorporate pheromone trail following into their food search algorithm.

10.15 Summary

In this chapter we have learned about classes and objects. The class concept provides a powerful paradigm for code reuse that is particularly useful for large programming projects. With the help of classes we can structure our programs as a set of independently solved subproblems (each having a unique name and stored in a separate file). Through inheritance, classes can be organised into convenient hierarchies that are easy to visualise. As a result, your programs will become easier to understand and even easier to modify and reuse.

You have also learned that during runtime your program becomes a collection of class instances called objects. These objects can interact with each other by sharing data and calling each other's methods.

10.16 Exercises

The final set of exercises that target your understanding of classes and other concepts covered in this book can be found at the following link: `https://claraworld.net/link/C10Ex`.

10.17 Epilogue

This chapter concludes our introduction to Java programming in Clara's World. You will have noticed that the Clara's World framework only offers a partial implementation of classes and has other limitations. It is now time for you to say goodbye to Clara and continue learning Java in other frameworks.

In your future learning endeavours you should start working with general-purpose Java frameworks, such as Eclipse[1] or NetBeans[2]. While these frameworks are not as visual and fun to work with as Clara, they are a great choice because they pose no limitations on what you can implement.

There is a lot left to learn before you become a professional Java programmer. We recommend searching for learning resources that provide an extended coverage of classes and object-oriented programming principles.

We hope that you found this book useful and that it helped you to fall in love with programming. We wish you all the best!

---

[1] `https://www.eclipse.org`.
[2] `https://netbeans.apache.org`.

Appendix A
Clara's World User Guide

Welcome to Clara's World, the online framework for teaching programming and problem solving in a fun way. In this appendix we explore the key features of Clara's World and explain common tasks related to completing your exercises. To visit Clara's World, please navigate to `https://www.claraworld.net`. Figure A.1 shows the home page of Clara's World.

Fig. A.1: Home Page of Clara's World.

At the Clara's World home page, you can find some essential information about the service and its partners. You can also try to solve one of the programming problems or see the instruction video on how to solve this problem. Clara's World is a robust yet easy to use programming environment. The next section will get you started in a few minutes, with the following sections providing more details on each step, just in case you run into problems.

© Springer Nature Switzerland AG 2021
A. Bogdanovych, T. Trescak, *Learning Java Programming in Clara's World*,
https://doi.org/10.1007/978-3-030-75542-3

A.1 Quick Start

Each good programming book has to have a *Hello World*[1] example. Check how easy it is to do it in Clara's World. You do not need to install any specialised software. All that is required is a modern web browser.[2]. Let's have some programming fun!

 All readers of this book have free access to the "Book" organisation. If you want to access problems covered in this book and the corresponding exercises, this is the organisation to select. Type "book2021" (without quotation marks) in the "organisation password" field when registering for the "Book" organisation.

The following steps show how to start working with Clara's World:

1. Visit `http://www.claraworld.net`.
2. Register a new account, selecting your organisation and using the email address of your organisation (see Section A.2). Some organisations (such as "Book") allow you to use your private email address, while other organisations restrict access to their resources to holders of email addresses from the organisation's domain.
3. If you are not a part of an organisation, but simply want to access the book problems and exercises, select "Book" as your organisation and type "book2021" (without quotation marks) as the organisation password. You can use any email address for registering with the "Book" organisation, however, please make sure that you provide a valid email address, where you will receive the activation URL.
4. Activate your account by clicking on the link in the email you received from Clara.
5. After activation, you should be automatically logged in, if not, please log in using your email address and password (see Section A.5 for further information about the login process).
6. On the homepage, select the "**Archive**" schedule.
7. At the bottom of the page, subscribe to your tutor. Do not worry if you do not know your tutor name, or your tutor name is not available. Please choose anyone; you can change this setting later (see Section A.6.1).
8. Select the "**Easy**" practical (see Section A.6.2).
9. Select the "**Hello World**" exercise (see Section A.6.3).
10. Read the exercise description (see Section A.6.3).
11. Type the code `System.out.println("Hello Clara!")` in the left part of the editor, just under where it says `// type your code here`.

---

[1] `https://en.wikipedia.org/wiki/"Hello,_World!"_program`
[2] Visit Clara's World page to see if we support your browser.

```
void run() {
    // type your code here
    System.out.println("Hello Clara!");
}
```

12. Run your code by clicking on the ▶ Run button (see Section A.6.3).

Fig. A.2: Incorrect Solution for the "Hello World" Problem.

13. Oh no! Your solution failed. In the exercise instructions it asks you to print "Hello World!", and not "Hello Clara!". See the error message in Figure A.2
14. Please fix your code, and make sure that there are no error messages at the bottom of the page.
15. Click the reset button ↺ and then the ▶ Run button. There is no need to press the save button ▣ , since all solutions are saved automatically on each run.
16. Enjoy the amazing feeling after completing a long set of instructions! Your result should look similar to what is shown in Figure A.3.

Clara's World allows you to create your own programming exercises. You can share them with the world, or invite your friends or colleagues for a programming challenge! Please navigate to the *Sandbox* schedule, practical *User Problems* and create your first exercise there. If you need help, please check SectionA.9 for a step-by-step guide.

A.2 Creating an Account

To start using Clara's World, you need to create your account. We require a valid email address, where we send you the activation email.

Fig. A.3: Hello World.

1. You can access Clara's World at `https://claraworld.net`.
2. To register a new account, select `Enter Clara's World` and then choose `Register`.
3. Please select your home organisation and use your organisation's email (e.g. name@organisation.org). If you are not a member of any registered organisation, please use the organisation "Book".

 Please do not use your personal email unless you are working with organisations such as "Book" that do not restrict access to their resources to a particular Internet domain.

4. If your organisation requires a password, please type it in the "`Organisation Password`" field. If you do not know the password, please contact the administrator of your organisation.
5. If you are registering to the "Book" organisation, please type "book2021" (without quotation marks) in the Organisation Password field. You can use any email address for registering with the "Book" organisation, however, please make sure that you provide a valid email address, where you will receive the activation URL.
6. Your password has to be at least seven characters long, but we recommend 12 or more characters. Setting easy to remember passwords such as "giant-mannequin-hero" works well on most occasions.
7. Click `Register`.

If there are no errors, we will send an activation email to your inbox and display the confirmation message shown in Figure A.4. If you do not receive the activation email within a couple of minutes, please check your spam folder. The email contains instructions on how to activate your account, either by clicking on the provided link or entering it in your browser's internet address field. After successful activation, we will automatically log you in.

Account successfully created! We sent you an email with instructions on
how to activate your account.

Fig. A.4: Confirmation Message after a Successful Registration.

A.3 Logging in

When you activate your account, we automatically log you in. On all other occasions, you need to log in using *the email you used to register for your account* and
your password.

1. Please access Clara's World at `https://claraworld.net`.
2. Select `Enter Clara's World`
3. Use your organisation email address and password.
4. Click on `Sign In`

After logging in, you will see a combined list of all schedules that are available
to all the organisations that you are a part of.

A schedule consists of the programmed list of practicals. Each practical
relates to a specific programming topic and contains one or more exercises.

If you are a member of the "Book" organisation, you will see the Book schedule and several public schedules, such as the Archive or the Sandbox. The "Book"
schedule contains all chapter problems and practical exercises.

`https://claraworld.net/link/book` is the direct link to the
"Book" schedule.

A.4 Recovering your Password and Verification

In case you forgot your email or password, please use the `Reset Password` link
on the login screen. Figure A.5 depicts the login with `Reset Password` and
`Re-send verification` links, positioned next to the `Sign In` button.

To recover your password, please provide your registration email, where we sent
you the email with password reset instructions. If you provide an incorrect email,
the system displays an error message. Please check your spelling if such an event
occurs (see Figure A.6).

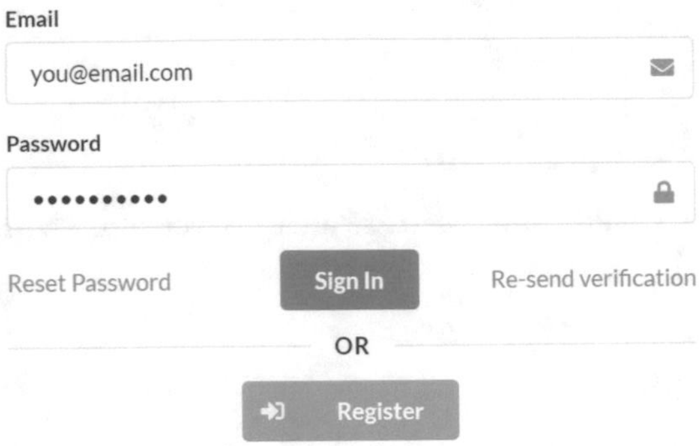

Fig. A.5: Login Screen with Password and Activation Recovery Links.

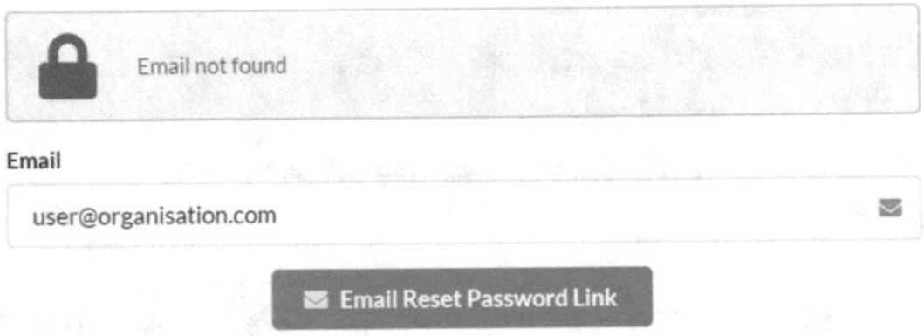

Fig. A.6: Password Recovery Screen with an Error Message.

To return to the login screen, please use the `Sign In` button and continue your login procedure.

A.5 User Home Screen

The user home screen provides access to the most exciting parts of Clara's World. On the left, you see the list of available schedules with all the awards you received for the given schedule. Please see Section A.6.1 for more details on schedules and what they represent. On the right, you see the list of latest notifications. Notifications often relate to achieving an award, receiving a mark or changing your position in the rankings. If this is your first time in Clara's World, you may not see any notifications. On the top is the main menu.

The top menu contains the following links:

- *Clara's World* will take you back to the Home Page, where you can find the list of your schedules.
- *User Menu* allows you to *Log Out* and view and modify your *Profile* information (see Section A.8).

The content of the top menu changes depending on the page you are visiting. For example, on the *Schedule* or *Practical* page, you can access leaderboards or

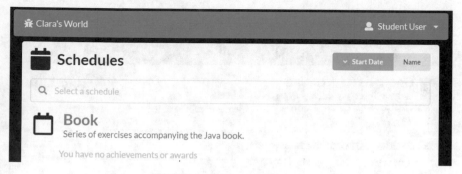

Fig. A.7: Home Screen for Logged in User on
`https://www.claraworld.net.`

timetabling information. Now is the time to explore the fundamental parts of Clara's World: schedules, practicals and exercises.

A.6 Schedules, Practicals and Exercises

Clara's World is organised into *schedules*, *practicals* and *exercises*. An *exercise* is a programming problem with initial code, description and one or more visual "boards" representing Clara's World. A *practical* is a collection of exercises with a common topic, for example, a practical teaching you loop statements, such as *for* or *while*. A *schedule* is a collection of practicals, usually created for a specific time period, such as a semester. Let us see how these three concepts help you stay organised and productive while having fun!

A.6.1 Schedules

Schedules organise practicals and exercises into collections, with the possibility to schedule the practical for a specific date. Often, schedules represent semesters (e.g. Autumn 2021), or organisations providing extra services (e.g. Peer Assisted Student Sessions - PASS, a student help network). You can access individual schedules on the home page of Clara's World (see Figure A.1). Once you click on the schedule header, you access the schedule details page, listing all available practicals (see Figure A.8)

Scheduled practicals are only visible from the admin specified date. Thus, during your semester, more practicals are added. Practicals can also have a *due date*, and you will receive a visual indication if the due date is approaching on the Practical page (A.6.2). You can filter practicals by name, providing your search string in

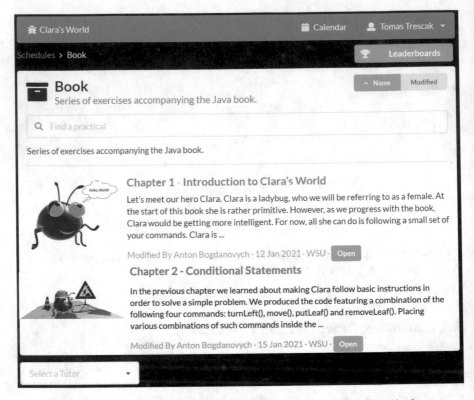

Fig. A.8: Details of a "Book" Schedule Listing Available Practicals.

the "Select Practical" input box. You can also sort the practicals by "name" or the date they were last modified. Sorting is particularly useful in schedules with many practicals, such as those allowing users to create their solutions (i.e. Sandbox).

You can access a practical by clicking on the name of the practical. But first, you have to select your tutor. If you access an exercise without a tutor subscription, you will receive an error message. In Figure A.8 you can see the "Select a Tutor" dropdown at the bottom of the page. Figure A.9 shows how to control changes after you choose your tutor.

Fig. A.9: Schedule Status with Tutor Subscription.

When you subscribe to your tutor, we provide you with the possibility to rate his or her performance. Rating is critical in organisations interested in feedback on the teaching performance of their staff. Your feedback is valuable and helps to maintain high teaching standards.

The remaining notable aspects of the schedule page are the "Calendar" and "Leaderboards" links in the top menu.

The leaderboards link will take you to the Leaderboards page (see Section A.7 on details of our ranking process). Please note that the leaderboards link is also context-sensitive. As a result, the link on the Schedule page will take you to the schedule rankings, while the link on the Practical page will take you to the rankings of the practical.

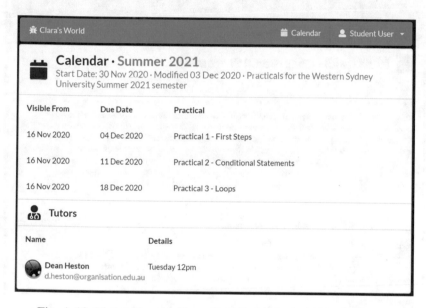

Fig. A.10: Timetable with Tutor Details for Spring 2020 Semester.

The "Calendar" link accesses the timetable information for the currently selected schedule. Figure A.10 shows the timetable for the Spring 2020 semester. In the top part, you see the list of three practicals. All practicals list their due dates. If a practical lacks a "Visible From" date, it is always accessible. In the bottom part of the timetable, you see the list of all tutors responsible for this schedule.

A.6.2 Practicals

On the Practical page, things are starting to be more interesting. Let us explore all the visual elements depicted in Figure A.11. Note that most of these elements help you to control and monitor your progress in the current schedule.

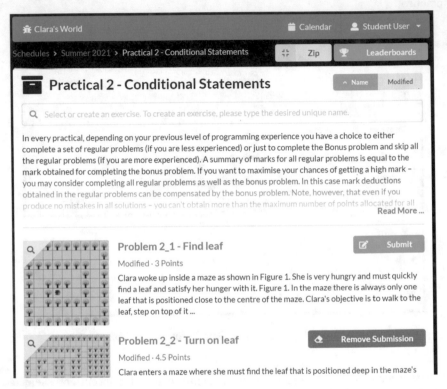

Fig. A.11: Practical Screen with the List of Exercises.

Download Zip

In the top part of the screen, under the main menu, you see the [⇅ Download Zip] button. This button allows you to download a zipped copy of all your attempted exercises. This button only appears if you tried and saved at least one exercise.

Leaderboards

Next to the Zip button is the Leaderboards button, which takes you to leaderboards for this practical.

Exercise List

Under the `Download Zip` button, you see the description of the practical and the list of exercises. Similar to the schedule list, you can filter the exercises by their name and sort them by date or by name.

Description

In the top part of the list, you see the instructions for the practical. Often, instructions provide the background story on what Clara is trying to learn, as well as the list of available commands. Please, expand the description by clicking on the `Read more .. ` link.

Exercise

Each item of the exercise list contains several important controls. First, clicking on the exercise image shows the instructions for this exercise. Second, after you attempt the exercise, you have the opportunity to **Submit** your exercise for marking or to **Remove Submission** and continue working on this exercise with the intention to resubmit it later.

> When you submit your exercise, the system creates a copy of your solution. Your tutor can only see the copy you have submitted. If you add any changes to your exercise after you submit your solution, your tutor will not see them. If you want to include the changes, you have to re-submit your solution (by clicking *Remove Submission* and then *Submit*)

Due Date

If the practical has a due date, you can see the visual indicator of the proximity of the due date. This indicator changes colour from green, when a due date is more than five days away, to orange if it is less than five days and red **Due 2 days ago** if the due date has passed.

A.6.3 Exercises

The exercise page is where the job gets done! It allows you to write and compile (i.e. check for errors) Java code in your browser, and automatically check your solution for completeness. Figure A.12 shows an example of the Exercise screen with the corresponding visual elements. Let us describe the functionality of these elements in detail.

Code Editor

In the left part of the page you see the Code Editor. It allows you to write and check the correctness of your code. Please note the red squiggly lines under the `mov()` and `turnright()` commands. These lines highlight the errors in your code. You can see the reason for the errors by hovering your mouse over the problematic code,

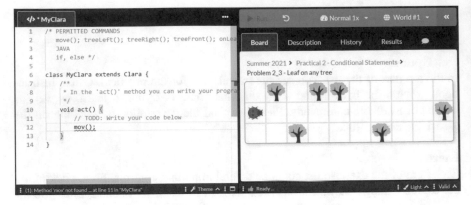

Fig. A.12: Exercise Screen with the Code Editor and the Clara's World View.

or in the status bar at the bottom part of the editor. The editor summarises and marks all error locations under its scroll bar on the right as red squares. The error summary is convenient for long code and helps to navigate to your first error easily.

> You can press the **F8** key to navigate to the first error in your code. Another helpful element of the Code Editor is the ⨍ Options ∧ button located in the bottom right part of the Editor's window. Here you can change the colour theme of your editor, choosing between *Dark*, *Light* and *High Contrast*.

Board View
In the right part of an exercise page you see the board controller. It contains five visual components, providing functionality to control the execution of your code, as well as to receive feedback on code correctness and quality. Next, we introduce them in detail.

Board Menu
In the top part of the page depicted in Figure A.12 you see the board controller menu. It has two parts. The left part shows tabs, allowing you to switch between the board view and the description of the problem. The right part is the board controller with the following buttons:

- ▶ Run button, executes your code and displays your changes on the board. This button is disabled if your code has compilation errors. You have to correct all errors before running your code.
- ↺ reset button works in two modes. Single click moves Clara back to her original location, allowing you to execute your code again. Double click also

resets all changes that you made on your board (e.g. changes of tree locations) to the original state of the problem.

- ⬛ button saves your code to the server. *Run* button also saves the code.

- 🐌 Normal ▾ speed dropdown sets how fast Clara is moving. The options vary from *snail* (0.1x) to *stellar* (50x) speed.

- World #1 ▾ world dropdown changes the active world, if your exercise contains more worlds. Your solution has to correctly work with all supplied worlds to be successful.

- 💬 discussion button provides the possibility to leave comments for your tutor, asking for help with your code or explaining some unusual aspects of your solutions.

- « back button takes you back to the practical page.

Breadcrumbs

Below the board menu, depicted in Figure A.12, are breadcrumbs, which provide convenient links to the schedule and practical to which the exercise belongs.

Spring 2020 › Practical 2 - Flow of Control › Problem 2_2 - No tree - no leaf

Fig. A.13: Breadcrumbs Feature Links to the Schedule and Practical.

Message View

Below breadcrumbs is a message view that provides you with automated feedback on your solution, both positive and negative. Figure A.13 shows the feedback on the successful solution, running correctly in all three worlds.

- World #1 completed in 13 steps
- World #2 completed in 11 steps
- World #3 completed in 23 steps
- Success! Your rating ★★★★★
- 7 lines of code. Three stars, Excellent!
- 47 steps (15 in average). Two stars, Excellent!

Fig. A.14: Message View Displays Automated Feedback on Your Solution.

Furthermore, the presented solution attracted five stars. Please see Section A.7 to see how we calculate the star ratings and rankings.

A.7 Rankings

Rankings provide feedback on student performance and, hopefully, motivate students to deliver high-quality work. We calculate rankings for each particular exercise, as well as calculate them per practical and schedule. Figure A.15 shows rankings for the Spring 2020 semester (these feature fictional names for privacy reasons).

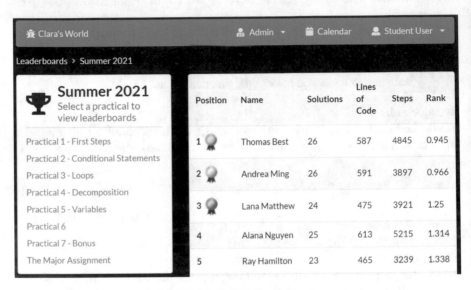

Fig. A.15: Schedule rankings.

Rankings depend on the number of lines of code in your solution and the number of moves and turns that Clara must make while executing it. Solving a solution gives you two different types of stars: (i) yellow stars for lines of code, and (ii) brown stars for the number of steps required to complete your solution. You receive stars based on a pre-defined maximum numbers of lines of code or steps to complete a given solution. For example, your solution must have a maximum of 20 lines of code for three stars, 25 for two stars and 30 for one star. These numbers are specified by your instructors during the exercise creation. We calculate rankings based on lines of code, using the following formulas:

- **Exercise Rank**: $e = loc/loc^{3star}$, that is the ratio of your lines of code to the three-star solution. If a user has not attempted the exercise, the rank is set to 3, which is the maximum number.
- **Practical Rank**: $p = (\sum_{n=1}^{m} e_n)/m$ is the average of ranks for m solutions in a practical. Please note that each exercise that has not been attempted adds rank 3 to the calculation of average (i.e. the rank of a practical where no exercise has been attempted is 3).

- **Schedule Rank**: $s = (\sum_{n=1}^{m} p_n)/l$ is the average of ranks for l practicals in a solution.

A.8 Profile

The Profile page allows you to personalise the Clara's World experience. Here you can also change your name, in case you made a mistake during the registration process.

 Please always use your real name; otherwise, your tutors may not be able to correctly mark your work.

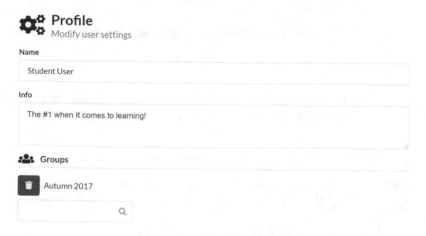

Fig. A.16: Customising User Details and Group Membership.

Groups

In the "Groups" section, you can join existing groups. For example, you can join a group of students from the semester "Autumn 2020" or a study support group. Joining a group allows you to view the content only visible to the members of this group. You can participate in multiple groups simultaneously. See Figure A.16

Editor

You can change the visual properties of Clara's World, such as the colour of the board, width of the division lines or tile size. Different colours can help if you have any visual impairment or just different visual requirements from those that are assigned by default. Please, see Figure A.17.

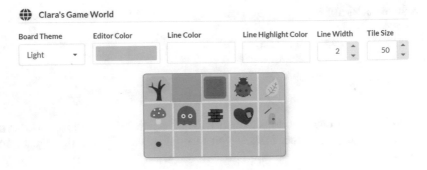

Fig. A.17: Customising World Options.

Fig. A.18: Customising Organisation Membership.

Organisations

You can join multiple organisations, providing the possible organisation password. You can also remove your registration in an organisation. Please see Figure A.18.

Fig. A.19: Customising Avatars.

Avatars

At the bottom of the profile page, you can change your avatar. The system displays this avatar next to your name during discussions. Please see Figure A.19.

A.9 How to Create Your Own Exercises

Do you like to challenge your friends or colleagues? Are you bored with existing exercises? Would you like to create your own challenges? Clara's World allows you to create new exercises and share them with the world. Each exercise comes with a leaderboard. As a result, you can create competitions or use exercises to teach others. Whatever your reason, Clara's World makes it easy. In this section, we explore the process of creating a new exercise, which we can summarise through the following steps:

1. Create one or more worlds, positioning Clara, trees, leaves or mushrooms on the visual board.
2. Create a validation for each of the defined worlds, allowing to check the correctness of supplied solutions automatically.
3. Optionally, in more advanced scenarios, modify the code and helper libraries.

Let's explore this process in a step-by-step guide, creating a new exercise, world definitions, validations and the necessary support code.

Step 1: Create an Empty Exercise

First, we need to create an empty exercise. In Clara's World, there are several schedules, which allow you to add new exercises. In this example we will work with the *Sandbox* schedule and *User Problems* practical[3]. Figure A.20 shows the empty User Problems practical. It is possible that when you visit this practical, there will already be quite a few exercises created by others.

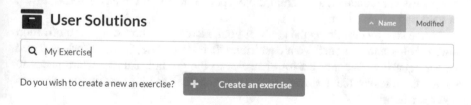

Fig. A.20: Creating an Empty Exercise.

Now, you need to type the name of your new exercise. In Figure A.20, we typed "My Exercise". If there is no other exercise with the same name, you will see a ➕ **Create exercise** button. Please note that if an exercise with the same name already exists, you will not see this button, but the filtered list of exercises with a similar name will appear. Please press the button, which will automatically save your new exercise and take you to the exercise administration page.

---

[3] https://claraworld.net/link/UserProblems

Fig. A.21: Exercise Administration.

Step 2: Describe the exercise

The exercise administration screen has two parts. On the left, you can see the *navigator* with the structure of your exercise and select individual components. These components are boards, board validations as well as general exercise settings. On the right, you see the *editor* of the selected component. In Figure A.21, you can see the general properties editor.

Each component provides specific actions (e.g. Add Board, Add Validation). You can access component actions from the dropdown menu in the navigator, or in the bottom part of the editor.

Please start by describing the goals of your exercise. A short story for motivation always helps, and humour is your best friend. In this exercise, Clara's World suffered an earthquake which shook a lot of leaves to the ground. Hungry Clara needs to move all the leaves that she finds back to her home. Exercise description uses rich text formatting.

It is a good practice to show a screenshot of the initial state and a final state of the world in the exercise description. You can either upload screenshots (or other images) directly in the rich text editor, or use the "Uploads" section. Please see Figure A.22, showing the Uploads section. Please try to save your exercise by clicking on the Save button or pressing "CTRL+S".

We should also provide estimates for the number of lines and moves that attract stars. Each estimate represents a maximum number of lines of code to achieve the award, e.g. 20 lines for three stars, 25 for two stars and 30 for one star. You can also provide the minimum number of lines of code to be used for flagging solutions that are implausibly short and automatically notify their creators about a potential problem with their solution. At this moment we do not know how to award stars and

Fig. A.22: Exercise Uploads.

how many lines are too few, since we need to first attempt the solution ourselves. That's why we leave this section for a moment, and instead, we create the board.

Step 3: Create a World

Creating the world is the most fun part of creating a new exercise. You have two options for how to add the new board. First, you can click on the dropdown icon next to "Boards" in the navigator (see Figure A.21). Second, find the Actions button at the bottom of the general properties editor. Now, please do the following:

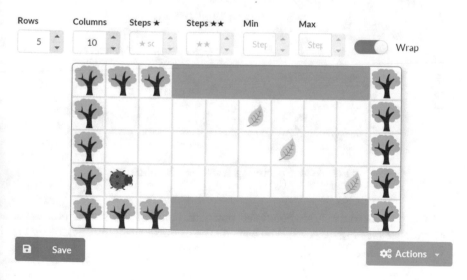

Fig. A.23: Definition of a New Board.

- Set the number of rows to five.
- Set the number of columns to ten.
- Please ignore the star rating for now.

- Turn off the world wrapping. World wrapping allows moving from one edge of the world to another. We do not need this in our exercise.
- In the right part of your screen, click on the "Tree" icon and then click on the tile where you want to place the tree. Please fill the world with trees as shown in Figure A.23
- If you make a mistake, you can drag and drop the tree to another tile.
- You can also delete trees by clicking on the trash icon first and then clicking on the tree you want to delete.
- Please repeat the process for leaves and water.
- It is time to position Clara in the bottom left corner. Once you put Clara on the board, she will be facing upwards. Click on her to rotate.

If you are happy with the board look, take a screenshot and upload it to the server either in the Rich Text editor or in the "Uploads" section. Once you upload your screenshot, please select this link from the Thumbnail image dropdown (see Figure A.24).

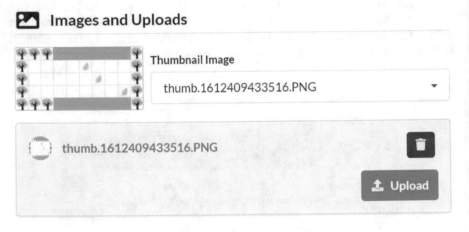

Fig. A.24: Specifying Exercise Thumbnail.

If you go back to the "User Solutions" practical, you will now see the preview of your exercise (see Figure A.25). You can edit the exercise again, by clicking on the edit button.

> If you do not see the exercise edit button, make sure that you enable the Edit Mode in the user menu. User menu is located in the main menu and has your name on it.

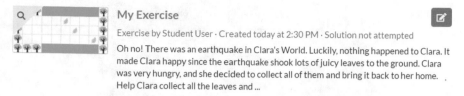

My Exercise

Exercise by Student User · Created today at 2:30 PM · Solution not attempted

Oh no! There was an earthquake in Clara's World. Luckily, nothing happened to Clara. It made Clara happy since the earthquake shook lots of juicy leaves to the ground. Clara was very hungry, and she decided to collect all of them and bring it back to her home. Help Clara collect all the leaves and ...

Fig. A.25: List View of Your Exercise.

Step 4: Validate the World

If we want to evaluate the user solution automatically, we have to provide one or more validations. We can validate a final state of the world or a text output provided by `System.out.println`. In our case, we will add a new board validation by clicking on the dropdown button next to "Board #1" in the navigator and selecting `Add Validation`. You can also use the `Actions` button in the bottom part of the board editor (see Figure A.23).

Next, we click on the dropdown menu of the new validation and select the item "`Add Final State from Board`". Again, you can use `Actions` button located at the bottom of the validation editor. Please see Figure A.26 for both options.

Fig. A.26: List View of Your Exercise.

You can add multiple possibilities for the desired final world configuration. In our case, we make do with only one, displayed in Figure A.27. We can also validate Clara's final position in the world by selecting the "Validate Position" checkbox. Since we do not care about where Clara is located after completing the exercise, you should uncheck it. Again, we take the screenshot and upload it to the server.

Step 5: Final Touches

We are almost done! It is time to solve your exercise and realistically set the star awards, both for lines of code and for steps. Make sure that all the star ratings are achievable. Also, use the uploaded images to update your description. Use

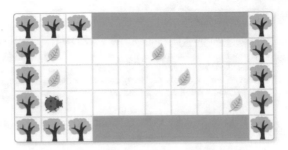

Fig. A.27: Validation View of Your Exercise.

Markdown notation to include images. Below is an example markdown code of the description from Figure A.25.

This description features two images that depict the initial configuration of Clara's World and its resulting configuration after correct program execution. A picture is worth a thousand words! Having such images in your exercise descriptions is very useful. We strongly encourage you to always include them.

And we are done! It is now time to share this exercise with friends and let the challenge begin! In the next step, we cover an advanced scenario, where you can provide a custom code for your exercise.

Step 5: Adding Custom Code

In the text editor section of your exercise, you can modify the code for your solution. The `MyClara` file is writable and allows you to leave commented instructions. If you want to add some hidden code with helper methods, you can add them to the `Clara` file. This file is locked and needs to be made writable by clicking on the `File` dropdown menu in the right part of the editor and then clicking on `Make Writable`. Now you can add any custom code to your solution. From the file menu, you can add other libraries or code interfaces. Make sure there are no compilation errors when you save your exercise.

References

1. Csikszentmihalyi, M.: Flow: the classic work on how to achieve happiness. 2 edn. The Random House Group Ltd, London, UK (2002)
2. Reichert, Raimond and Hartmann, Werner: Unterrichtsmaterial fuer den informatikunterricht. https://www.swisseduc.ch/informatik/ (last visited 25/01/2021)
3. Sahami, M.: CS106A - Programming Methodology Course. Stanford University. https://see.stanford.edu/Course/CS106A (last visited 25/01/2021)
4. Prensky, M.: Digital Game-Based Learning. Paragon House (2007)
5. Koster, R.: Theory of fun for game design. O'Reilly Media, Inc. (2013)
6. Roberts, E.: Karel the robot learns Java. Department of Computer Science Stanford University (2005)
7. MIT: Scratch programming environment. https://scratch.mit.edu (last visited 04/01/2021)
8. Kölling, M.: The greenfoot programming environment. ACM Transactions on Computing Education (TOCE) 10(4) (2010) 1–21
9. Code.Org: Introductory learning resources for children. https://code.org (last visited 04/01/2021)
10. Pothole.Info: The pothole facts. https://www.pothole.info/the-facts/ (last accessed 11/01/2020)
11. Madli, R., Hebbar, S., Pattar, P., Golla, V.: Automatic detection and notification of potholes and humps on roads to aid drivers. IEEE Sensors Journal 15(8) (2015) 4313–4318
12. Zimmerman, H.M.: Pothole repair machine (January 24 2006) US Patent 6,988,849.
13. Rohlfshagen, P., Liu, J., Perez-Liebana, D., Lucas, S.M.: Pac-man conquers academia: Two decades of research using a classic arcade game. IEEE Transactions on Games 10(3) (2017) 233–256
14. Ricci-Tersenghi, F.: The solution to the challenge in "Time-Reversible Random Number Generators" by Wm. G. Hoover and Carol G. Hoover. arXiv preprint arXiv:1305.1805 (2013)
15. Cui, X., Shi, H.: A*-based pathfinding in modern computer games. International Journal of Computer Science and Network Security 11(1) (2011) 125–130
16. Hagelbäck, J., Johansson, S.J.: Using multi-agent potential fields in real-time strategy games. In: Seventh International Conference on Autonomous Agents and Multiagent Systems (AAMAS), 12-16, 2008, Estoril. (2008) 631–638
17. Ng, J., Bräunl, T.: Performance comparison of bug navigation algorithms. Journal of Intelligent and Robotic Systems 50(1) (2007) 73–84
18. Togelius, J., Karakovskiy, S., Koutnik, J., Schmidhuber, J.: Super mario evolution. In: IEEE Symposium on Computational Intelligence and Games, IEEE (2009) 156–161
19. Hooge, C.: Preface to college physics. BCIT Physics 0312 Textbook (2016)
20. Conway, J.: The game of life. Scientific American 223(4) (1970) 4
21. Hartman, G.: Fundamentals of Matrix Algebra (Third Edition). Virginia Military Institute (2011)
22. Hölldobler, B., Wilson, E.O., et al.: Journey to the ants: a story of scientific exploration. Harvard University Press (1994)
23. Dorigo, M., Bonabeau, E., Theraulaz, G.: Ant algorithms and stigmergy. Future Generation Computer Systems 16(8) (2000) 851–871
24. Deneubourg, J.L., Aron, S., Goss, S., Pasteels, J.M.: The self-organizing exploratory pattern of the argentine ant. Journal of Insect Behavior 3(2) (1990) 159–168
25. Sutariya, D., Kamboj, P.: A survey of ant colony based routing algorithms for manet. European Scientific Journal (2013)

Printed in the United States
by Baker & Taylor Publisher Services